GOOD-BYE TO ITHACA

BOOKS BY LOUIS GOLDING

Fiction

Forward from Babylon
Seacoast of Bohemia
Day of Atonement
Store of Ladies
The Miracle Boy
The Prince or Somebody
Give Up Your Lovers
Magnolia Street
Five Silver Daughters
The Camberwell Beauty

The Pursuer
The Dance Goes On
Mr. Emmanuel
Who's There Within?
No News from Helen
The Glory of Elsie Silver
Three Jolly Gentlemen
Honey for the Ghost
The Dangerous Places
The Loving Brothers

To The Quayside

Short Stories

The Doomington Wanderer   Paris Calling
Pale Blue Nightgown

Verse

Sorrow of War
Shepherd Singing Ragtime
Prophet and Fool

The Song of Songs, Rendered as a
    Masque
Poems Drunk and Drowsy

Travel

Sunward: Adventures in Italy
Sicilian Noon
Those Ancient Lands: A Journey to
    Palestine

In the Steps of Moses the Law-Giv
In the Steps of Moses the Conqu
Louis Golding Goes Travelling
Good-bye To Ithaca

Belles-Lettres

Adventures in Living Dangerously
Letter to Adolf Hitler
We Shall Eat and Drink Again
    (With André Simon)

James Joyce
The Jewish Problem
Hitler Through the Ages
The World I Knew

Sport

Louis Golding's Boxing Tales   My Sporting Days and Nights
The Bare-Knuckle Breed

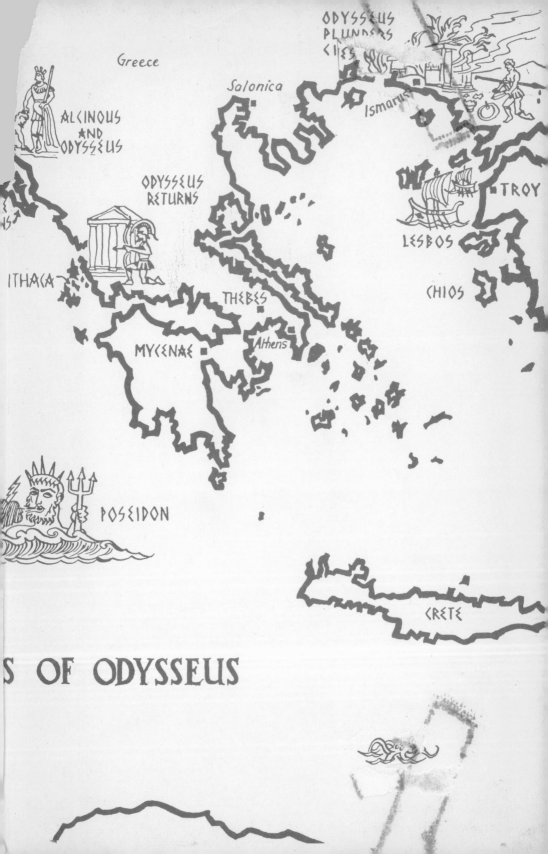

Greece

ODYSSEUS
PLUNDERS
CITIES

ALCINOUS
AND
ODYSSEUS

Salonica

Ismarus

ODYSSEUS
RETURNS

TROY

LESBOS

ITHACA

CHIOS

THEBES

MYCENAE

Athens

POSEIDON

CRETE

S OF ODYSSEUS

Old man of Palaeokastritza, domain of Alcinous

GOOD-BYE TO ITHACA

by

LOUIS GOLDING

THOMAS YOSELOFF

NEW YORK • LONDON

Thomas Yoseloff, *Publisher*

11 East 36th Street

New York 16, N.Y.

Thomas Yoseloff Ltd.

123 New Bond Street

London W. 1, England

Printed in the United States of America

FOR

LEV AND JANE ZEITLINE

AFFECTIONATELY

FOR

DR. LEV ZEITLINE

GRATEFULLY

Setting out on the voyage to Ithaca
You must pray that the way be long,
Full of adventures and experiences.

You must always have Ithaca in your mind,
Arrival there is your predestination.
But do not hurry the journey at all.
Better that it should last many years;
Be quite old when you anchor at the island,
Rich with all you have gained on the way,
Not expecting Ithaca to give you riches.
Ithaca has given you your lovely journey.
Without Ithaca you would not have set out.
Ithaca has no more to give you now.

Poor though you find it, Ithaca has not cheated you.
Wise as you have become, with all your experience,
You will have understood the meaning of an Ithaca.

C. P. Cavafy
(Translated by John Mavrogordato

CONTENTS

LIST OF ILLUSTRATIONS

LIST OF ILLUSTRATIONS

CHARTS

CHAPTER ONE

The Adventure Begins

I WAS a very small boy when I first became aware of Odysseus and his voyages. It may have been from "Lady Kathleen" who in the early years of this century produced a series of "Penny Books for the Bairns" and devoted one of her volumes to the hero. Or perhaps it was Miss Pollitt of Standard Three in my Manchester Elementary School who first ·uttered in my hearing the magic words, Troy, Ithaca, which have always exercised over me so compulsive a fascination. But when my voyages to Ithaca actually began I was about twenty, and it was during the course of that other war. I was asked would I like to go to Salonica. Salonica? But that was Greece, or, at least, it was Macedonia. One would go out through Mediterranean and Aegean waters. It would probably mean Athens, too. Yes, I agreed with delight, and went forth on the first of my voyages in the wake of Odysseus.

That was not the idea of my sponsors, of course, and I, too, had a good many other things to think of. But as the Messageries Maritimes liner, the *Ernest Simon*, passed the Aeolian Islands on the starboard bow, my heart thrilled at the thought that I was now, so young and so soon, in Odyssean waters. Perhaps Homer himself as a sailor-boy had travelled among those islands, and it had been pointed out to him that the island here, the one made visible by the fiery flame that capped it, was Aeolia, the home of Aeolus, Lord of the Winds. "Look. You see? It floats," said the old salt who was spinning yarns to the deck-hands. And indeed that day, too, in 1916, it seemed to be floating, the water was so blue and volatile. "There's a wall of bronze all round it," the old man said, "and the cliffs run up sheer from the sea."

We did not go near enough in the s.s. *Ernest Simon* to see if the wall of bronze was still there. But it was enough to know that if Homer meant by Aeolia any actual island, it was possible he meant Stromboli, the island before my eyes.

So Odysseus sailed from Aeolia for his home, Ithaca, to a favouring wind, with all the winds that might have hindered him safely stowed away in the leather bag Aeolus had given him, tightly secured with a silver wire. And nine days later there he was within sight of the beloved island, its vines and olive trees, its high hills starred with rock-rose, and the goats leaping from ledge to ledge. But what must the foolish sailors do but open up the bag, and let out the winds, and fill the whole sky with tempests. So they are driven back in reverse to Aeolia, and the long round of adventures must begin again. There will be giants in the Laestrygonian land, there will be the witch Circe in the island of Aaea. There will be a siren-singing island, and a place of Wandering Rocks. Only when Odysseus and his men, but not all of them, have survived these dangers, will they reach the still more dangerous monsters, Scylla and Charybdis.

We, however, in the *Ernest Simon* were driven by steam, and had no bag of winds to play around with. We reached Scylla and Charybdis not many hours after we left Stromboli, we entered the Straits of Messina, in fact. "A dreadful place," says that old salt to the boy, Homer, a long time ago. "Hold your fingers crossed, everybody!" Then he tells them the ghastly story of Scylla with teeth large as barns, and the arms and legs of the sailors of Odysseus sticking out all ways. "And if you get by Scylla," the old rogue goes on, "then it's Charybdis that'll suck the salt sea down in the way she has, and you all with it, as likely as not."

But if the sailors of Odysseus had a bad time, the boy Homer was luckier, and so were we, though monsters quite as horrid as Scylla and Charybdis lurked under the innocent waters. We reached the Malta group of islands, of which both Malta itself and Gozo, the second largest island, have been identified with Ogygia, the island of Calypso, though why Gozo, too, has been specified I have not been able to discover. It was on the shore of Ogygia that Odysseus was washed up, the last survivor of his headstrong company, who had impiously devoured the sacred oxen of Helios, in the island of Thrinacia, that is Sicily. On the island of Gozo-Ogygia, Odysseus stayed seven long years, for the nymph fell doting on him, and promised him eternal youth if he stayed with her for ever. Agreeable though it may have been for a time, at length the affair palled on Odysseus, and under pressure from Olympus the nymph was forced to let him go. I have heard the sentiment echoed by present-day British mariners that seven years of Malta would be a lot too much. We in the *Ernest Simon* left after a day or two and made for Greece. Northward, far from our course, the Ionian Islands were strung out along the west coast. Beyond Zante there was Cephalonia. Beyond Cephalonia was Ithaca.

"*Ithaca!* I've come as near as this," I told myself. "Some day I'll come nearer."

We berthed in the Piraeus for a day or two, which must have been the harbour for Athens in the time of Odysseus, too. We went to Athens. We went on to Salonica, and stayed there for some time. It seemed even further away from Ithaca than Manchester had been and though the distance between Salonica and Troy, the other focal point in the Odyssean journey, was roughly the same as the distance between Salonica and Ithaca, Troy seemed further away than any pale planet. Turkey, an enemy country, lay between. And on the way to Troy was Gallipoli, with all its legions of dead, and its legions still dying.

We stayed in Salonica for some time, and I was aware that eastward along the Thracian shore was, or may have been, Ismarus, the city of the Cicones which Odysseus had sacked in the first of his adventures after he started home when the Trojan wars were over. It was not practicable at that time, in 1916, to go hunting the Cicones so, after some months, I boarded the s.s. *Ernest Simon* again, and made for Marseilles, her home port. She got there, and set out once more for Salonica, but did not arrive. Like many another brave ship in that war, and in another war to come, the *Ernest Simon* came to grief. A fate befell her, and in the same waters, not unlike the fate that befell my hero's blue-prowed ship after she left the island of the sun, where the unfortunate episode took place of the slaughter of the god's cattle. Some god destroyed the *Ernest Simon*, too, using an up-to-date thunder-bolt.

I got back from Salonica without mischance by sea or land. Some day, I told myself, the war will be over. I will come back again, sooner or later, however many years it takes me, to this blue and golden world surrounded by the flat and circular waters of Ocean stream, the world of the Lotus-Eaters, Circe's world, the world of Nausicaa. I will find my way to Ithaca.

It was not till the late spring of 1953 that I reached Ithaca at last, having spent many more years on my journeys than the arch-Ithacan himself. Only a month or two after I left the island, an earthquake cracked the houses of the villages like so many match-boxes. Not in my lifetime, at least, will it be the same place. In one sense it can never again be the same place. But there are two Ithacas, and one of these is more permanent than mountains, which can slide down into the sea. That is Homer's Ithaca, which I saw.

CHAPTER TWO

Athens to Aulis

I

THE Athenian bays were like cauldrons of Reckitt's-Blue dye simmering against the copper rims of coast. The Cadillacs and Studebakers slid like molasses on the broad, shining road. As you approached the city you had the feeling that the walls had a new wall-paper and the roads a new sort of road-block, made up out of pressed dollar notes, white in this country, not green.

The first sight of the Parthenon was sudden and disappointing, as it so often is. So it certainly had been to me that time I first set eyes on it, in 1916, a jawful of yellow teeth. Then I approached by the grubby little Piraeus train. The air was brown with the reek of smoke from tanneries and soap factories. Then, suddenly, the Parthenon was visible, through a window where some-one who did not know how to spit properly, had spat. If I had been younger, or older, I would have wept.

This time the first sight of the Parthenon was not a jawful of yellow teeth, but a ballerina's tinsel-encrusted coronet in the Metropolitan Opera House (so it was phrased by Edward who was with me throughout the last journey). The whole city looked as prosperous as Manhattan, with elegantly-gowned women every-where, Athenian as well as American, and the shop-windows as brilliantly dressed as Madison Avenue. In the best confectioners the Parthenon repeated itself in marzipan, with mammoth chocolate Easter eggs interspersed, combining thus the classical and the Christian motifs. The combined weight of the glossy paper-backed twenty-five cent books on the kiosks launched with dollar aid to expound the American dream, could hardly be less, I thought, than that of the Parthenon itself.

Yes. In the big squares, the big streets, the big hotels, it was an Athens quite taken over by the U.S.A., as once the Macedonians had taken it over, and in their turn the Romans, the Goths, the Turks. And sooner or later, as those others went, the Americans will go, too, when high politics demand it, carrying off their aircraft-carriers and command-cars and the seamen's trunks crammed with dollars. It might be next year, though that is not likely. It might not be for ten or twenty years. And what will happen then, I wondered, to the expensive blocks of flats that are going up everywhere and the dazzling highways which are so much too grand for the indigenous traffic?

But there was one detail in the ensemble which I welcomed for its relevance to the Odyssean task I had so long been engaged on. I mean the U.S. sailors that sat at every café table in the Square of the Constitution, their long Texan legs extending stiff over the pavements. For Odysseus doubtless gave shore leave to his ships' crews when they put in here *en route* for Aulis; doubtless they, too, sat about in the hot sun, knocking back rather more than was good for them. Captain Odysseus, himself, I suppose was paying his respects to his devoted Athene over there on the Acropolis, in the Erectheium, the great palace sacred to the worship of her foster-son, the Athenian hero, Erectheus. It was to the Erectheium, so Homer tells us, that the Goddess fared at a later stage of the hero's history, when she left Odysseus behind in the genial land of Scheria, and then crossed the broad sea, and came to Marathon, and the broad streets of Athens— broad then as they are now.

It was, perhaps, the season of one of her mysteries, the *Procharisteria*, at the beginning of spring, when hymns were sung to celebrate the resurrected seed. Or perhaps the high summer festival of the *Sciropheria*, when the priests marched in procession from the Acropolis, under the shade of protecting parasols. And now it was Holy Week, the season of the Christian mysteries. And as Good Friday lengthened, Manhattan removed itself further and further away. Over in the Church of the Metropole, the Eikon of the Christ, deposed from the Cross, had lain since noon on a flower-engirdled bier, flanked by tall yellow candles. All day the faithful had come and gone to pay homage. And now, in the late evening, they were carrying the bier out of the church, the processions were forming, they were moving forward, a candle in every hand, upon their journeys through the streets and squares of the city. The crowds were thick upon every pavement, on every balcony, behind every window, these, too, holding aloft their candles. Nearer and nearer came the sound of funeral marches, very slow, quite heartbreaking. They were playing the second movement of Beethoven's Eroica Symphony, the shining helmets of the flanking policemen accentuating the steely discords. The music was wry, out of both time and tune, so that somehow it became abstracted from the country and the century, even the musical culture, from which it had emerged, and sounded as appropriate to the dirge for Christ Crucified, as it

B

might have done for some Greek deity similarly slain, similarly to be born again.

In that formalizing air, the clothes of the moving mourners, so completely of our own day, did not intrude upon the sense of antiquity, nor the uniforms of the armed forces, nor the Boy Scout shorts, not even the frock-coats and striped trousers of the high government officials. The superb vestments of the priests glimmered and glittered across the liquid air like a treasury scattered over the sea-bed after the vessel that carries it has been split wide open on a submerged rock.

The procession came to a halt beside us at the pavement's edge. A priest stood there, almost bent double by the load of an enormous cross. The mouth was pulled far down at the corners and twisted quite out of line, the eyes were immobile in the distended sockets. It seemed like a mask where a craftsman in papier-mâché had combined all he knew of ecstasy and anguish. The procession unfroze at length, and the priest moved on. But the face haunted me all night. I awoke again and again to see the lightless glass eyes and the mouth knocked sideways with grief. And here was morning; here, between the line of wall and window-curtain was sunshine thrusting through like a fence of swords. The priest's face was still there; or it was again there. The eyes moved healthy in the sockets and the lips smiled.

I stared astonished for some moments till I realized it was a matter of earth *and* heaven. For it was Easter Saturday morning. At the stroke of midnight his Lord would be risen again. Happy belief, I whispered, happy believers.

Already the streets were a-scramble with people laying in their provender for the feast days now to come; the rich folk in the Street of Churchill buying their vast chocolate eggs, as ornate as if Fabergé had made them; the poor folk buying their chicken-laid eggs, hard-boiled, blood-red; and all the poor quarters loud with the bleating of doomed lambs that were being dragged forward by one leg in preparation for the paschal sacrifice.

In the afternoon a hush fell on the brooding white city. Even the American sailors seemed to drop their voices. But after nightfall the air became restless. Soon the procession to the Church of the Metropole would be forming, the King, his Queen, and all their ministers would set forth, a great multitude. Now the loud-speakers gave tongue, now and endlessly for the next two or three hours rendering the National Anthem with a tinny and distorted voice. In between the verses some officer screamed instructions with a near-Hitlerian hysteria which was probably only physiological. The bells were ringing with such violence you wondered would they be torn from their bolts in the steeples. In the Church of the Metropole the royal party had reached their appointed places. First singly, then in whole constellations, the lights were switched off, the candles were blown out. Only the oil lamp that burns perpetually before the image of Christ on the High Altar still burned. Now at last from behind the altar screen a priest emerged, carrying a single white candle, newly lit. "Come!" he intoned. "Take light from the everlasting light!"

So from the priest's candle the candles of the multitude were lit up again. The lights were switched on. The congregation moved out into the open air. Then the cry went forth in ever-widening circles of sound, like a stone dropped into still water, over to the last confines of the city. "Christ is risen again! He is indeed risen!" The fire-works hissed and crackled, the bells swung and clamoured, the crowds at length dispersed homewards, the young elegants with plastered hair along with the old men mumbling ceaselessly through toothless gums: "Christ is risen again! He is indeed risen!"

In every direction the dissolving procession flickered and faltered like a thinning drift of fire-flies. At the foot of Mount Lykabettus I caught sight of one equipage that holds me in memory still entranced; an ancient Ford, preserved as immaculate as any dynastic Rolls-Royce, and seated in it a gaunt company of black-veiled old ladies, as many as the car could carry. Each of the old ladies held a candle aloft as the car proceeded with infinite stateliness. An old black-coated chauffeur, as old as any of the old ladies, held the wheel in his left hand, and a candle in his right hand. The only answering glow in all that blackness was the flame of the chauffeur's candle reflected in his gleaming brass buttons.

We wound our way up next day, being Easter Sunday, towards the Parthenon through a steep huddle of Turkish houses which by some miracle had escaped the incessant fires that have ravaged the city. Pausing to shelter a moment from the dust and the hot glare, we looked over a low wall, and there we were back nearly two thousand years. Deep below us the lines of the old Roman Forum were as clear now as they were then. On the fringe of the Forum, the olive trees, whose remote forebears had perhaps once given shade to a Roman senator's family, and before that to the family of a Greek architect, and perhaps even our hero from Ithaca had paused here for a moment to wipe his forehead on his way up to the Erectheium—the olive-trees now sheltered an Athenian family that was preparing its Easter repast. Using the drum of an ancient column for a table, they sprawled waist-deep among masses of golden marguerites.

"Who are they?" they whispered, catching sight of us. "They are strangers." It seemed preposterous to them that strangers should be forced to take their luncheon alone on this great day. A young man was sent to summon us without ado; for such was the ancient Greek quality of *ksenia*, and such it still is to-day, whatever other changes may have taken place. First, as soon as we were settled, they gave us scarlet eggs, and we set to work doughtily to smash our eggs against theirs. For the egg was held by the early Christians to be cram-full of blessings, as indeed it is, but the blessings can only be let loose when the egg is smashed. And perhaps, too, a more august symbolism is involved, the letting loose of Christ from his tomb, for each time the egg-top came away, there was a pious exclamation: "Christ is risen! Yes, indeed, Christ is risen!"

But by this time the first hot dish was ready, the *mayeritsa*, a spiced stew of lamb's innards. Then we toasted each other in glass upon glass of *ouzo*. Then an old crone, moving erect as any figure on a Greek vase, brought in a great flat basting-plate in which half a lamb was sizzling. Then we got down to it, washing down our titanic portions with libations of resinated wine. We had honey-cake, and goat's cheese whiter than snow, and tiny cups of Turkish coffee. We made speeches at each other in various languages, in which our sentiments were radiantly clear, though our speech was a little thick. Then we slept gently for an hour or so, cushioned among the marguerites, with the olive branches making an exquisite tracery between ourselves and the westering sun.

These are the great occasions of travel in the classic lands. They are not set down in the travel books. They cannot be stage-managed by the travel agencies. But perhaps to places like this one, and at such a time, the old gods still come back occasionally and people incline their ears towards a voice which has not actually spoken. Perhaps that momentary blurring of the sunshine was Athene herself, not a cloud, for no cloud was to be seen. We were on her own hill-side, where her ivory and gold had once shone far and free. And she may have been curious to know why, between the *ouzo* and the *rezzina*, the name of her hero had been so insistently invoked.

II

It is beyond belief that on his voyage from Ithaca to Aulis Odysseus did not disembark for supplies of water at Athens, that is to say, at the port for Athens. For ancient travellers travelled only by day and their cargo space being so limited, loaded at night where there was some convenient source of water.

Odysseus disembarked, then, from his ship. Edward and I disembarked from our aeroplane. Truth to tell, I had the feeling that Odysseus would not have been shattered at the sight. He would merely have felt that one of the gods, Hephaestus probably, had invented a new sort of chariot in his smithy on Olympus' top, and was paying a visit to his son, Erectheus, whom Athene also loved greatly. If it pleased Hephaestus to give a couple of mortals a lift, who could argue with him? If Odysseus had been present on the tarmac and seen the passengers emerge from the belly of the aeroplane, the spectacle might even have planted in him the seed from which some years later the idea of the Wooden Horse was to flower. Always assuming that it *was* Odysseus who was responsible for the idea of the Wooden Horse, as some of the ancients believed, though Homer himself tells us no more than that he was one of the passengers.

Or it might have occurred to Odysseus that Daedalus had invented a full-scale flying-machine, to take the place of the wax wings which he had fastened round the body of his son, Icarus, when the young man sought to escape from Crete; those wings with which, as Daedalus had warned the boy, he must not fly too near the sun, or they would melt. And the boy did, in fact, fly too near the sun, and the wings of wax did melt, and Icarus duly fell into the sea.

"It did not happen *this* time," one could fancy Odysseus muttering there on the tarmac, into his still-youthful beard. "But you can't tell what the future holds in store. Icarus must have been rather surprised too. But I suppose it'll be all right, if they consult the omens, and make the proper sacrifices."

Well, there we all were in Athens. From here Odysseus and his sailors sailed off to join the grand fleet at Aulis, and I felt it would help the mood and the impetus to go to Aulis, too, though I had been there before. There were several ways of doing it. One could take a boat up the Euripus channel between the mainland and Euboea, and get off at Chalcis, on the island side of the swivel-bridge, and thence cross to the two bays, separated by a rocky ridge, where the vast Achaean fleet was once assembled.

Or we could get there by train, on the main line to the north, changing at the tiny station of Skimatari. Or one could go by road by way of Thebes. We went by Thebes, partly because our passages were booked for Istanbul, and time was getting short; partly

because I had already made the sea-journey; partly because I
wished to pay my respects to an illustrious Semitic grandee, I mean,
Cadmus the Phoenician, founder of the city of Thebes, inventor of the
alphabet and the art of working in metals, who clearly incarnates a
Semitic influx into Continental Greece in the dim centuries when
there was, or may have been, a Mycenaean influx into Syrian Asia;
but chiefly because the name of Thebes is charged with such over-
tones of awe and tragedy, Thebes the theatre of the agony of Oedipus,
that I felt it an insolence to think of by-passing the place.

The car was troublesome, and our time in Thebes was short,
which is worse than no time at all. Some three or four miles beyond
the dun pear-shaped town lifted on its citadel, the car broke down.
We got out and tried to start it. But it would not start. Half an
hour went by, an hour. Edward almost entombed himself inside the
engine, he was so fascinated by the situation. It seemed inconceiv-
able that so many profoundly organic things could be wrong with an
engine which, only three or four hours ago, had found it possible
not only to start, but to move for quite a number of miles. I, too,
was well at ease in that fresh warm air, in the blessed Boeotian
countryside of wheat and vines, of fig-trees and olives, and westward the grey hills climbing towards Parnassus. I hoped there
would still be time to stroll for an hour along the twin Aulis beaches,
filling my imagination with the becalmed fleet of ships, the blue-
prowed, the crimson-painted. Perhaps even I might have the good
fortune of the young Cambridge scholar I had met in Athens who
not long ago had kicked up a most exciting sherd among the shells
and pebbles. Or did he say that he and his colleagues were digging
a kilometre or so away at the site of the Artemisium, where
Agamemnon had sacrificed that poor girl? (Or had just been about
to sacrifice her, for some held that his hand was stayed by Artemis
herself at the last moment, and a hind put in her place, exactly as the
hand of Abraham was stayed by Jehovah's angel at the last moment,
when he was about to sacrifice his son, Isaac, and a ram was put in
his place.) I found it difficult to concentrate for the garden beyond
the windows was fretted with flowers like a mill-race with foam, and
the bees were having a great time. "Let me show you," the young
scholar was saying, as he opened a small tin cigarette-box, and
tenderly removed from a shroud of cotton-wool the small terra-
cotta fragment it contained, part of a dedication-plaque, he thought.
"You see? This is a helmet here. Pure Homer. Behind it these are the
tips of spears, probably the warrior's bodyguard. But the important
thing is the lettering above: — sonos, we think, the genitive of a

name. Then γ *epist* —, the beginning of the second name." It was all of importance, I gathered, in the dating of the Homer poems, and a useful contribution to the debate as to whether the poems were orally transmitted or were written down. The poems were later than had been thought, and the Greeks had mastered script earlier. "These bold fine strokes . . ." the young scholar was saying. The water hissed softly on the almost English lawn. The roses in the borders knocked at their sheaths like tiny birds inside their shells. "I beg your pardon," I said guiltily. "These fine bold strokes?"

The young man resumed . . . "Definitely the work of some-one who had not recently learned the art of writing and painting. As for the type of spear . . ."

The driver pressed the horn on his ramshackle car, there on the road between Thebes and Aulis. "We'll make it!" proclaimed Edward. We got into the car and advanced a hundred yards, then stopped once more with a grinding and a groaning. "That's torn it!" the driver said, in the Greek version of the phrase. A mile or so away the electric-diesel train winding through the valley hooted sardonically. Out of a cloud in our rear a bus came snorting towards us. "For Chalkis!" our driver said tersely. "You'd better take it!"

We took the bus and got within three or four miles of the coast. The water was not yet visible, but it would be visible from the next rise, or the next. Then suddenly the bus stopped sharp as at some invisible barrier, like a horse shying at a visible fence. We got out. Everybody got out. Some betook themselves to the roadside and sat chirping among the wheat-stalks like grasshoppers. I was one of these. Some disappeared below the underside of the bus, like beetles. Edward was one of those. When he emerged an hour later, he assured me that the bus was going to remain there for some time.

"I'm not surprised," I observed. "I saw a crow fly in over my left shoulder."

"Well?"

"It's exactly as it should be. We're becalmed at Aulis, like our predecessors. On the landward side."

"We might thumb a lift," he said hopefully. There might be a third, and even more complicated, breakdown.

"To Athens," I insisted. "The fleet sails for Troy in a few hours."

CHAPTER THREE

Hellespont

I

THE s.s. *Abbazia* of the Adriatica line, in which we sailed from Athens for Istanbul *en route* for Troy, was about as different from the scruffy tramp steamer in which I last sailed through these waters, in the late twenties, as the tramp steamer was different from the ships which carried Odysseus and his island band some time earlier through these same regions. The tramp steamer had been less comfortable, but the passengers were enthralling in ways they do not enthral any more. In the first class the men were all millionaires who between them owned the world's casinos, the women were all Mata Hari. In the third class easy ladies looked through clouds of gold hair at their Levantine *maquereaux* with jewel-encrusted fingers. There was one dapper little Albanian who proposed to carry out, at cut rates, as many murders as I cared to order.

Mediterranean sea-travel is not as friendly as it was then, or so primitive as it was when Odysseus set forth from Troy and disappeared·into dim blue legendary distance.

For now it is as hard to get out of a country as to get in. Odysseus and Telemachus would have endless trouble with their visas. So would the wandering gold-toothed men and gold-haired ladies of the years between our own wars. So they stay where they are, and the Mediterranean liners take on a less adventurous sort of passenger.

Up in the first class of the s.s. *Abbazia*, all day long the American business-men consumed highballs, and the spectacled ladies from the Women's Clubs discussed next winter's lecture programmes. The third class was full of earnest German students from Munich lecturing each other on Byzantine art with a great scratching in note-pads and rummaging in text-books. The mood was different in the second class, with a group of hearty young Englishwomen who looked as if they had just breezed in from the hockey-field. They were going round the world on their Treasury allowances, which involves prodigies of manipulation—"knitting", they called it. Somehow they managed to see Rome on seven-and-sixpence, and were flushed with triumph over their achievements in Athens, which they did on six shillings. They had four more Continents to do.

They will "knit" their way through to triumph—those glorious girls of the bull-dog breed.

All next day we sailed through the entranced Aegean waters, and even the business-men deserted their highballs to gaze on the contours of the islands, as exquisitely sculptured as gems, and hardly larger.

"Ah, there it is! There!" Just off-key the secretary of the hockey-club murmured the famous verses and her eyes filled with tears.

"If I should die think only this of me,
That there's some corner of a foreign field
That always will be England."

The other girls crowded round her, trying not to scuffle for the field glasses. She thought she was pointing to the island of Skyros, where Rupert Brooke lies buried, but she was pointing to Strati, I think, or perhaps by that time Lemnos. But what did that matter? The young Apollo, golden-haired, might well have died on any of these islands. All the Englishwomen, and several Americans, furtively wiped their eyes.

The evocation of the ghost of Rupert Brooke had induced in us all an elegiac mood. There was sadness in the air as we approached the Dardanelles. Dark above the dusking water stood Cape Helles, where so many good lads fought and fell and lie there still. Sharp eyes, but not mine, detected their monument. Over at the opposite extremity was Cape Sigeum, and close by, the harbour where the Achaeans beached their ships, and poured out upon the plain, and drew up to beleaguer Troy, the ruins of which still stand on a gouged-out hillock only two or three kilometres away.

If Odysseus had his rights, it would have been there, at Cape Sigeum, we would have disembarked. But for the s.s. *Abbazia* that would not have been practicable, and there were passengers with other obligations than to Odysseus.

Mist gathered as we drummed slowly along the Hellespont. I was happy to think my Odyssey must take me to Istanbul, a city I had not yet visited, before I could tranship for Trojan land. I recollected, moreover, that there are certain commentators on the poem who place a number of the episodes, including the business of the Sirens, *east* of the Dardanelles, not west. (One of these was one von Baer, a Russian naturalist, of whom Norman Douglas speculates that this may have been "a kind of patriotism" on his part. It is "a kind of patriotism" we have become more familiar with recently.)

I imagine that the chief ground for this line of thought is the fact that Odysseus is stated to have sailed from Circe's island to the land of the Cimmerians, and there is no question that the Cimmerians were a historical people who lived at one time on the northern shore of the Black Sea, until they were driven thence by the Scythian hordes into Asia Minor.

The trouble is that the poet, or Circe, explicitly states that the land of the Cimmerians is a day's sail southward from Circe's island in the breath of the North wind, and that is difficult to reconcile with any location for the Cimmerians either on the North or the South shore of the Black Sea. Or, perhaps it is no trouble at all, for in the countries of the Odyssey there is no compass saving the poet's own mind. At any rate, if we were not sailing in the wake of Odysseus, we were in the wake of the Argonauts, those earlier Achaean adventurers, and there must have been a town in the place where Istanbul stands to-day, where the Argonauts watered their ships; for the Argonauts will have hugged the Northern shores, to keep well out of the clutches of the mysterious Amazons, or Hittites, or whoever they were, who invested the Southern shore.

An arc of light was strung out southward under the indigo hills. What place was that? That was Chanakkale. In order to reach Troy, it was to Chanakkale we would have to come later, after the *Abbazia* had landed us at Istanbul, to an anchorage where many of the ships of Priam's Trojan allies must have unloaded their crews of fighting men.

"*Ja, ja, hier links haben wir Sestos,*" a German voice, inextinguishably expository, floated up from the deck below. "Here on the left we have Sestos. On the right, it was once Abydos, now Chanakkale. Here swam Leander to his *Schatz*, his sweetheart, Hero, to her tower opposite. But it was no tower. It was only *Mythus.*"

Despite my addiction to attested truth, I was rather irritated to learn, at that moment, in that charged darkness, that the pale glimmering arms of Leander had never in sober fact cloven these swiftly-moving waters. The knowledgeable voice continued. "Here also swam across the English Lord, the Byron." My heart hovered in mid-beat, apprehensive. Was the English Lord also *Mythus*? No, he, at least, was history.

"What was that? Did he say Byron?" The English girls caught at the name, as if it were a dark feather floating by the tips of their fingers. Yes, yes, they remembered. Byron who evidently from this point had swum the Hellespont a century and a half ago. "Where?" they asked. "Where?"

The deck-steward was non-committal.

"*Li!*" he said, without pointing. "*Dunque!*" There, finally, from some invisible beach, the poet trailed into the water, and, kicking free with his good foot from the stubborn element, gave himself to the sea, free as the fish beneath or the birds over it.

"Here also," expounded the German voice, "between Sestos and Abydos, the Xerxes made his boat-bridge. But the tyrant was driven back. Europa was saved."

I could not help reflecting on the time to come when a later Xerxes was to strike from inside Festungeuropa.

On our starboard bow we left Chanakkale behind. Just beyond the sea-wall a large ship lay close to, a fine white-painted ship glimmering above the dark amethyst water. She was a Swede. Yes, a Swede. What was she doing there, not moving? Was it because she drew too much water for Chanakkale harbour? But surely. There was something odd about her bows. Yes, that was it. A great hole was gaping there.

Then slowly, like a wisp of smoke rising through the deck-boards, from nowhere at all the knowledge seeped into all our ears. The ship was the Swedish ship, the s.s. *Naboland*. Only a few hours ago that staved-in bow struck a Turkish submarine, issuing from behind Cape Nagara, that point there. She went down with a loss of seventy lives, eighty, no-one can say yet. There they lie, the poor youths, like our own drowned youngsters of the *Truculent*, the *Affray*—perhaps here, under our very keel.

We continued our voyage along the narrow straits, the tourists to their hotels, the peasants to their cabins. The crew members of the Swedish ship would sooner or later be on their way again to their little scrubbed houses in their Swedish home towns. But these lads under our thudding engines would not disembark in Chanakkale again, or Istanbul, or Izmir, to throw back a glass of *raki* in the seamen's bars, or to exchange photographs of their families with their mates, as sailors far from home do all the world over.

The mist thickened as we entered the Sea of Marmora. All night long the fog-horns called out to each other from ship to ship, and the moaning buoys lamented over sunken rocks. At length dawn came, but the mist only slowly dispersed. We were in the Bosphorus. Now at last the mist was totally gone, though the sky remained grey. The pageant of Istanbul defiled, white and grey, brown and grey, the ancient fortress walls, the great domes of the mosques set in the skiey hedge of their breathlessly thin minarets, the peeling gimcrack

palaces of nineteenth-century grandees, the sheds, the office buildings, the warehouses. Now at length we hove over to port into the
crowded waters of the Golden Horn thrust between flat-lying
higgledy-piggledy Istanbul, and Pera knee deep in dust, tottering
over, only just not sliding into its own gutters. A sack meandered
lolling along the water under the scuffling sea-gulls. One half hoped
it was the body of some long-ago Sultan's wife whom he had dis-
carded in a fit of pique, and the lady was now at last rising up from
the glimmering depths. Or perhaps it is older than that (I permitted
myself to speculate). Perhaps in that sack is the Golden Fleece which
Jason and his Argonauts went to acquire, sailing eastward through
these waters a long time ago.

The rationalizers of myths had said, even in antiquity, that if
you laid down a sheep's fleece in auriferous waters the wool would
trap the gold-dust, and from that beginning the whole complex and
beautiful legend started. At this day it is not known whether there
actually was a gold field in Calchis on the Southern shore of the
Black Sea, where the dragon of King Aeëtes guarded the fleece, and,
aided by the wiles of Medea, Jason captured it. In fact, most of the
gold the ancients used came from the regions later called Transyl-
vania, lying north, not south, from the Black Sea. But who knows
where the emporium was in which the gold was assembled? At all
events it is not unlikely that that was the sort of golden fleece that a
later generation of Greek adventurers sailed to capture, the generation of Menelaus and Odysseus, and the poets gave it the name of
Helen, the golden woman. But their kinsmen, the Trojans, had
taken possession of the town of Troy upon the hill that commanded
the narrows; and the Trojans demanded such preposterous dues
before the Achaean ships were allowed to pass through, that the
Achaeans determined to pull the place down. It is, of course, not
impossible there was a Golden Helen in Troy as well as a Golden
Fleece in Colchis, and neither one nor the other was the whole of the
matter. No-one will ever know now. The sack floating and bobbing
beyond the bows of our ship kept its counsel. The sea-gulls squawked
and scuffled as the sack passed from view. It was probably only a
sack of bread-crusts that some chef had at last decided he would
have no use for.

Istanbul is one of the cities that quickens the blood when you
merely utter the name of it. You can count yourself no collector of
cities till you have it there, safe in your pouch. But you must have the
sun for your first sight of it, I thought, or it will yield only slowly

whatever enchantments it has in store for you. And perhaps you must not approach it through shifting mist, with fog-horns keeping you awake all night, meditating morosely how young men pointlessly die in the prime of youth while statesmen round the green tables align themselves now in this formation, now in that, as Jooss so angrily traced in his ballet of between the wars.

We were well inside the harbour, with a chugging of tugs all round us, and a hooting of sirens from other ships impatient to be away, when suddenly such dry-eyed meditations as these were broken by an Olympian thunder. It was as shattering as if supreme Zeus himself had spoken. We turned to behold an enormous American aircraft-carrier, its decks crowded with jet-planes like a barley field with locusts. The sound I had thought to be the thunder of Zeus was the titan clamour of a jet engine being revved up, or hotted up, or whatever they do with jet engines. The shocked hill-slopes of Constantine's ancient city thundered back their protest.

"What is it all about?" I asked Edward, who is much nearer to the jet age than I. It was a terrifying prelude to raucous symphony of this city, with its *obbligati* for muezzin and klaxon-horn, brothel-pimp and fishmonger.

Edward proceeded to explain with enthusiasm. It was some mysterious business of using the carrier's superstructure as a sail, by directing the exhaust gases of the engine against its side. It was hoped thus to turn the ship round in the limited space they had there, in the crowded harbour. The process was not very clear to me. I only knew that the bones of the Sultans must have moved uneasily in their tombs.

II

The Customs officials, being Turks, talked Turkish. Had we been Schliemanns, we would have talked Turkish back, for it was precisely with the idea of talking Turkish back at Customs officials that the greatest of the neo-Trojans had mastered the language, taking some two weeks over the job, or maybe three.

But being no Schliemanns, we showed our papers instead. A blessing upon papers! I don't think it really matters what is written, typed or printed upon papers, so long as they are presented with an air of imperious confidence. It may be useful that they should bear some sort of stamp, the rubber sort or the sort you lick. And of course seals are particularly valuable. But let them be *papers*! And let them be *presented*!

The Customs people, the passport people, the currency people, were in a very awkward frame of mind that morning. We would have kicked our heels in the customs-shed for hours, as most of our fellow-passengers did. But, as I have said, we presented "papers".

A taxi was waiting for us out in the cobbled roadway. I don't mean it had been ordered for us, merely that we were predestined for each other, that ancient taxi so terribly up-to-date in its decoration. Once you had opened the door, replaced the door on its hinges, and allowed the vehicle to settle after the tremors caused by your subsidence into the seats, you found yourself facing a unique collection of ultra-modern decorative appurtenances, some stuck on to the windows, some nailed, clamped or glued on to the dash-board, others hanging by threads or chains from the steering-wheel, the gear-lever, or the struts in the roof. Plastic was the dominant material, as in the pink plastic-encased and blue plastic-bound miniature Koran, but there was a good deal of aluminium, as in the hanging model of an aeroplane. There were rexine flowers, feather dolls, celluloid bells and fans, and several musical instruments. The driver himself was a young man with large dark eyes, hair slick as a seal, and five gold teeth, which remained on exhibition in his swivelled-round head practically the whole time he drove us from the harbour to the Galata Bridge, and up along the dangerous steep slopes of Pera. His heart was as golden as his teeth, for we had not been in the taxi half a minute before he had presented me with a bunch of violets and Edward with a bag of sweets. Before he allowed us to descend at our hotel he insisted on celebrating our health in a café. We looked apprehensively at the taximeter, but he assured us with a wealth of gestures and a rolling of the great dark eyes that taximeters do not talk the language of love, and no-one loved anyone as much as we loved each other. We drank a great deal of Turkish coffee, devoured a good many lumps of Turkish Delight, but sooner or later, as we all knew, with embarrassment, the question of fares would have to be raised. Tears trembled in the driver's eyes as he at last broached the subject, somewhat obliquely, with melancholy reference to his mother who was dead, his wife who was dying, and his five children who were in a bad way. At length he demanded a sum so preposterous we sat there gazing at him stiff and speechless. With the help of the gendarmerie and the British Council, the least of their services to us, the affair was some time later liquidated.

An equivocal city, Istanbul, we had already decided, a city in suspension, like the Prophet's coffin, suspended between the old and the new, the west and the east. Where else could we have seen that taxi, or such a battleship as we looked out upon next day from the harbour quayside? A true "collector's piece" you might call it, if you were in the habit of collecting battleships. The mind went back instantly to pictures of the German Grand Fleet at the Battle of Jutland, with the prow curving outward at the waterline, the tall elaborate masts like the masts of sailing-ships, the three tall ungainly funnels; a tale we heard that day epitomized this ambivalence. It is a true tale, I believe. An I.T.G., an Important Turkish Gentleman, a Minister, in fact, was returning from an Important Mission abroad. Large numbers of his fellow countrymen had gathered at the airport to do him honour, in particular the Trades Union to which he was attached. A group of his top Trades Union officials had a ram with them, a very handsome fellow, with a coquettish blue rosette behind his ear.

"What's that for?" asked the senior official of the air-line that was carrying the I.T.G. He was English. His heart was thumping apprehensively.

"You know very well," said the Trades Union official severely. The Englishman had an idea. He had been in Turkey long enough for that. But he was hoping he was wrong.

"Whatever it is, can't you do it at your own offices?" he asked. "Or use ours, if you like? What about using the Minister's own home, maybe?"

"Certainly not," he was told.

"But what about the other passengers? It's going to upset them, you know."

The Secretary shrugged his shoulders. The other passengers did not concern him. And anyhow, it was a *very* Important Turkish Gentleman. There was nothing else for it. The Englishman went to the control tower and radioed to the pilot of the approaching aeroplane that the other passengers were to be detained inside the aircraft for some twenty minutes after landing.

In the meantime the ram had been led out on to the tarmac to await the I.T.G.'s descent from the clouds. There were still ten minutes or so to go, so the Treasurer of the Trades Union took out a steel comb and combed the ram's wool carefully, till it looked even more beautiful than before. At last the I.T.G. touched down. The steps were trundled up to the door of the aircraft, the door was opened and the I.T.G. began to descend. In the same moment, with a dexterous movement, the ram's throat was slit, amid a roar of

acclamation from the crowd. The Important Foot came down upon
a pool of blood. From the windows of the aircraft a couple of dozen
chalk-white western faces looked out upon the solemnization of the
marriage between east and west, old and new, the ram and the
aeroplane.

We were sitting at a café in the Taksim, the main street of Pera,
the more modern section of the city, as we heard this tale. A Turkish
lady was stepping out, wearing a ravishing confection that might
have come from Paris itself, if there had been less decoration, if the
material had been silk rather than satin, if the silk stockings had not
gleamed with so brassy a shimmer. Her mother's face, certainly her
grandmother's, had been hidden behind a black yashmak whenever
she appeared in public, if she ever did.

In the café behind us they were playing some dance-music—
Gershwin or somebody—a little out of date but quite sophisticated,
thoroughly western. In the café alongside, the radio was delivering
the official Turkish programme, male and female voices singing to
primitive instruments we could not identify. We had heard that song
and tune every hour of each day since we arrived in Istanbul. It may
actually have been a different song and a different tune. But it
sounded the same, terribly gloomy, very limited in scope, rendering
all the monotony and tragedy of the bare Anatolian spaces. Somebody murdered my girl. So I murdered his two brothers. So they
came to our village at the dead of night and it went up in flames. So
I called out my brothers and cousins . . . It was the song these Turks
were singing when the Crusaders met them at Acre and Kerak. It
was the song they were singing some centuries later when they lay
outside the walls of this very town, and at last captured it, and laid
it waste with fire and sword.

Yes, it is a queer city, where one is never quite on balance. I
mean quite literally. I wandered round the corner from the café. A
vast new Packard was almost sliding down a cobbled slope of one-in-
four, rubbing the flanks of a horse so decrepit it hardly looked like a
horse any more. It was dragging a brakeless and desperately over-
laden cart and the hooves maintained their grip on the frightful
slope only with extreme difficulty.

Across the street the "Rita Hayworth U.S. Navy Nicht Club"
extended a welcoming banner across the cobbles. A few yards away
the U.S. Navy was further assured: "Pigal welcom you Sailors,
Kabare, dancing stuff visit aile Night." Then fifty yards along the
street another sort of welcome awaited another sort of votary. We
entered a small mosque. Ahead of us ran a couple of business-men,

Athens: The Parthenon

Along the Hellespont

Istanbul: Across the Galata Bridge

complete with homburg and brief-case, taking off their shoes as they ran, as if they had an appointment with Allah and his Prophet, and they were afraid they would be late for it. The old men were already at their prayers, raising and prostrating themselves with such agility that you wondered whether there were any bones inside those loose envelopes of desiccated flesh. In a deep twilight, on the raised platform where females are segregated, a handful of old women were immobile, curled round upon themselves like the foetus in the womb, their foreheads stuck as with a gum, upon the faded carpet. It was as if they, too, had made an appointment long, long ago with the Prophet, and he had never turned up, and all the rest of the world had forgotten about them.

For these are the women whom the more recent Prophet, Kemal Ataturk, the creator of Modern Turkey, has not emancipated, despite all his prodigious efforts to secularize his country, he who made Sunday the day of rest, Latinized the tortuous script, abolished the fez and the yashmak. As for those women who believe themselves emancipated, who walk the streets in high heels thin as minarets, and at endless evening receptions wear a *décolleté* for which their husbands of an earlier day would have had them sewn up in sacks, I wonder if they are as emancipated as they think. I went one night to a wedding reception at the smart Karavanserai Rooms. I had never met so profound an air of gloom. Two comedians were trying to entertain them. The air was heavy with unshed tears. The band played. Nobody danced. Everyone sat and stared gloomily. One got the impression that in their heart of hearts the men hated seeing their wives thus exposed to public scrutiny. The women would really have preferred sitting in their cosy harems, eating endless Turkish Delight, and twittering like happy canaries. The music went round and round. The tears did everything but flow.

Kemal Ataturk died too soon, I told myself sadly. Had he lived as long as Churchill or the late Mr. Stalin, he would have left this city and this land in a better equilibrium. I consoled myself in Santa Sophia, and the Blue Mosque, and the Mosque of Suleiman the Magnificent, though Heaven knows that they are no place for a traveller to linger in whose prime concern is the wanderings of Odysseus, who chafes at the bit each day he is kept away from the embarkation for Troy. But I cannot refrain from recording one or two of the less trumpeted splendours.

As, item: two out of all the fabulous riches in the show-cases of the Seraglio. First—the squat figure of a Sultan shaped from a single great pearl. Under a palanquin of striped red and buff enamel

C

he sits, the palanquin surmounted by a crescent moon made of diamonds and rubies, from which rise five diamond feathers bound by an emerald girdled with gold thread. The pillars supporting the palanquin are spirals of emerald and rose-pink enamel. He sits on a green and gold enamelled cushion tasselled at each corner and wears turquoise breeches, the cushions lying on a rose-pink enamel base. In his hand is the drawn gold thread cable of his narghileh. Before him lies a gold wire basket in which a translucent amethyst pannier holds a gold-wrapped bouquet of rubies and emeralds. Two: Below the Sultan crouches his blackamoor, who wears a thick-crusted turban of diamonds spitting with sharp rubies, the turban surmounted by a diamonded crescent. His bolero is made up likewise of diamonds packed with rubies. His trousers are of pearl, he wears diamond putties. He is no end of a blackamoor, of whom even so dazzling a Sultan may well be proud. A group of raggle-taggle Anatolian soldiers passes by, their greatcoats sweeping the dust of the cold stone floor. It is all theirs, all theirs, Kemal Ataturk has handed it to them. Their noses are blue and their hands puffed with cold. It is a very cold day. Beyond the windows, through a flurry of petals flung from the twisting fruit trees, you look out on the leaden-grey waters of the Bosphorus, scored with wind and current.

Those items, then, from the Seraglio. These items from the vegetable and fish market behind our hotel: pale green leeks as large as truncheons; purple cabbages unveiling bosoms more luscious than roses; orange carrots diminishing towards their jade green tops; artichokes like green begonias; cauliflowers spuming like water amongst rocks; glowing globes of apple-sized radishes; sliced ivory pumpkins baring peach-coloured midriffs; anemones stuck coyly between baskets of courgettes resting on beds of cabbage-leaves; painted eggs clustered like clumps of scarlet roe; plump chickens hanging, their heads wrapped in electric blue paper; the shell-fish, *tarak*, opening, shutting, like winking negro eyes; sharks' fins for parrot cages encompassed by paper rosettes; a rosy glow from candles stuck deep inside barrels of apples so that each is a great bronze lantern; tiny paraffin lamps behind jars of honey that bloom like blobs of amber; groves of hanging salami wrapped in acid-green, coral-red, tinfoil covers. Everybody selling something, buying something, or at small tables, eating, drinking, as if this were not any day in the week but the night before the Day of Judgment, and there will be no eating or drinking any more. A man moves over to us with a hanging aquarium of mussels. Another competes with a pile of shrimps in a great scoop painted sealing-wax-red and shaped like the oblong shield of a Homeric warrior. A small rat-faced, bare-foot boy will not be out of this saturnalia. He carries about hopefully a battered cardboard lid on which are displayed five or six grubby caramels. A fishmonger hard by is attracting a *kalkas*, a huge nodulous flat fish, wielding his battleaxe knife with a great to-and-fro flourish and a chatter-chatter on the brass plate, as of starlings on telegraph wires.

This was the Eve of the day on which Allah enjoined Mohammed to take the Moslems in his care and show them the right way. It was also the evening of the day on which we were to sail for Troy. We sat down to celebrate the double occasion at a restaurant in a coign of the market-place. Over us extended the blossom of a pink oleander, which looked like paper in the hissing light. As we waited for the grilled sword-fish we had ordered, a youth came up from behind a bank of tulips massed on a base of carnations, and weighed out a quart or two of shrimps, scooping them from the Homeric shield where they lay against the sealing-wax lacquer. There followed a plate of *apikoglu*, dry cheese-cakes, which the faithful devour in great quantities on this day, as, on their own occasions, Christians devour Hot Cross Buns and Jews Pockets-of-Haman, stuffed with poppy-seed. The *apikoglu* were washed down with divers glasses of *raki*, raised to those heroes of the Iliad we most looked forward to meeting at Troy, and on Scamander's banks. Now came sword-fish, flanked by a Kavaklideri, a pleasant Turkish-type hock. For dessert there was a dish of nuts in deep honey, with a glass of the banana liqueur they make in this Moslem land, Prophet or no Prophet. Not even the pigeons of the Hotel Konak would have awakened us next morning, if we had not given orders to be awakened before the crack of dawn . . . those regrettable pigeons of the Hotel Konak which of all winged creatures in my experience I remember with least pleasure. In fact with so little pleasure, I feel I must spare a moment for anathema before I leave Istanbul.

Our rooms looked out on the narrowest of courtyards, less a courtyard than a shaft, less a shaft than a chimney. The other court-yard of the Konak was protected from the affliction by a stout roof of wire netting stretched between the top floors. Not ours. At all hours of the day the pigeons flew in to the shaft, flew out again—those ululant amorous pigeons, those beady-eyed splenetic pigeons, crop-gorged, puff-bosomed, immeasurably conceited. Even at night there would be pigeons clucking or somnambulating in nightmare. If one had been a Fabre with a special devotion to pigeons, how supreme a vantage-point those windows of the Konak would have provided, as the pigeons flickered and fluttered from window-ledge to eaves, to projecting gutter, back again to eaves and window-ledge; as they cooed in each other's ears; as they pecked affectionately for fleas in each other's necks! Even we, who are no Fabres, began to recognize them apart, to find distinctive modulations in their cooing, to hate them with a differentiated as opposed to a mass hatred. How pleasant it was to see Johnnie (as we called him), who always led the early dawn chorus, open his beak, get a mouthful of rusty rain-water, spit it out, and relapse sulkily into his neck-feathers! What fun to see Minnie collect offerings of straw and seed for her para-mour! What tale-tellings went on, what thievings, what adulteries! What a joy it was to say good-bye to them, that very early morning when we set off for Troy!

III

Homer has made Odysseus very much an individual. But of course there is an Odysseus type, of which there have been speci-mens in literature both before and after the days of the King of Ithaca. In London a Turkish man-of-letters revealed to me the existence of a Turkish Odysseus who goes back, he assured me, a long time before the Greek one. He didn't know much about it himself, Dietz was the authority. Dietz had written a book called *The Book of Dede Korkut*, this Dede Korkut being a Turkish trouba-dour, though he was not clear of what epoch. Anyhow, the original manuscript was in Dresden, where one could consult it as soon as the opportunity presented itself. Dede Korkut's work was divided into twelve sections, one of which is called "Tepegöz", that is, "Cyclops", no less. It is the "Tepegöz" section which Dietz compares with the Odyssey. He holds it is considerably older, and the inference is that somehow Homer had access to it. I gathered further, that some year or so ago another MSS. had been found in the Vatican, by a certain Rossi, who published a photostat of six of the twelve books with the University of Rome, as well as a translation.

There were one or two other indications, contended the Turkish scholar, that Homer was in touch with the Turkish epic. There is, for instance, the description in the Iliad of the way they roasted meat on skewers. "When the thighs were burned up, and they had tested the inner parts, they carved the rest into small pieces, pierced them with skewers, roasted them thoroughly, and drew them all off."

With excitement I made enquiries about the work in Istanbul, but could get no satisfaction. We would have to go to Troy, after all. And the way to Troy is by Chanakkale, the small port we had passed to starboard as we steamed up the Dardanelles some ten days or more ago.

It was probably fairly easy to travel there in the period between the wars. But we had been warned in London it was anything but easy now. In fact the country on both sides of the straits is a high-voltage military area, and since the end of the second war it has been extremely difficult to get a permit to go wandering in those parts, at least until lately. When I arrived in Istanbul I applied for permits through our Embassy in Ankara, sending copies of those comforting "papers" with which I had been fortified in London. I found, how-ever, that I myself had introduced a slight complication into the matter. Over in England, the Authorities had, some time earlier, arranged for me to go on a short cruise in a submarine to gather material for a novel I have in mind. It was an exhilarating experi-ence, and when a journalist asked for a sketch of my plans, I told him I had been so happy in H.M.S. *Tiptoe* I hoped it might be possible for our British Naval Mission in Athens, when I reached there, to arrange for my transport in a submarine to the shore of the windy plain of Troy. What could be more fitting, I asked, than to follow in the belly of a Steel Horse where a Wooden Horse had gone before?

It was a remark recorded with more seriousness than I had intended. I was at once flattered and chagrined to discover they knew about it in Ankara. However an assurance came to me that I need not consider myself *persona ingrata* in Troy. Favourable advices would be sent to the authorities in Chanakkale.

So (as I said) one would have to get to Chanakkale, and pre-sumably by one of the coasting steamers that take in the small ports. I went into the office of a well-known travel agency and requested information from a young man, a Greek, I thought he was. He did not hear me, though he was disengaged. He stood behind his counter, thinking. I asked again, a shade more loudly. He permitted his long-lashed eyes to rest on me a moment.

"Where you say?" he murmured.

"Chanakkale."

"Where?"

"Chanakkale. *You* know. The port in the Dardanelles, on the south shore."

"I never hear from it."

"You get off there," I said, "when you go to the ruins of Troy."

Did I see a flicker of hostility in his eyes? Was he descended from

a fanatical Achaean who detested the very sound of anything
Trojan? Perhaps not.

"We are not interested," he said remotely, "in that sort of
travel." At that moment an American business-man came in, of the
broad-shouldered type, in a loose Palm Beach suiting, wearing a
Panama hat circled with a cross-hatched blue and silver hat-band.
He was even smoking a cigar. He was the sort of client for whom you
fix up air travel to Colombo or Bermuda, with first-class hotel
reservations. You probably give him advice about the stores he
should patronize and arrange his evening entertainments. He almost
certainly had his wife, Shirley, with him, back at the hotel, and
perhaps his two daughters.

The young Greek's eyes glowed like lumps of amber with the sun
behind them. He almost, not quite, rubbed his hands.

"Good-morning, sir. Yes, sir?" he said with the voice of a Hotel
Konak turtle-dove.

The Senator opened his mouth, but the words were not given
time to leave it.

"I said I wanted information about Chanakkale," I exclaimed
loudly and firmly. "Excuse me, sir," I added, turning to the Senator
from Wyoming. (Everything was becoming very clear and specific.
By now I knew exactly what the young assistant did in his off time
to supplement his income.) I bowed. Mr. Hiram K. Bubenshacher
bowed, too. He was rich, but his manners were good. I turned to
Dimitriados again.

"You are not interested in that sort of travel?" I said icily. "You
are not interested in Troy? You have never heard of Homer? Give
me the manager!" I demanded.

I was given the manager, but I soon saw I was being fobbed off
with an assistant-manager.

"I want the chief manager," I insisted. "The chief manager in
all Turkey." Employees in all directions were beginning to look
apprehensive. A messenger went out. A telephoning went on.
At last I was escorted to an office on the first floor, where I met the
chief manager in all Turkey. I showed him my "papers", with
special reference to those in the Turkish language. He apologized.
From one drawer he produced a box of Turkish Delight, from
another a box of cigars. He sent out for coffee. He brought from his
drawer folders crammed with schedules. He studied them profoundly, extended his studies by telephone, cajoled, threatened,
waved his free hand. At last he returned to me with a distillation of
the information he had gleaned.

"There will be a boat leaving for Smyrna in ten days. It will call at Chanakkale on its return."

My heart sank.

"That won't do," I said. "It is too late. Please try again." Nothing was too much trouble. There was more Turkish Delight and a good deal of note-taking on pads. It was the fifth conversation which was the triumphant one. He beamed all over.

"You don't say?" he asked the unseen partner in the conversation. (That is what I judged the words to mean.) He *did* say, apparently. The chief manager turned, rosy as an apple. "You go by bus!" he proclaimed.

"Bus?"

"Yes, bus!"

And, of course, why not? People on both sides of the water come up from the country and go back again. Perhaps one crossed to Skutari in Asia and went westward along the southern shore? Or perhaps westward here, direct from Istanbul? Yes, that was the way, of it. Early in the morning one took a bus at the Sirkeçi station for Gallipoli. One arrived there eight hours later, and found one's way somehow, by taxi or boat to Maydos. At Maydos one hired a motorboat to take one across the straits to Chanakkale. It was as easy as that.

We thanked the chief manager profusely. He had taken a great deal of trouble in our behalf. We had also eaten a lot of Turkish Delight.

"You've not gone yet?" asked the British Consular official. The time was that evening, the place the lounge of the hotel.

"We're going to-morrow."

"Be there in good time. You never know when they move off."

"Could one get tickets in advance?"

"The shipping-offices will be closed now."

"Shipping-offices? We're going by bus."

"By bus?" The official opened his eyes. "You mean by Gallipoli?"

"That's right. They worked it out at the agency there."

"But you haven't got a permit, have you? *I* don't know about one."

"No, we haven't."

"Do you want to be hanged, drawn and quartered?"

"Not particularly."

"It's just as much a military area as the other side. But they've been advised about you at Chanakkale. It should be all right. Go by boat, gentlemen. What day is it? Oh yes. There's a boat leaving to-morrow. Eight o'clock."

"We'll go by boat," we said humbly.

"Oh by the way——"

"Yes?"

"There's been an earthquake in those parts lately. Did you know?"

"Vaguely." We had heard of an earthquake round there, but it had not been associated especially with Chanakkale.

"You won't be comfortable," he warned us.

"So long as we get there," we said.

Next morning we asked the hotel clerk to tell the taxi-driver to put us down at the office of the Chanakkale-Smyrna line.

"Make sure he's got it right!" I insisted. "The office of the Chanakkale-Smyrna line!"

The clerk repeated it to the driver, the driver repeated it to us. "The office of the Chanakkale-Smyrna line!"

We got into the taxi and bumped down the steep streets towards the quayside. Beyond the bridge the fabulous domes supervised the city and its Faith like enormous djinns. The Battle of Jutland cruiser in the Golden Horn looked hopelessly anachronistic; as it might have been the transport which long ago carried to Troy the Trojan allies, the warlike Cicones, the Thracians whose lands are bounded by the swift-flowing Hellespont, and the Paeonians with their curving bows.

The driver deposited us at an office building on the waterside.

"For Chanakkale?" we demanded, making sure.

"Chanakkale!" he confirmed enthusiastically.

We entered the offices, which were mainly stone-masons and carpenters. The flooring was either rubble or wet cement, which you traversed on planks. On dry islands baulks of timber were being sawn, partitions were being assembled, glass was being cut, paint was being mixed. But there certainly was a small area at the far end of the building devoted to clerical activities, with a counter, a dais with several chairs, and a proliferation of telephones like fungi round a tree-stump. Behind the counter was a well-dressed clerk in a blue-pin-stripe suit.

We negotiated the hazards and addressed him. He was very busy with files and carbon-copies and things.

"We want two tickets for Chanakkale, please."

"Chanakkale!" he repeated, and nodded. He requested us to take two chairs on the dais. "Coffee?" he asked. We were not interested.

"The boat *does* leave at eight?"

He nodded, but the eye was unresponsive. I was talking French. I had a feeling he did not know the language. I switched over to elementary Greek, and pointed to the fingers of the clock. "Boat—leave—eight?"

"Eight!" he repeated.

"What about tickets?" I apparently did not have the right Greek word for tickets. I pointed to the papers on his desk. "Chanakkale! Tickets!" I repeated.

"Yes, yes!" He indicated the chairs. One inferred if one would only sit down, the ticket matter would adjust itself. We sat down. The minutes passed. It was now seven-thirty. Even with the tickets in hand, we would still have to find the boat. Clouds of grey dust moved around disconsolately. There was a great noise of sawing, hammering, planing, grinding. I noticed for the first time that the long wall behind the clerks was decorated with an immense mural portraying Mercator's projection in bright colours. The countries were cunningly outlined in raised metal contours. It was all done in an ultra-modern manner and with the best craftsmanship. I say I noticed the mural for the first time, because somehow I did not realize it belonged to the room I was in. It was like the ultra-modern opera house which they have begun some years ago and have not money to finish, and when they have finished it, they will have no operas for it, and if they perform Western operas they will not have the ears for it. It was like the smart Turkish ladies, and the smart men's shops advertising "English Tweet". It was contemporary Turkey, left suspended by Kemal Pasha in mid-air, no longer there, not yet here.

I took a grip on myself. There was no time for rumination.

"Chanakkale!" I called mournfully from my exile on the dais.

There was now another clerk behind the counter. The two put their heads together.

"Yes, yes!" repeated the first clerk.

"What do you mean yes, yes? I want my tickets!"

"Café!" the two clerks said in unison, and clapped their hands. At the doorway a small man with the paraphernalia of shoe-shining appeared, then at once disappeared. The swishing of wet puddles of cement continued, the hammering of nails.

"Chanakkale!" I called again. "Tickets!" I was like a curlew calling in a moorland.

"Telephone!" said the second clerk in a sudden onrush of inspiration. He disengaged one of the telephones from the cluster, and talked into it, then stopped talking.

The shoe-black now appeared. He had laid down his brushes in favour of a brass tray, supported by three twisted brass supports held from the hand like a weighing-machine. Beside it a little brass vase held anemones. Very pretty, but we were worried about our tickets.

"Tickets!" I shouted, with more spleen than before. "Not coffee! Chanakkale! Ship!"

The two clerks looked helplessly at each other, then put their heads together. They emerged from their conference some minutes later, with an expression of enlightenment on their faces.

"Oh, tickets!" they confirmed. "Ship! Chanakkale!" Then they got back to their pink copy-sheets again. I could stand it no longer. I flung away from my chair on the dais and hurtled against the counter.

"What the hell!" I roared. "The ship leaves in five minutes! I want those tickets for Chanakkale!" I think I was talking Turkish now, using a number of dreadful Turkish words I had no idea till that moment that I knew.

The shoe-black leaned over towards the clerks, the clerks consulted with the shoe-black.

"Oh!" said the clerks. "They want tickets for Chanakkale!" They saw it all now. "Take them! Quick!" they insisted. "Or it will be late!" It was a minute to eight. The shoe-black sped ahead of us. He was wearing bright blue breeches patched with a bright red moon. Apart from the blue breeches, the next few minutes were a blur and a nightmare, with our luggage knocking sharply against our knee-caps. So we raced half-way across the dockside area, thrusting aside hawkers, policemen, Customs men, cycles, carts, cars, and reached another office at last, the right office, very cosy and efficient. We got our tickets in no time, then raced back to the quay-side again, to the pier where the Chanakkale boat was loading up; the *Gidis*, her name was, an old steamer built, maybe, at the turn of the century, with a curving prow and a bowsprit reminiscent of the old tea-clippers. But for some time I was hardly in a state to appraise her, my breath laboured as if I were Ixion himself, and the eyes were nearly dropping out of my head.

"Is all right," a kindly passenger assured me at the barrier. "In two hours. Then she go." He pointed to a towsle of soldiers shuffling along the quay towards a barrier. They were obviously going to hold things up for some time. The barrier had two openings, one for ordinary human beings, the other for livestock and soldiers. The soldiers looked a great deal like livestock, except for the fact that many held hands. In just the same way they ambled and drifted along, or suddenly quickened their gait in a round-and-round flurry. Every minute or two they clotted at the gap in the barrier, like sheep entering a sheep-dip. Once inside, the job was to get them to form in line. One gaping youth, with huge shoulders and ears like wings, seemed to have not the faintest idea what it was all about. Breaking line once, then a second time, he shambled forward to stare at this fantastic thing, this ship. None of them had seen a ship before (I learned later) except when they took the midnight ferry across the narrow water a night or two ago. The officer in charge suddenly lost his temper and kicked the man's rear furiously again and again. The face remained quite impassive.

They were an uncouth collection, with their shoes like soaked cardboard, their uniforms traversing thirty shades of khaki from straw-yellow to nigger-brown, pea-green and mole-grey, their safety-pins and bits of string for buttons, their parcels wrapped in frayed bits of sacking. It is no concern of mine, God knows, how the Turkish War Office dresses its recruits, but I was conscious that the spectacle was making me feel not only embarrassed but quite angry. Is there any excuse, I wondered, for demeaning youngsters by making them look such scarecrows? Or is it merely a technique, a discipline? I saw Turkish soldier-prisoners in the other war, and I have seen films of Turkish soldiers fighting of late in Korea, and they do not look in the least like this. And that day in the Dardanelles, as I rubbed shoulders with them and talked with them, or tried to, I perceived there was a good deal more of the mastiff or the bear in them than of any tamer animal. I told myself that in those deep-set slightly slanting eyes one could glimpse the soldier who has been so feared since his first appearance in the battlefields of history; one could trust men like these to keep intact behind their brawny shoulders the frontiers of the country Atatürk has confided to them.

The harbour was very crowded that morning. In addition to local ferry-boats, harbour dredgers, cargo-boats, caiques, coasters, police launches, motor barges, schooners, there were a great many foreign ships. The American aircraft-carrier was back again, with two destroyers. There were several up-to-the-minute Italian-built passenger vessels, with delicately curving bows and streamlined funnels and superstructure. There was a solitary British cargo vessel, very clean and trim, built on strictly business-like lines. I could make out a solitary seaman with his back up against a stanchion, bent over a newspaper. I had no doubt he was working out his football pools, though the paper was an old one, and his coupon would certainly not arrive in time. He was keeping his hand in, in the supreme religious rite of the English week. That was enough for him. And there was one more steamer riding alone at anchor, with so wide a space round it it seemed that other ships were giving it a wide berth, though perhaps that was fancy, or coincidence. It was a handsome vessel with a pearl-grey hull, electric-welded, very modern. It had a cream-coloured funnel with a red and black band. It flew the Turkish flag at the mast-head, and the Swedish at the stern. It was, in fact, the s.s. *Naboland*, the ship which had rammed the Turkish submarine ten days or so ago. The hole in the bows just above the water-line looked larger, more naked and horrid, than when we had first sighted it in the mist and the darkness off Chanakkale. A little fleet of inquisitive skiffs ran busily round it, like Capri boats come to survey the Blue Grotto, or blow-flies clustering round a stricken beast.

It was a sad sight. A picture of the ship's captain thrust into my thoughts, not for the first time, his head on his hand, his red beard splayed on his chest. He was a sad man, wherever he was. I tried to concentrate on the great city now falling behind us, the long grey line of walls topped with infrequent cypresses, the bastions of the Seraglio, Santa Sophia with her minarets and dome, the shops, the offices, the fretted wooden houses that somehow have not yet been destroyed by fire, this city that in these few days had ceased to be a background in a spy-story or a backcloth in a foreign-speaking play, that had ceased to be merely aesthetic or history and had become flesh-and-blood. At last the mosques, the harbour, the tragic Swedish ship, were invisible. As I moved to go over into the saloon, my eye caught sight of a typed news-sheet on the notice-board: *The captain of the Swedish ship,* Naboland, *which sank the Turkish submarine in the Dardanelles, causing the death of 83 members of the crew* . . .

The feeling came over me that wherever we moved in these regions we would be attended by the ghosts of eighty-three dead men and one still alive, all of them waiting with set mouths for the moment when steel ground against steel and the midnight water came in, tumbling and rolling like a school of porpoises.

Every inch of space on the forrard and aft well-decks and along the passageways was crowded with the soldiers we had taken on, looking as close-packed and furry in their greatcoats as a grove of

nettles by a churchyard wall. Then, when we had left the Islands of
the Princes on our port bow, and the waters of Marmora opened up
before us, suddenly from the forward hatches we heard a strumming
at an instrument, and a man's voice singing to it, singing with all his
dazzling teeth, with a beautiful candour, and a heart-breaking
sadness. Then a soldier beside him played a sort of shepherd's pipe,
emitting a thin, high sound, like midges above reeds. The instruments seemed like things outside time, having been fabricated by the
players themselves out of such bits and pieces as you might find in a
remote village in the high plains. One was a sort of banjo, *cün büs*,
they called it; the other was a pipe, a *zurna*, cut from an amber-
coloured wood, with a tin horn at its end. I felt that music like this
might have been heard long ago on board those earlier ships sailing
to strengthen Troy, when King Priam sent word to his allies that he
needed the help they were sworn to give him. For the Achaeans
were massed at Aulis and any day now their scarlet and blue prows
might be sighted beyond Samothrace. So they sang their songs of
kidnap and rape and murder, always, to the untutored ear, so much
the same song. Then in an hour or so, or it might have been less, or
it might have been much more, somehow a space of a few feet was
cleared on the choc-a-bloc hatch and a soldier rose from his haunches
and did a solo dance of incredible intricacy, the other soldiers
clapping their hands in time, sharply, loudly, like machine-gun fire.
Then it was three soldiers spontaneously rising and dancing together,
shoulder to shoulder. The man on the right had his right hand
upraised, waving a strip of rag in time with the music, his left hand
resting on the right shoulder of the next man. The man in the
middle had the right hand upraised, the left arm on the shoulder of
the third. The third man, too, had the right hand upraised, the free
left arm balanced against his hip. Then this third man detached
himself from his fellows, did a *pas seul*, then came up sharp, as if a
rope had been thrown round his ankles; then the second man did his
pas seul, then the first, all in such perfect rhythm you could believe
they had danced together since childhood, though probably they
had not set eyes on each other till a day or two ago. Inside that
clumsy and dishonouring clothing their bodies became precise and
heroic, while all the time the player on the *cün büs* sat over against
them, singing out of the white flare of his teeth.

So the noontime hours went by, and the music tinkled and died,
and the soldiers sat leaning against each other's backs, dozing. One
group devoted itself to a three-man job of shaving, one supplying
the beard, one holding up a sliver of mirror and a mug of cold water,

and a third wielding a rusty razor. I saw a soldier wander into the first-class part of the ship, very unsure of himself, and puzzled about the strange things he saw. Here people did not lie about on bare planks. They had small rooms to themselves. They had taps. Yes, you pressed them, and water came out. One of the cabins thus visited was a woman's. There was a powder-puff on a ledge and a pink plastic hair-brush. She had put out a silk dress on her berth. The soldier reached his hand forward to see what the feel of the garment was. It was soft and strange. He savoured it between finger and thumb. Then he tittered. "Mustapha!" he called out, to a friend who was not far off. Mustapha came. He, too, fingered the thing and tittered. Then both shambled back again to their mates, to tell them of the marvels they had seen.

The hours lengthened. So did our shadows as we leaned over the deck-rail. The contours of the hills of the southern Marmora were now softened to velvet. It was time now for the faithful to turn to Mecca, and after an earnest consultation as to the direction in which Mecca lay, a small dark hook-nosed soldier detached himself from the rest, went up on the top deck, took his boots off, bent his legs under him, touched the boards with his forehead, and began to mutter his prayers. Now and again he raised his head, still muttering, the sunset washing his eyelids with golden water.

I wondered how soon some, at least, of the other soldiers would join him at his prayers up there on the empty top deck, for certainly there was no room on and around the hatches to bend your legs under you and touch the boards with your forehead. But none did, not one. A few were still singing, one or two dancing, some went on nibbling at lumps of bread hard and grey like sea-raddled limestone. The man on the top deck was isolated, like a dark and uncouth fish in a tank. Why was this? I asked myself. These peasants were far too simple to be self-conscious about reciting their prayers in public. Had Kemal Ataturk's attempt to secularize his country achieved a much more radical success than the anti-god zealots in the new Russia? I did not think it was that. I had a feeling that they had hardly heard of Kemal Ataturk in the aboriginal wilds whence they had been brought; that even Mohammed to them was comparatively a new and alien name, that their affinity was rather with those more ancient stocks on the fringes of pre-history, the Hittites on the southern shores of the Black Sea, and the more fabulous peoples on the northern shore, Cicones and Cimmerians.

As I stood there reflecting on these matters, someone had sighted a mysterious black creature leaping out there from the violet and pale green waters. The singing and dancing petered out. Everyone rushed to the port rail. Out of the depths jumped a whole school of dolphins, glistening in the sunset. "Ah-ah-ah!" sighed all the young men with one voice. It was exactly like children when fireworks suddenly explode in glory at the top of the sky, though this marvel was from the depths of the sea. Even the young man praying had no thought for the Prophet. His body was still turned to Mecca, but his head was twisted towards the portent, the prayers frozen like foam upon his lips, and his hands curved and stiff like the paws of a stuffed beast. "Ah!" they went again, the wonder shining in their eyes. It was not for nothing they had travelled in cattle-trucks for weeks from their villages and homesteads in the dusty Anatolian plains.

It was late. The sea was an infinite shoal of mother-of-pearl mackerel, sliding towards the west. As the sun lit up one after another an endless succession of cliffs, the top of each cliff in turn was bright as copper, cut off sharply from the dark isthmus that led to it. Then the water seemed to turn within the shores that contained it and slip over its shoulders a garment of daffodil yellows and breathless egg-shell blues. In a second the garment had slipped again. The sun now projected a bar of brassy light that lay like a column just below sea-level, and the water poured over it and did not quench it. The Asian ridges were diaphanous, pulsing like the throats of birds. And now at last there was no sun. The European ridges were glaciers and the ice was frozen wine. Like the ghost of the dead day, like the ghost of the soldiers who had died there, a mist rose thin and forlorn along the foreshores of Gallipoli.

We went down and had supper. They put *kuzu kizastmasi* before us, and *zeyten yagle cali fasulye*. I cannot recall what those dishes looked or tasted like, though I imagine, perhaps mistakenly, the *fasulye* are beans. For it was the mystery of Mehmet, the waiter, that absorbed me, Mehmet with whom I talked German, who, therefore, was more mysterious than if we had had no speech at all in common. He was not a Turk. The face was flat and Mongolian. He had been born in the Crimea, a Russian subject. The skin was smooth and pale, like a bean that has been kept for years in a jar in a preserving spirit. He may have been twenty years old, he may have been fifty. Time seemed to have ignored the eyes as well as the skin. The Nazis had come to the Crimea. He had worked for the Nazis, because he hated the Russians so fiercely. But his dead tone and mouth and eyes so completely failed to commit him to his hatred, that we felt he perhaps hated the Nazis and loved the Russians. He went off with the Nazis to Czechoslovakia, and after the expulsion of the Sudeten Germans found himself a Western German in Munich. Brazil suddenly entered the story, as if Brazil, Munich, Tashkent, Lahore, were all the same place in a world without differentiation and without dimension. He was now a Turkish subject, he said. One felt that if some-one turned a ring on his finger, he might be a Russian again, having been born a Russian; or perhaps a Portuguese.

The Captain in charge of the soldiers dined at the same table. He had lost one of the stars on his shoulder-strap during the day, and the loss made him look as unkempt as the rudest of his soldiers, so spick-and-span was the rest of him, the black-beetle hair, the warm mahogany shoes, and the seed-pearl teeth, where a tooth-pick ran ceaselessly in and out, in and back again, like a mouse in a cage. Beside the Captain was an official in the Customs service, rather seedy now, getting on in years, but doubtless in his day he, too, had been as spick-and-span as the army officer beside him. He had, in fact, been an officer in the Turkish Navy during the other war, and seemed to resent his lost splendour. He had not only been a naval officer, but the captain of a destroyer that had rammed a British submarine. He recalled his feat, true or not, with extraordinary relish. It seemed to reconcile him somehow to the destruction of a Turkish submarine many years later, in almost the same waters. "There were no survivors," he said. "Not one." He grinned all over his face. "But that is a long time ago now. We are friends. We are happy. We are twenty-one million people in a country big enough for fifty. We are a western people." At that moment the radio embarked on another threnody, as ghoulish as anything we had heard that evening.

"You'll have to learn new songs," I said. "What's that one about?"

He listened, with evident distaste.

"It's all about the sufferings of our people," he explained at length, "those that were left behind in Macedonia after the Greeks . . ." He found difficulty in stating the thought. After the Greeks had driven out the Turks, he meant. He clapped his hands, and summoned Mehmet. Some minutes later, the radio was switched off and a gramophone-record of a Beethoven quartette was relayed in its place. It was a scratchy record, but it was Beethoven, it was the west. "Ah!" he murmured, and blew a cloud of cigarette-smoke through his pursed lips.

Istanbul: The market

Istanbul:
The harbour

We went up on deck. There were no stars. The mountains of the southern shore were like a dark backcloth slung behind an already lightless stage. A few lights north and south winked red and white. We went below and drank coffee. It was Chopin now, not Beethoven. Time moved slowly. It would be well after midnight by the time we arrived, after one, probably. Where would we be spending the night? There must be an inn or two in Chanakkale. Would they be open so late? Would they, after the earthquake, be in any state to take in travellers? We began to be a little disquieted. It would be a comfortless night, on the quayside, among the dust and rubble. We dozed a little, then went on deck again. We were in the Dardanelles now, the southern shore close to, the northern not far off. A shaggy heap stirred like a sleeping hound on the well-deck, then a second, then a third. The soldiers were coming up out of their sleep, as if to a voice whispering in their ears. A light glared and turned away and glared again. It was at last the eastward beacon of Chanakkale. More lights traced the further curve of the harbour. The soldiers were now crowded thick against the port rail, whispering and muttering.

"This is another fish than dolphins," I said to myself, "that is exciting them now." The skin creaked on my scalp.

"Down there!" the soldiers whispered, and pointed to the depths with their blunt fingers, where their kinsmen were, the drowned sailors.

Now, at last, some half-hour later, we were drawn up against the quayside of Chanakkale, once Abydos on the Trojan shore. Only an hour or so away, before a favouring wind, was the harbour by Scamander's mouth where the Achaeans disembarked, and the ships heeled over sideways on the reedy sands. There, among the first, Odysseus jumped down lightly from his beached ship, giving orders to his men about the stacking of the oars, and the slaying of a sheep, and the getting out of the wine-jars. And as they went about their duties, the weary warriors looked upward to the stout walls of Troy upon its hill, the city where Helen was, the city that must be laid waste.

But that was long ago. A quick eddy of air blew in from the mystery of the sleeping town. Was it merely fancy that I smelled the sour dust of earthquake? A solitary crane standing out against the sky looked like some archaic war-engine left lying around from some old war. A few surly harbour-men made the boat fast and brought up the gangway. The cries to and from the waterfront did not break the silence so much as deepen it. The core of the silence was a tall and burly man standing shrouded in a huge coat at the water's edge, almost as tall, he seemed, as that crane. It would not have been strange to see that monolithic man crested with a helmet and carrying a spear, and to hear oneself calling out to him: "Ho, Aeneas! What news of the fighting? Or are you perhaps Hector?"

It was not a helmet he wore, but a bowler-hat. And it was he who spoke first.

"Hello! Is your name Golding?"

My heart leapt with delight. The senders of signals between Istanbul and Ankara, between Ankara and Chanakkale, had done their work well. We would not sleep that night among the dislodged paving-stones and fallen roof-beams.

"Yes, yes!" I proclaimed eagerly. "Good-evening! I mean, good-morning!"

"Good-morning!" the tall man said.

We stepped ashore. Our feet touched Homeric earth.

Over from Asia as we disembarked from the Hellespont, the tall man put out his hand.

"The name's Millington," he said. "I look after the graves."

I started. "The *graves*?" I cried. "The *graves*?" But there couldn't be any graves to look after any more, excepting deep in the buried cities, under one Troy and another Troy and another, graves still unexcavated by Schliemann and Dörpfeld and Blegen, graves perhaps never to be revealed to the light of day. As for Homer's Trojans, they had no graves, most of them. They were encalcined in the burning city, and then the survivors fled southward to Cilicia, or westward to Italy, and became known by other names. And Homer's Greeks, were they not burned in pyres and buried under barrows? Were these the graves the tall man looked after, on the plain between Troy and the sea?

"The Imperial War Graves Commission," the tall man was saying, "a number of years now." He pointed across the opaque night to the peninsula yonder, to those graves where Sol Benjamin of Cheetham Hill Road still lies, and Mortimer of Radley and Queen's, among those I myself knew, and many thousands more I did not know.

"I've got them to fix up a room for you," he went on, "at the Bakri Sefd. I'm single-handed, or I'd have put you up myself. But I've brought a little whisky for you." He patted his pocket. We were walking on towards the harbour-front buildings. Quite a number of them, so far as we could make out, were broken off sharp, like a biscuit, or a bone. "We'll take it neat. I'm not sure about the water-supply yet."

We walked up one street, then turned right on another, the main street of the town, everything very shattered and hurt and mysterious, like a beaten dog licking its wounds in a black kennel. Then we took our whisky neat in the lounge of the very-much-knocked-about hotel, full of earthquake-dust and new cement and bundles of bedding. It seemed to us it would hardly have been more adventurous to sleep out in the open.

"To that old man in that book of yours," said Mr. Millington. "What did you say his name was?" I think I knew who he meant and I told him. I never loved the old man so much, greeting me this way with a nip of whisky on the fabulous Troad shore.

"To Helen," I said. We drank to Helen. And, of course, to Odysseus.

"I understand you want to go to Troy," said Mr. Millington.

"Yes," I murmured. "That's what we're here for."

"And you'll want to see my cemeteries, too, at Helles and Anzac." It was obvious he took great pride in his cemeteries. "And I was thinking of going over to the place where the collision was, behind Nagara Point. You know? The submarine!" I knew. I knew the disaster would be flapping its wings in these parts for many a long day. I knew not even Troy would keep the submarine out of my mind for more than a few hours at a time. "They say the steamer was coming up too fast. On the other hand, the submarine was too far over on the Asiatic side. She'd been on manœuvres with Mountbatten." He was shocked about it all, but excited. There had not been so much excitement in Chanakkale since the early twenties —and he had been here then—when the small force commanded by General Harrington sat facing the triumphant army of Kemal Pasha that was thirsting to pursue the beaten Greeks into Thrace and at any moment there might be war again. And all these years Mr. Millington had been tending the well-being of bodies quietly dead, almost forgotten. Now young men had died again, suffocated in the depths of the sea. Perhaps a few, perhaps all, would never lie in a tidy plot, with an evergreen springing at their feet, and a head-stone to say who they were.

"The Swedish captain is here," continued Mr. Millington, "to answer questions. He's in hospital. He's taking it pretty badly. Maybe you'd like to see him and give him a word of sympathy."

"If he wouldn't resent it——"

"I'll find out. Good lord. Look at the time. I'll be leaving you. Good-night."

"Good-night. And thank you, Mr. Millington."

"Don't thank *me*," he insisted. He may have meant our mutual friend from a book, or it may have been H.M.'s representative at Ankara. He took off his Achillean frame, hardly clearing the lintel.

We turned in. It was rather a grim room, but the only one towards the sea that had been more or less put to rights. One of the walls was still damp with cement. The beds were like railings round one of Mr. Millington's graves, with coverings like a slab of stone. The window-frame behind my bed was leaning lopsidedly from one of its hinges. During the night a terrific wind blew up. Across my disturbed sleep I could hear that window-frame jerking and tugging like a huge mastiff at its chain. At last it woke me. I struck a match, or tried to, to consider the matter of that window-frame again. It could hardly be any lighter, I thought, than a grand piano. I got up at last and moved my bed into the middle of the room. I fell asleep again, the window-frame still groaning, the wind howling. The water hurled its black billows between the walls of the Hellespont. The branches of the forests on Mount Ida creaked. In Troy few slept, for it seemed that matters must surely come to a head soon. The armourers sharpened their swords and refined the tips of their spears, but they looked ill at ease. Outside by the Greek tents the horses whinnied and stamped their hooves. Over the camp-fires men sat huddled together. Then suddenly all was uproar. There was a splintering of wood and walls were crashing down and women were screaming and babies whimpering at the breast. And in the light of fires the plumes of the Achaeans were themselves like flames as the heroes ran through the narrow streets yelling dreadfully and smiting left and right with their swords.

"She's down! She's done for!" I cried as loud as any.

"Who? What?" Edward demanded, on the edge of panic.

But I was awake now. It was not Troy that had fallen. Troy had fallen long ago. It was that window-frame that had torn loose from its hinges, and had come down exactly where my head had been.

CHAPTER FOUR

Troy

I

IN the grey and blustery morning the Straits seemed even straiter than they are, and beyond the nipped white wave-tops old Mohammed's castle across there in Europe seemed within swimming distance. If the swimmer were Byron, of course, who from his house behind the headland (now a petrol-station) had achieved the feat, though it was not easy, not easy at all.

We got a Turkish coffee-cup of warm water each to shave in, and were grateful for that, in a hotel that the earthquake had handled like a foot treading on a match-box. Then we went across the street for our breakfast, in a place that, further west, would have been called a milk-bar. Breakfast was chiefly a dish of sheeps' trotter soup, unexpected but nourishing, with a couple of raw eggs to nourish you still further. Bread was almost impossible to get, but when it came there was jam to spread on it, made out of rose-petals. There was coffee. By this time Mr. Millington was with us. He had arranged for a car to take us to Troy, but the engine had gone wrong, it would not be ready for some hours yet. (I should state that all these journeys in the wake of Odysseus were bewitched by engines that went wrong, even when they were engines that had had a fairly blameless history till I appeared on the scene. They did not have to wait till I sat down in them. As soon as it was rumoured I was in the neighbourhood, their tyres went flat, their brake-linings seized, or their steering-wheels snapped like the ribs of an umbrella.)

There was no progress to report on Mr. Millington's own boat-engine. Beside a half-stripped lorry outside our milk-bar two puzzled mechanics were screwing and unscrewing bolts. Altogether it was a bad day in the Troad for Daedalus, if it is he who is the tutelary deity of the internal combustion age.

The Captain of s.s. *Naboland*, Mr. Millington told us, would be grateful if we spent a minute or two with him later. In the mean-time, we would pay our respects to the chief civic official who would have been called the Bey once, I suppose. Beyond an Italianate clock-tower we came out on to the waterfront. The tents of the earthquake victims steamed in the rising sun. Behind their wind-

53

raddled gardens stood the villas of the merchants, with their fretted matchwood cornices and window-ledges, and geranium cascading over from classical urns and troughs.

We came in some minutes to the Bey's premises. Under a large portrait of the first President sat the Bey, a distracted young man, whose stomach kept rebounding lightly from the edge of his table, like a balloon nosed by a dog. He had a lot of extra work on hand with the earthquake, and had forgotten his tie and collar, but he had exquisitely kept hands with no bones inside them, and finger-nails like cultured pink pearls. Turkey is a democracy, now, of course, and people kept on coming in and out without being announced, to make suggestions or complaints, or to say nothing at all, just to make sure that everyone knew about Turkey being a democracy. We had coffee once, then again, and I suggested to our friend that it was perhaps time we left, because the Bey was obviously very busy. We were told that it would be the height of bad manners to go so soon, so we had more coffee. The Bey knew no other language than his own, and we none of that, so conversation was sluggish. Then our friend told a funny story in between visitors. If confined to one language, it would have been even more successful than it was, but it kept on slipping between the two languages, and its final point was a play on words, in English. We laughed, and the Bey, correctly assuming the story was finished, laughed too, the stomach rebounding from the edge of the table again and again. No, we would not have more coffee, so now we went. Mr. Millington went to see how the engines were. We could go for a stroll in the town, he said. He would send a boy for us if the car was ready. There would be no difficulty in finding us. So we went strolling through Chanakkale. I was anxious to be on my way to Troy, if only because the way to Ithaca lay through Troy. In Troy I would, for the first time, get to grips with Odysseus. He had, after all, been long enough in Troy to leave an impression on the place.

But it was no good getting impatient. Turkey was still Turkey, despite the colossal statue up the street of Kemal Pasha, with the flared skirt of his bronze overcoat, and his heavy bronze binoculars, a bronze that looked like solid cod liver oil. So we went strolling through Chanakkale.

Chanakkale, I should explain (the full Turkish form is Chanak-Kalessi), means Fortress of Pottery, of which both the Fortress and the Pottery still survive. I suppose some of the soldiers who had travelled with us from Istanbul were already installed in the local Fortress, which stands on the spit of land beyond the southern curve

of the bay, and is still a going concern. Its opposite number on the
European side is only a shell, but is more imposing to look on, standing as it does on rising ground, and has a more imposing name,
Kilid-ud-Bahr, Key-of-the-Sea. Both are in the Venetian style, as
the great mosques are in the Byzantine style, but they were built by
the great Turkish Conqueror, Mohammed, after the capture of
Constantinople; for, being in possession of both sides of the straits,
it was now possible to command the situation with his shore guns.

I said the Pottery of Chanak-Kalessi still survives. It has been
stated that the Pottery once enjoyed a considerable reputation, but
that it is now decadent. That is an understatement. The pottery,
chiefly vases now, which they make in several establishments, com-
prises objects of a hideousness such as I have never met before, even
in nightmare. Many years ago, in Bologna, I think it was, where
I had seen some particularly frightful frescoes, I tried to draw up a
Gallery of the Ugliest Objects I have Ever Seen. There were those
frescoes, a plush arm-chair, a collection of wax exhibits designed
to warn the young of the dangers of incontinence. The Vases of
Chanakkale could have held their own with any of these, and had a
startling similarity with the last. It is extremely difficult to describe
anything well, things beautiful as well as things ugly. But a writer
deliberately exercises himself in the description of things beautiful.
There are few who exert themselves in the exact and fastidious
description of things ugly. I will not try, therefore, to describe those
Chanakkale Vases, and believe I would fail if I tried—the colours,
the shapes, the textures, the swellings, excrescences, proliferations.

Who bought the things? The merchants and shop-keepers? That
is not impossible. I should imagine the peasantry, chiefly. But the
pottery made by and for every other peasantry in my experience
has had some virtue, often more than the objects produced by
sophisticated hands. Can the ghoulish tastelessness lead us to any
profitable speculations regarding the mental or aesthetic levels of the
Turkish peasantry and the Turkish people as a whole? One remembers the celebrated mosques, and many of these, certainly the
earliest, were the work of Byzantine architects. But Sinan, the
maker of the glorious mosque of Suleiman the Magnificent was a
Turk? True, but he was a Janissary, therefore presumably not of
Turkish blood, and he himself informs us he studied in Santa Sophia.
One remembers Turkish carpets, illuminated manuscripts, paintings
behind glass? The primal inspiration is to be found elsewhere than
in Turkey, chiefly in Persia, of course, one of the most supremely
gifted of the nations. One is happy to accede the delicious Beykoz

glass objects, but would they have been there if there had been no Venice? One hails, too, the exquisite painting of the eighteenth-century Levni and his school, but the Turkish experts themselves admit the strong influence of Western models.

Perhaps the aesthetic glories of the Turkish people are still to be, for these people who have been little but peasants and soldiers for so long show now a startling readiness to make new explorations in other fields. It can be said, maybe, that the new regime has effected a too sudden and too violent dislocation of all their mental and spiritual processes. Things are forced to build themselves up in a year which should flower slowly over decades.

Do such musings help to explain the horror of the Chanakkale pottery? Probably not. Writing nearly a century ago Schliemann makes a reference to those crockery-shops on the shores of the Dardanelles where there are immense numbers of earthen vessels with long upright necks and the breasts of a woman, and others in the shape of animals. That sounds very much like the contemporary monstrosities.

"In spite of their gilding and other decorations" (Schliemann tells us) "these vessels cannot, either in regard to quality or elegance of form be compared with the Ilian terra-cottas, not even with those from a depth of ten feet; but still they furnish a remarkable proof of the fact that, in spite of modified political changes, certain types of terra-cottas can continue in existence in one district for more than 3,000 years."

And, indeed, close to where Chanakkale stands now, long long ago stood the town of Abydos, which is numbered in the Iliad among Priam's allies, lorded over by Asius, whom his big and glossy horses had carried there. No-one can say whether some of the terra-cottas which were made in Chanakkale-Abydos are among those which have been disinterred in the successive layers of Hissarlik-Troy, but how indestructible pottery can be, we found for ourselves that morning in Chanakkale. For whereas walls have been smashed in the earthquake, roofs brought tumbling down, pavements opened, those dreadful vases had ridden the storm like sea-gulls. I could not help wondering what general conclusions some later Schliemann, three thousand years from now, would come to regarding the Troadic ulture of this epoch, when his spade upturned the first layer of Chanakkale pottery.

The streets in the rear part of the town were more like bazaars

than streets, with their windowless shop-fronts and the proprietors
sitting cross-legged on low straw stools. The earthquake had been
more light-handed here. The merchants were Jewish, for the most
part, the young people dapper and alert, the older ones serene and
unhurried. I would like to have believed them the offspring of
restless Hebrews who had wandered down from the Judaean hills
and married Phoenician girls, and some of their offspring had gone
sailing westward in Phoenician ships, as far, say, as Djerba, the
Island of the Lotophagi. Indeed, one old man, by name Saraf
Avram Penso, sat in the dark rear of his store, stuffing himself with
halva, with something of the oblivious bliss one would associate with
a draught of lotus, out there by the yellow sands. But it was Ladino
he talked, the language of those Jews who, having been expelled from
Spain by the Inquisition in the late fifteenth century, settled on the
shores of the eastern Mediterranean, above all in Salonica, and there
flourished finely for centuries till the Nazis destroyed them.

But Salonica was Greece, of course. Chanakkale is Turkey.
Monsieur Avram and his townsmen gave the impression that they
had been there when the shipwrights of Xerxes were fastening his
myriad boats together, bow to stern, to bridge the Hellespont; they
had had bolts of Phoenician purple cloth to sell, and filigree gold
earrings, and red leather sandals. They had sold those same things
to the Turkish soldiery when they were defending the Gallipoli
narrows, and to the British troops a few years later, when Harrington
faced Kemal Pasha. When the Nazis transported their kinsmen from
Dedeagatch and Salonica to the Balkan death-camps, they were only
dimly aware of it, if at all, as they are only dimly aware of the
ingathering of their brethren from all the wide world in the small
new State of Israel, not far off. And still over their counters they
sell the same merchandise, silks and spices and glistening black
olives. But now they sell radio sets, too, and electric irons.

And I suppose then as now the storks made their nests on the
wide brick eaves, those nests which look like large flat cakes, or like
cart-wheels. Indeed, Saraf Avram Penso told us that in these
regions the peasants actually provide old cart-wheels for the storks
to build their nests in, and that the storks pay rent in return, a
feather for the first year, an egg for the second year, and for the third
year a small stork . . . or if not a stork, a baby.

How delightfully disproportionate the storks looked on the
low roofs of Chanakkale, to eyes accustomed to roof-top birds as
being no larger than starlings or swallows! They were out of scale
in the same way as those saints or princesses in Gothic paintings who

emerge from the tops of towers and are as big as the towers themselves. How pleased with themselves they looked, how superior to the pigeons, strutting along the eaves, or the sparrows lodging on the lower twigs of their nests! How conscious they seemed of their own popularity among humans, the females sitting on their nests with necks curved like the necks of swans, the males standing with both legs rigidly parallel, or one leg tucked under the body, and the whole heavy torso held aloft by a single leg as thin as a glass rod! How handsomely, when a slight puff of wind blew, did the feathers above the chest blow out, like the plumes in the helmet of a Guards Officer during a royal parade! And when a stork launched himself from his own roof-top to fly the few yards that separated him from the opposite roof, what a flapping and clacking there was! With so large a space of sky obscured you could have thought the roof-top itself had taken flight!

"You wouldn't believe it," observed Monsieur Avram, handing each of us a third lump of *halva* in the bowl of a spoon, "but when the storks come back after winter is over, they collect at the Mosque of the Sultan Ahmed, then fly off to their old nesting-places." Monsieur Avram winked. He didn't believe it, either. These Anatolian yokels might, but not he, this Sephardic merchant whose ancestors had been doctors at the Courts of Aragon. "They also say that twelve years ago in the country behind Izmir there was a great battle between the storks and the eagles. It went on for weeks and weeks, and finally the storks drove the eagles away. It may have happened. I only believe what I see with my own eyes." A shadow fell across the strip of light at the threshold. "Ah, Mr. Millington!" It was our friend. Greetings followed in Turkish. "The gentlemen will have some more *halva*?" That was the last thing in the world the gentlemen wanted. We bowed and withdrew. The car would be with us in less than an hour, we learned. We would have time for lunch.

"I'm sorry about the Captain," he said.

"The Captain?"

"The Swedish Captain of the *Naboland*. He's thought better of it. He sent a message he'd rather not see anybody. Tomorrow, maybe, he says."

Yes, of course. The Captain of the *Naboland*. I got a sudden startlingly clear vision of him, lying in his bed in the hospital, now passionately anxious to assure the world he was totally innocent of any fault, now racked with misery for the sorrow the misadventure had brought to so many people.

"We'll see," I said. "Maybe we'll have time." But I knew we

would not. In such a case it is better that even close friends keep their distance. We went to the restaurant. In the window two small flayed kids faced each other with exact symmetry, like two heraldic beasts in an escutcheon. The blood seemed to be still pulsing along their capillaries like neon lighting, though it had ceased to flow hours ago. In their eye-sockets one wore a blue paper rosette, the other a pink. The idea was to stimulate the appetite. Between them, the *halva* and the flayed kids made us less fervent about our lunch than we should have been, even though it included that noble dish of *gear samesi* (I think it is called) of beaten liver and rice and boiled pine-kernels all served up in a casing of lamb's tripe and all that washed down with wine from Tenedos.

There was another little matter that impaired the appetite. I was sitting on the side of the table that commanded a view into the street. I became aware quite early of a mysterious figure pacing up and down the pavement outside the restaurant. I would say shuffling rather than pacing. He was tall, round-shouldered, and wore spectacles, and a long dark jacket that was almost a frock-coat. Every now and again he approached the door, peered in, hesitated a moment, then walked on. Of course, he may have been waiting for someone who had not turned up. Then why did he not come inside and wait for him? Were we under observation? I wondered. What a bore that was going to be! I understood we had one policeman already to look after us, and really we were quite undangerous people.

At last the gentleman entered. Mr. Millington turned round, smiled affably, and introduced us. This was Mr. Tanyel. Would not Mr. Tanyel sit down and have coffee with us? Mr. Tanyel was a schoolmaster, but he was more than that, he was an author, too. Mr. Tanyel beamed through his glasses, and brought from an inner pocket a copy of the current issue of the local magazine, *Canakallexi Sesi*. The cover was decorated with a drawing of a fine upstanding Turkish soldier, grasping a long unpleasant-looking bayonet. "*Yasak!*" proclaimed the soldier. But Mr. Tanyel's contribution was entirely pacific. It was about Troy, and Paris, and Helen, and the Golden Apple.

"An offering!" he said. "One Troy-loving author to another!"

We were delighted. The car still bided its time, so we set to work then and there to translate the article, a labour concluded in Oxford later. I present the charming sentiments in the concluding passage:

> "*I have no doubt that when we bring near to the Turkish imagination this world of inspiration to which foreign writers and painters have given*

*their hearts, we shall enrich our artistic life with new sounds and colours.
Now, whenever I go to Kumkale, every shepherd's pipe I hear on
those plains of Troy, which present a new beauty within the green-hued
dawn, seems to me to be wailing the dirge for an ill-starred love which
cost the downfall of a civilization."*

Still the car was not there. So we talked about storks. To our
delight we found Mr. Tanyel knew a lot about storks, too. He had a
great addiction to them. From him we learned it is believed that if
storks leave their nests in a great state, and start building in trees,
then there will be war. If they desert a whole region, then there will
be plague. There are peasants who believe that storks were men
once and that in Egypt, that land of fable, during the winter storks
become men again. It is also believed, he said, that if the birds are
clean and white when they arrive, there will be much sunshine, but
that it will be a year of storm if they are dirty. "If they do not arrive
at all?" I asked. "Then it is the end of the world."

Luncheon was over now. Still no car. So we went to have more
coffee on the balcony of a large house on the sea-front that described
itself as the Toring Kulüb—the Touring Club, we realized, in a
flash of divination.

And then at last it came, with a honking of wild geese it came,
the chariot upon which we were to set out for Troy. A slight spiral of
smoke circled upward through the fissures of the bonnet, looking
not unlike the smoke which rises from an altar in the first stages of
a burnt-offering.

It was an old car, predominantly still a Citroën, but it had never
been a large car. It already contained a policeman who was there to
see we did not photograph the military installations *en route*. He
was big, and so was the driver. Mr. Millington is big and tall. I am
big but not tall. There was room to be found for Edward, too. Somehow we wedged ourselves into the small Citroën. Three small
maidens stood hard by on the pavement, swathed to the feet in
cinnamon wrappings, each holding a tall pale green leek aslope over
her left shoulder. Their bronze expressionless eyes were as large as
pennies. I turned to Mr. Millington to ask the Turkish for how are
you. I turned again. They were not there. It was as if one of the gods
had lifted them by the hair and set them on Mount Ida.

We were on the road now. On our right was a cinema where a
hoarding displayed in tomato scarlet and paprika yellow two pairs
of mammoth lips pressed close. *Kauli Ask* the film was, Bloody Love,
a present-day Turkish film. That might well have been, I thought,

the title of the more celebrated story played out in the prehistoric city whither we were now chugging and puffing in a chariot almost as prehistoric.

We crossed at once a sandy and distraught river, said to be the Rhodios we hear of in the Iliad, that fritters away in the "yellow shallows" of the bay. A few old-time German howitzers were manœuvring along the reedy fore-shore, and the black-bloomered black-wimpled washerwomen went on imperturbably beating their clothes under the muzzles by the water's edge. The loose gravelly road, dusted over with earthquake siftings, wound steadily upward into a country shaggy with heath and sea-pine and vallona oak. Close-packed euphorbia lashed out, hissing at our broken-backed mudguards. On the coast at our right had been the ancient pre-Homeric town of Dardanos, from which the narrow waters of the straits derive their present name. It also provided the name by which Homer sometimes talked of the whole Trojan force. For these Dardanians had crossed the Hellespont at about 1700 B.C., and had sent out a clan to occupy the hill later called Hissarlik, building there a settlement the scholars were to describe as Troy Five. Dardanos was an obscure little place, but it has managed to perpetuate itself in a way that some more resplendent old towns have not, towns which now are as anonymous as the sands which cover them.

We were ascending the Erenkoi Ridge now with a good deal of choking and spluttering, but I was aware of a pleasure bordering on elation as I reflected on the poetry which invests each syllable and letter of place-names like this of Dardanos-Dardanelles, with so immense an ancestry. I recalled two other instances from this same region. The whole of this corner of the promontory, we are informed, became known to the Egyptians in the time of Thutmose III as *Asy*, a little later to the Hittites as *As-su-va*, and to the Greeks as *Asia*, while the city built on Hissarlik by the Dardanians was known to the Hittites as *Ta-ro-i-sa*, to the Hellenes as *Troia*.[1]* To ourselves, of course, it is known as Troy, Homer's Troy, Golden Troy. I recalled, too, an instance which had enchanted me during certain journeys in the Nile Delta. I had to find my way to a minute village called San el Hagar. I knew that the "San" of this dim present-day name is like a fossil in stone, involved in the Hellenistic name of "Tanis", which had been a fine place once in the time of the Ptolemies; that it is involved, too, in the name, "Zoan", which we meet in the Bible, where (the Psalmist tells us) "the Lord had wrought his signs in Egypt, and his wonders in the field of Zoan". I knew finally that the

* For reference see H. Peake and H. J. Fleure, p. 238.

name is ultimately derived from the name of a place called "Sekhet Chan", which we meet in the hieroglyphs of Egyptian monuments some three to four thousand years ago. A fair lineage, I thought when I got to San el Hagar, for this handful of mud hovels by the breathless backwater.

I wrenched my mind away. This was not the Nile Delta, it was the Troad. And we had reached the summit of the steep rise, at a village called Erenkoi. And here, on a terrace, looking down on steep escarpments west and north was a café, an officers' café. And there would be coffee here, said our policeman.

There was more than coffee, there was one of the most heart-shaking panoramas I have ever gazed on, the more mysterious and moving as the driving cloud now obscured, now revealed, its tremendous elements—north of us the narrow echoing waterway, the Dardanelles, along which the ribbed alligator of the Gallipoli peninsula prolonged its spine; behind us the great dark slopes of Ida; on the sky-line full in sight the islands of Tenedos and Imbros. And in between the whole Trojan plain, the Homeric streams mazily traversing the marshy levels all the way to the grey electric sea, the plain of Scamander where "clan after clan poured out from the ships and huts, and the earth resounded sullenly to the tramp of marching men and hooves, as they found their places in the flowery meadows by the river, innumerable as the leaves and blossoms in their season".

Yes, and there, rising humped and gap-toothed not far from the sea's edge, glimpsed for the first time across a near-by confusion of rusty earthquake-contorted roofs, there was the hillock of Hissarlik, once crowned (though it was a lesser hillock then) with Tall Troy and its towers, Troy known also as Ilion.

So we sat on the summit of the hill of Erenkoi, sipping our thick cups of coffee, on the same hill-top (so the tradition is) as the one where Paris awarded the fateful apple to Aphrodite, for which reason it is called Kallikolone, the Hill of Beauty; the same hill where later the gods that were on the side of Troy and Priam, sipping a more volatile nectar, were gathered around Lord Phoebus, and Ares, Sacker of Towns, gazing on the battle below, while Poseidon, the dark-haired god, assembled the opposite party, the gods friendly to the Achaeans, to watch the battle from the lofty earthwork between Troy and the sea, that had been made for Heracles, "as a place of refuge from the great sea-beast when it came up to attack him on dry land".

We moved off, with a clamour and emission of mist hardly

paralleled since those old days, over a red-ridged country, where the
storks paced ceremoniously along the furrows and the bright-
scarfed women moved slowly, hoeing the tawny earth between the
rows of beans. The women did not look Turkish, nor did their
men, chopping up the gnarled roots of holm-oak piled up to fuel
the odd bee-hive-shaped ovens that stood beside the gimcrack homesteads along the road. As the men moved, the seats of their trousers
swinging loose and heavy, I remembered when and where I had
first beheld trousers like those. Long years ago it was, in the camps
near Salonica. What luggage they carried now I did not know. Then
it was generous loads of bully-beef tins, and tins of Maconachie
jams and stews, and a dehydrated potato the horror of which I
recall to this day. And indeed these were all colonists, refugee
Muslim Bulgars who had fled from Thessaly, chiefly, when the New
Order of Moscow had moved in on their native land.

The landscape was now more Aegean than Anatolian in character, oleander and myrtle, olive and rock-rose, with unfolded
thyme softening the stony outcroppings. Then, some kilometres
further along, we saw beyond the car's bouncing bonnet a rusty
painted panel stuck high up on a drunkenly reeling sign-post. To
TRUVA, the sign-post said, 6 kilometres. Truva, which is Troy as the
Turks write it. The sight of the name set up inside me a sudden
spatter of bell-music which had its visual counterpart in as sudden a
lift and frolic of gold-finches.

Here at last, so short a distance away, so unexcitedly announced,
was Troy, where the heroes were gathered in two hosts and set up
against each other, and most cunning of them all, and by no means
the least valorous, fought Odysseus, my old brave. Who had put that
sign up? It looked so antique one played with the thought that it was
one of Hector's R.T.O.'s directing the Phrygian contingent to H.Q.
But that was unlikely. The place was not called Truva then, and the
Latin script had not been invented. Not even the Greek script, not
by many centuries . . . or so it has been thought until only quite
recently.

Had the relevant Ministry at Ankara put it up? It was too
casual even for Chanakkale. They show little excitement about
Troy at the Fortress of Pottery, no postcards for sale, no souvenirs,
no novelties. Was it a left-over from the time of Schliemann, to
direct his workmen across the plain, during the twenty years when
he was in charge of those archaeological operations which can well
be described as a subsidiary Iliad? Or did Dörpfeld (who has been
described a little cynically as "Schliemann's greatest discovery")

—did Dörpfeld put it there, when he took over from him in 1893?
Or could it have been Blegen and his associates, who took the spade
from Dörpfeld's hands in 1932 and used it royally till 1938, when the
shadow of war rolled up and blanketed the hill?

Perhaps it had been improvised by my literary friend, the schoolmaster from Chanakkale? Or the schoolmaster from the small
village whither we now proceeded, the village of Chiplak more than
half-way to Truva, on the very edge of the plain. There was certainly
a school in Chiplak. For a dozen children stared at us curiously,
dressed in the elementary school uniform, the black smock, the
perforated plastic collar introduced by the new authorities, a uniform that makes you think for a moment you are in some French
village. But the mosque by the roadside is not French, with its small
squat minaret. Nor is it wholly Turkish, even. Embodied in its
fabric, and in the fabric of many a humble building for leagues
around, are blocks of squared marble which must have been carted
off from the Hill of Troy in the off seasons, when the archaeologists
were not at work, ever since Schliemann dug in his first spade.
Beyond the mosque the street narrowed and its whole width was
occupied by a massive Middle West tractor, which seemed perverse
on the road to Troy. But after a great deal of manœuvring we were
through and across. We rumbled unsteadily over a loose plank
bridge. It was the river Simois we were crossing now, not much of a
waterway, practically nothing at all, and what there is of it soon
seeps into a marsh. Further on, beyond Hissarlik now full in view, a
line of reeds traced the course of Scamander, that does, in fact,
manage to get to the sea. Trivial trickles both of them, Simois and
Scamander, but being notes, or themes rather, in the superb
orchestration of the Iliad, they reverberate in men's ears not less
resonantly than Volga or Mississipi or the Yellow River.

II

I did not spend more than a few days on the Hill of Troy and in
its environs, yet the experience stands outside all computation by the
clock. Of this Odyssean adventure, Troy and Ithaca were the two
pinnacles, the two foci. I had been thinking of them, and striving
towards them, for many years, and my experiences in both places,
whether as in the one case measurable by days, or as in the other case
measurable by weeks, must colour all the years that remain to me,
as the anticipation coloured the years that went before; and more

Hellespont: The Bebek Bay

Hellespont: Sole postulant

Soldiers aboard for Troy

than that, whatever disappointments or frustrations may lie ahead in the years to come, I will be able to say I have been to Troy and to Ithaca, and know that I carry with me a certain measure of fulfilment. To recall Cavafy:

Ithaca has given you your lovely journey.
Without Ithaca you would not have set out
Ithaca has no more to give you now.

Poor though you find it, Ithaca had not cheated you
Wise as you have become, with all your experience,
You will have understood the meaning of an Ithaca.

And, of course, Cavafy would have said that Troy is implicit in Ithaca. It is the greatest of all the adventures that happen to you on that "lovely journey".

In places like the two I am speaking of, awareness is on many levels, layer upon layer, like Hissarlik itself. But I think three main levels can be separated, though level is an inexact word. The awarenesses are not horizontal, but vertical, and, though vertical, are folded into each other, like the interfused gases in a pillar of smoke, and they are the awarenesses of the senses, the mind, the spirit.

What is the sensuous experience? You are crossing the scrappy marsh plain, which here and there clots into tufts of reed and the sedge called galingale. A dot-dot-dash of willows marks the course of two hardly discernible water-channels, and those are Scamander and Simois, you tell yourself. Solitary elms and tamarisks, wind-blown, lean back from the sea-winds. Due west the sea's edge is marked by broken dunes, grass-muffled. You wonder whether sea and wind piled them up, or have they formed around what is left of barrows raised over the burned bodies of heroes long ago. The tang of brine is in the nostrils. From the country east and south, in fact from the Mount Ida massif behind you, a series of low ridges feel out towards the narrow coastal plain. The nearest ridge steepens slowly, and its termination is Hissarlik, which you are now approaching obliquely. It is a mistake to conceive Hissarlik as an isolated hill standing up dramatically with flat land all about it; though it is difficult not to think of it in those terms; for did not Hector run three times round Troy with flaming Achilles hot in pursuit of him? Yet who knows? Perhaps long ago the end of the ridge was truly a lone fortress with a deep dyke on the side where now the unbroken

E

ridge extends, and time and earthquake have filled in the hollow
on the side away from the sea. Yet the steepness of the seaward-
facing cliff and the command the site has over the two waters of
Aegean and Hellespont, must always have made it inevitable for a
fortress to arise there, a *pergamos*, an enclosure. (During the latest
epoch the Turkish word Hissarlik, derived from an Arabic root "to
enclose", perpetuates this same meaning.)

Some hundreds of yards from the abrupt escarpment where the
ridge ends, already the work of the archaeologists is visible. Further,
the trenches are deeper, the artificial cliff-sides higher, the knobs of
piled earth become themselves fair-sized hillocks. The pointed slag-
heaps of the Five Towns, your mind ludicrously announces. You
blink, and shake your head. Burslem is not born yet. Nor London.
Nor Rome. Not even Athens, or it is just a few reed-thatched huts—
hardly more important than Chiplak.

You ascend the slope, and the long grasses are damp about the
ankles. The earth heaves, as if a breed of giant moles had been at
work; or a whole cemetery full of grave-diggers. In square pans of
naked grey earth small handfuls of purple and white forget-me-nots,
dark purple bee-orchids, double yellow daisies, royal purple vetches,
pads of thyme, lie about, like untidy heaps of crude jewels in a
jeweller's working trays. Small wild hollyhocks fling their white
bells about, making no sound.

Now the senses are not enough. The mind hastens among the
scattered blocks of marble, to the round drums and shafts of columns
prostrate or raised on their bases. The mind takes part in the digging
with the corps of scholars, or on its own chooses an apparently
undisturbed parcel of earth, thrusts in the spade, turns up sherds and
fragments of images; or reveals a lintel, a hearth-stone, a slab of
antique wall.

Hissarlik can be likened to a film recording a vast stretch of
human history. But it is not only a film of multiple exposures, epoch
superimposed upon epoch. It is a film which plays backward. The
first city you come upon as you approach from the east when the
slope is easiest, is also the most recent in time, the Greco-Roman
city of Novum Ilium. Comparatively recent though that city is in the
enormous time-register of the Hissarlik settlements, there was no
trace even of that on the windy hillside when Schliemann first came
to the Troad to find out exactly where Troy had been. Indeed, those
scholars who admitted that there might have been a physical Troy
outside Homer's hexameters, following Lechevalier who visited the
site in 1781, generally placed it on a high hill called Buna-bashi

some five miles south, where the Scamander issues from a sheep gorge into the plain, and there are two streams, a hot stream and a cold, or so it was said, which could be identified with the hot and cold streams the poet locates under the walls of Troy.

But there on Hissarlik, with inspired divination, or at most acting on the most cursory hint, Schliemann set to work. In a sense Schliemann had been working on the problems of Troy, from the day when his father in a small town in Mecklenburgh had shown him a picture of Troy town burning on its hill, and Aeneas fleeing from the ruins. "I shall some day go to that place," the small boy said to himself, "and dig among those burnt ruins, and perhaps I shall find gold." He was born a poor clergyman's son, became an office-boy for a wage of a few shillings a week, and in course of time became a Homeric scholar, a redoubtable linguist, a very rich man. All he was and had he devoted to the excavation of those burning ruins, whose flames had been extinguished long ago, but still burned inextinguishably in his head. There are many renowned ghosts who haunt the uneven crest of Hissarlik, and among these Schliemann deserves an honourable place. Another illustrious excavator, Sir Arthur Evans, wrote these words of him, which it would not be unfitting to see inscribed on one of the marble slabs that lie about on the hill-top: "I have myself an almost uncanny memory of the sparse, slightly-built man—of sallow complexion and somewhat darkly clad—wearing spectacles of foreign make, through which—so the fancy took me—he had looked deep into the ground."

But in this narrative the time has not yet come for a Schliemann epitaph. He has only just dug his first spade into the top soil of Hissarlik.

First then, he unveiled Novum Ilium, then digging deeper and deeper with immense courage, resolution, and with vast expenditures, he unveiled some seven or eight cities more, till at last he got down to virgin rock. More recent archaeologists amplify this number considerably, and while admitting that cities of importance can hardly have numbered more than Schliemann disentangled, they enumerate no fewer than forty-six successive settlements, which prove how imperiously this city commanding the Hellespont where it debouches into the Aegean, imposed itself generation beyond generation.

It would be too simple to say that these settlements lie superimposed on each other, though some certainly are. Others were placed on the *same* level as their predecessors, almost as soon as that was permitted by the dying down of the natural or man-made fires which in some instances destroyed them. Sometimes the top of the hillside was drastically levelled to simplify the new job of building, with materials carted or dug up from preceding settlements. Earthquake must have disturbed the order again and again. And old Schliemann, heroic Schliemann, increased these confusions by the precipitate enthusiasm of at least his first diggings. It seems likely that, as the centuries and the millenia succeeded each other, the terrain near the original crest became more and more confused, more liable to subsidence. The temptation would be to build further and further from the crest.

Novum Ilium, the first city to be revealed on Hissarlik, fades completely from history during the fourth century. But it flickers interestingly on the backward-moving film for a number of feet. On the mosaic pavement of the uncovered palaestra a naked helmeted warrior, holding his shield before him, attacks with his spear a furious man-sized bird from the aviaries of fable. Two naked boxers deliver a right-arm cross each to the other's chin, in a style as modern as Harringay Arena, or the field of yellow-green young wheat beyond the edge of the diggings. Further along the slope is a small Roman theatre where I sat on a bench for a little time trying to give form and feature to the ghosts that brushed my shoulders: the small Roman officials listening to the great plays with something of the awe of Americans listening to Shakespeare at Stratford-on-Avon, and the rather scruffy local inhabitants kow-towing to them in the hope of unloading the latest cache of fake relics of the Wars of Troy. Perhaps Novum Ilium was a less meagre place than the ruins suggest now. The rumour was current in Rome that both Julius Caesar and then Augustus had the idea of transferring the centre of the empire to Ilium. Later an illustrious builder got to work on the project.

"Before Constantine gave a just preference to the situation of Byzantion" (as we read in a sonorous passage in Gibbon), "he had conceived the design of erecting the seat of empire on this celebrated spot, from whence the Romans derived their fabulous origins. The extensive plain which lies below ancient Troy towards the Rhoetean promontory and the tomb of Ajax, was first chosen for his new capital; and though the undertaking was soon relinquished, remains of unfinished walls and towers attracted the notice of all who sailed through the straits of Hellespont."

As the film winds backward, more than one renowned figure flashes briefly on the screen: Caracalla lays votive wreaths on the tomb of Achilles (which may have been that mound there, by Kum Kale, Land's End, washed by the sea-spray of both the Aegean and the Hellespont). Augustus before him confirms to Roman Ilium the ancient privileges of Greek Ilion, and adds to its territory. Christ dies, and is born. They are even less aware of these events in Ilium than elsewhere. Alexander has crossed the Hellespont, and is about to fight, or has lately fought, the famous battle of the Granicus, which will redeem the Greek cities of Asia Minor from the Persian tyranny. Shining like one of the sunlit marbles of the great temple of Athens on the Hill of Troy, Alexander makes sacrifices to the Goddess and does obeisance to the heroes. He anoints with oil the pillar on the tomb of Achilles, crowns it with a wreath, then he hurls his garments from him, and runs round the tomb, naked and transfigured. He is not only the descendant of Achilles. He feels he is himself Achilles— as well he might. The natives invest him with a Trojan panoply; and this (they insist) this is the very shield Achilles wore when he came up out of his tent to avenge Patroclus. But alas, the object is hardly likelier to have been the shield of Achilles than the Treasury of Priam which Schliemann was to discover twenty-three hundred years later, not many yards away, and only a few yards down, was in truth the Treasury of Priam.

The film unwinds for the few feet which cover another century or two, while we move along the hill-top sliced and flattened by an earlier generation of Ilium-builders. Here are the piled drums of a Corinthian column, there is the fragment of a plinth or entablature, where you may read in the grey light a mysterious word, or the fragment of a word: –Oloula. As Alexander will later cross from Europe into Asia, so now an earlier general, Xerxes, prepares to cross from Asia into Europe. But first he must ascend into the Pergamos, the Fortress of Priam, "since he had a longing to behold the place", as Herodotus tells us, like many others since his time, and many before it. And, "when he had seen everything, and inquired into all particulars, he made an offering to the Trojan Athene, while the Magians poured libations to the heroes who were slain at Troy".

The handle turns, the spades dig. We go back to Troy Eight, as the archaeologists enumerate it, a Greek city founded by Aeolian settlers, a city which sees the erection of that famous temple to Athena where so many illustrious visitors in centuries to come will pay their devotions, and heap hecatombs of cattle upon the altar of the Goddess. Yes, a Greek city. The last Trojans have migrated from it long ago. Now it can be said that finally, irretrievably, Greek King Agamemnon has defeated Trojan King Priam.

Once more to work. The film runs; it runs for dark centuries. We walk a few yards, we scramble down a few yards more. These ruins, of this city, are Mycenaean at last. Here at last is indisputably Troy (if anything is indisputable in these fields of shadowy speculation). And it is during this interval, these dim centuries, that our great golden Homer must have visited the Troad and stood upon this self-same hill. It is hardly believable he did not do so if he lived at all, unless those two superbly organized and idiosyncratic poems came together haphazard like two fields of daisies. He must have stood here, within a few yards this way or that, like the heroes of the bygone times he celebrated, and the devout lovers of his poetry in times to come.

Though nothing is certain regarding this man, yet not all is vague. Hardly less is known of him than of Shakespeare, even though in the case of Shakespeare a scratchy signature exists on an obscure document or two . . . this though in the age of Shakespeare printing had already existed for over a century, while in the age of Homer not even writing had been invented. (At least this has been the consensus of opinion till now, despite the mysterious and solitary reference in the Iliad to "a folded tablet" on which were traced "a number of devices with a deadly meaning".)

Yes, no poets ever spoke with more immediately recognizable a voice than these two, Shakespeare and Homer, unmistakable as those voices we heard on wartime radio to which no faces had ever been attached. Yet though Shakespeare and Homer as poets have subdued time, as mortal men they were born somewhere, they lived, they lay down and died. Shakespeare came from green fields in Warwickshire, Homer from a sea-port in the Troad, or from one of the islands that lie near to its shores. He knew far too much of the sea in all its moods not to have been born within perpetual sound and sight of it. And, like Odysseus, he was a traveller, all the way to those fringes of the known world beyond which extend mystery and marvel. How should he not have visited Troy, and at some time been to Ithaca, when to his muse Troy and Ithaca were the most important places in all the world?

So another shade is added to the host moving hither and thither upon this hill-top, he who sang the shades that had been, and summoned all the shades that were to be. What sort of a city can it have been where Homer's living feet moved? It would be possible to begin to answer the question, if it could ever be decided in what century Homer actually lived, and it seems unlikely now that that will ever be done. But it certainly was only the ruin of a city, and it is probable that several strata of ruin even then were interposed between the living Homer and the city whose drama he was to celebrate. Only one thing is sure. You must dig down to ruins from the Mycenaean time before you reach Priam's Troy, for it is the Mycenaean time which is the world of Homer's heroes. The archaeologists who followed Schliemann tabulated the Troy of the Iliad as Troy Six. But it has since been established that they, too, were wrong, for Troy Six was destroyed primarily by earthquake, not by the fire of a victorious army. It was a smaller city, Troy Seven A, planted on the massive earthquake-tumbled ruins of Troy Six, which was Priam's city, if Homer was not fabricating some fabulous city of the moon, spinning it from his entrails as a spider his web.

So the great wall here that the diggers have laid bare (I said to myself) is the wall that protected Hecuba and Andromache; through these gates the champions went out of the city and returned; on these altars the gods were worshipped; they drank their wines and ate their roasted meats from these sherds we now dislodge with the toe of the boot as we scramble over raw necks of earth and down steep-shovelled gullies.

The diggers get their hands to the shaft of the spade again. We go down from Troy Seven A, to Troy Six and Troy Five. Troy Five is hardly more than a tribal settlement, yet traces endure of a wall so massive it can be equated in the mythic pattern with that "lofty earthwork" which Athene, and an earlier generation of Trojans, had made for Hercules.

Already, then, with this wall, we are in an earlier stratum of Greek mythology than the Iliad is concerned with. Our spade goes deeper, to primitive proto-settlements which go back ever more remotely through the mists of the Bronze Age, to Troy Four, Troy Three, hardly more than clusters of a few farms.

But Troy Two tells a different tale. The second of the cities built on Hissarlik seems to have been at least as powerful as any that went after, surrounded by so massive a wall, and pierced by such broad gates. It is possible to trace the square room of a chief's house, a *megaron*, of exactly the same style as the *megaron* in Mycenae where a thousand years later Agamemnon is to lord it, and the *megaron* in Ithaca where Odysseus is to teach so fearsome a lesson to licentious princelings. Here, in Troy Two, a type of pottery worthy of the chief's house will be disinterred, and a collection of bronze that would have been notable in any age.

But it was not the bronze in Troy Two, nor the size of the rooms in the *megaron*, that caused Schliemann to believe that here, in Troy

Two, he had come to the heart of his matter, Homer's own Troy. It was not the clear evidences that this place had been destroyed by fire, for he was well aware that several of the succeeding settlements had been so destroyed. It was the breath-taking discovery of "Priam's Treasury", as he called it, in a thick layer of ash under an angle of the building he identified as the "House of Priam" close by the "Scaean Gate". There in seventeen hoards he discovered eight thousand seven hundred gold objects, gold masques and rings and diadems, gold necklaces and plaques and a fine gold goblet. "Eureka!" he cried. "I have found the diadems of Priam and Hecuba, the rings and necklaces of Helen, the goblet Hector drank from!"

He managed to get his Treasury away from Turkey to Greece, where for a long time the relatives of his beautiful Greek wife hid it in their attics and cellars. A painful tragi-comedy followed, for he found it almost as difficult to dispose of the hoard as it had been to locate it. The English, French and Italian authorities would not accept it, either because the price asked was too steep, or because they did not wish to compromise themselves with the Turkish authorities under whose noses, the stuff had been spirited away. He addressed himself to the Russians also. "I promise you" (he wrote to a Russian correspondent), "to give Russia preference over all other countries, for I made my fortune there." The Russians also refused the offer, and "Priam's Treasury" finally went to Berlin, where it was one of the chief glories of the national collections. When the bombing of the city started, the gold was moved to a bunker in the Zoological Gardens. In course of time the Russians entered the city and destroyed the bunkers. But it is unlikely that they did not examine the bunkers first, and carry away whatever was of value in them. Nothing is now known of the whereabouts of Schliemann's and Priam's Treasury, not a single ring, a single brooch, has been traced. It is possible that Schliemann having long ago given Russia "preference over all other countries", his option has a little circuitously been taken up.

A fate even more grotesque, if not quite so mysterious, has befallen the ceramics discovered in the same deposit as the jewellery. "These objects had been evacuated during the war to the small town of Lebus, near Frankfort. Here they were under the guardianship of some employees of the Berlin Museum, and had been packed in big cases and deposited in a castle belonging to a Junker of Brandenburg extraction. The townlet of Lebus never knew it had the honour of being entrusted with these treasures.

"The war ended, and in 1945 the museum administration asked

for the restoration of the cases, which was refused by the military authorities. The castle had been declared public property and was to be 'socialized', but it fell instead into private hands, and this new owner, before demolishing it, sold all there was to be sold without touching the cases. Ignorant of what was in them, he then abandoned the house, which was left derelict. In 1948 a native of Lebus got married. It was the custom to organize, on a wedding eve, a *Polterabend*, a boisterous party of carnivalesque character, of which an inseparable feature is the breaking of china or pottery against walls. But immediately after the war pottery was scarce; certainly none was available for the happy event.

"A peasant then remembered the big cases in the castle, and made up his mind to open them to see if they contained china. Joy! Pots, pans and vases were found in quantity and unpacked. They were just what was wanted for the *Polterabend*. After the party the rest of the mosaics and similar pieces were built into some kitchens and stables.

"A little later an employee of the Berlin prehistoric museum went to Lebus to see what could still be saved. The Mayor having refused permission to allow her to do so, she had the clever idea of offering sweets to the children if they would bring her objects found in the cases. She had not reckoned with the commercial sense of the young people of Lebus who, to get more sweets, made the fragments smaller still, and it was only by offering a larger bait that a few pieces were secured intact."[2]*

As for the gold objects known as "Priam's Treasury", it is no consolation to know that Priam's gold was not Priam's at all. The great wall, the foundation of Priam's House, are not Mycenaean, but Cyclopean, put together ages earlier by crude men out of lumps of crudely squared rock. The remote ancestors of both Trojans and Greeks were a long way yet from leaving their far-off Scythian steppes, with the horses and the bronze swords that were to overwhelm the indigenous populations wherever they found them. There would be no Troy lorded over by King Priam and assailed by King Agamemnon for a thousand years or more.

Yet even under Troy Two the spade has even yet some crafty digging to do. It must dig through no fewer than ten settlements, before it reaches the vestiges of the mud-bound wall put together out of irregular blocks of stone which is the chief feature of Settlement One, Troy One.

Now at last the spade clinks against the virgin rock. The tale

*For reference, see Acknowledgements, page 237.

has gone back to its beginning. The tale will go forward some day
to a blind poet singing, and all the generations of human history
listening, enchanted.

I wrote earlier that the experience of Troy is on three levels
(though I insisted that "levels" is an inexact word)—the physical,
the mental, the spiritual. Obviously they overlap, or interfuse, but
the time comes at last when you forget the bee-orchid in the grass
and the eidolon in the rubble, the shelves of books you may have
read or you now vow you must read. You are left only with the
Poet and the Poems. The spirit takes charge.

You are standing on a hill where forty-six cities and settlements
were built over a span of time extending to nearer five than four
thousand years. Of all these, Homer's Troy is the only one that has
any meaning for you. In the incomparable music of the poet's
hexameters, with their inexhaustible variety of rhythm and movement, the hexameters are like breezes in the waterways or like
thunder among the hill-tops, a thousand pictures and a thousand
more are made visible behind the eyes; while behind the ears an
infinite variety of quiet or tumultuous noises are made audible,
horses champing in the fields of clover, horses yelling as they are
driven into battle, ordinary soldiers in the barracks of Troy or by
their bivouacs in the plain recalling old encounters, renowned
heroes cracking the air with the terror of their battle-cries.

Sky, sea and land are populous with presences. The gods are
hastening, or have already arrived, from the top of Olympus, to
look upon and take part in the great endeavour. The Achaean ships
are coming in from Aulis, or they are beached already, there upon
the sandy shore, or assembled, so many as there is room for, in the
Harbour of the Achaeans by Scamander's mouth, and some will be
ablaze, for things are already going ill. Somewhere there, where it
is all marshy scrub now, and sea-thyme and mint and clover, are the
tents of Agamemnon the overlord, and of his associate princes, aged
Nestor, cunning Odysseus, gallant Ajax, and the rest. Somewhere
withdrawn is the tent of Achilles, where darkling he holds aloof from
the battle. In between is the plain where the chariots crash and the
bronze finds its mark. Here, on the citadel, in this house, or the
next house, Andromache embroiders flowers on her loom, or holds
her small boy, crowing, at her shoulder; perhaps she lowers him to
the cobbles to teach him his first steps, while Hector strides off, for
out there on the plains between the citadel and the protecting wall
the Achaeans have builded, the battle that has languished has

flared up again. But Hector does not dare to turn his head, as he goes clanking off with his girded sword and his two spears, and the horse-hair plume streaming from his helmet. This is the palace where, in peacetime, old Priam and Hecuba and all their sons sat down to dinner; and then Paris went visiting to Argos, and brought Helen back, and a troop of sorrows came with her. Here she is in her palace, "at work on a great purple web of double width, into which she is weaving some of the many battles between the horse-taming Trojans and the bronze-clad Achaeans in the war that has been forced upon them for her sake". She rises, and goes out by the Scaean Gate. Look! These are the hollowed blocks into which the gate-posts were set. Now she reaches the watch-tower, where the old men are sitting, "like cicadas perched on a tree in the woods chirping delightfully". Now they see Helen coming to the tower, and lower their voices. "Who on earth," they ask one another, "could blame the Trojan and Achaean men-at-arms for suffering so long for such a woman's sake? Indeed, she is the very image of an immortal goddess."

Then there may have been a pause, I think. A moment or two later the old men resume the conversation, a little petulantly! "All the same, and lovely as she is, let her sail home and not stay here to vex us and our children after us."

But it was not Helen of Troy I had come to evoke, here on Hissarlik Hill. Nor Paris, her lover, nor doomed Achilles. It was, of course, my friend, the wanderer, Odysseus of Ithaca. I who was wandering in the wake of Odysseus, would do well to spend a day or two here, where he was to spend ten long years.

Did he? Was there in fact an actual Odysseus? Of course, the question is exactly of the same order as those others we have glanced at from time to time. Was there a Troy? Was there a Homer? The philosophers of mythology are at pains to prove that he was a metempsychosis, or one of the incarnations, of this or that deity. He has been identified with Hermes, and with his own enemy, Poseidon, who dies at winter; that is, he goes venturing to the limit of the western seas, and even descends to the underworld; then, in the springtime, returns to his own land. He has been explained as a solar myth, the sun who disappears and returns again to free Penelope, his wife, from the suitors; or, alternatively, he is a god of the fields, and his wife is the moon-goddess, whom he abandons but embraces again on the night of the new moon.

Such questions as these it is up to the folk-lorists to decide, and

it is in the nature of the case that they can never be decided with
finality. But is it impossible that, if they are right, the legends that
had then arisen in response to the pressures of primitive feeling, may
have attached themselves to an actual man who seemed to incarnate
one or more of these myths?

Was there an actual Homer? Encouraged by many stalwart
voices, I say yes. Was there an actual Odysseus? Still with un-
becoming firmness, but with a little more diffidence, I again say
yes. He is presented to us by Homer with such convincing freshness
and particularity, that the reader feels it is not merely the poet's
dramatic genius which is presenting to us so four-square a character;
we feel also that Homer, too, was certain that such a man actually
existed, however long before his time, somewhat as he presented him.
It is exactly the same feeling as we get when we consider Hamlet.
We say: there *was* a Prince of Denmark. We say: there *was* a Prince
of Ithaca. It has been pointed out that the heroes of the Trojan War
were either descendants of a certain Aeolus, with fairly long pedi-
grees, or were grandsons, in some cases great-grandsons, of Zeus
or some other god. In other words it was only for a limited number
of generations the heroes knew who their forefathers were. When
knowledge ceased, they provided themselves with a god-ancestor;
not out of vanity, like that which, in later societies, caused com-
moners who had done well for themselves to create fictitious pedi-
grees of nobility. They were the people who had raised themselves
above their fellows. By force of arms, and guile, which was hardly
less respected, they had become masters of lands and herds and
women. They felt it was not at all improbable that it was a god who
had sired their breed. For, after all, gods were not very different in
kind from themselves. They had more privileges and talents. Above
all they were a good deal more mobile. That was about all.

The names of these heroes sprung from gods are recorded only
in poetry, and later in drama and lyric. But one or two have a
historic existence that seems to be confirmed outside that volatile
air, and in the dryer records of another people. The name of
the one most pertinent to this tale is Atreus, the father of Agamemnon and Menelaus. The archives of the Hittite monarchs, who
reigned over large parts of Asia Minor for some centuries before
1200 B.C., have been discovered in the squalid little village of Boghuz
Keui, the site of the one-time Hittite capital. One of the inscribed
clay tablets which constitute these archives records an attack on a
Hittite province by a certain Attarissyas, ruler of Ahhiyava. It was
first announced by Farrer, a Swiss scholar, in 1924, that this same

Attarissyas is none other than this same Atreus. As for the country
of Ahhiyava of which he was the ruler, it had long been concluded
that that was Achaea. Other scholars bent their ears to the vowels
and consonants as locksmiths to the tumblers of a lock. Raising
their heads, some cautiously confirmed the pronouncement. It was
deduced further, both from certain passages in the Iliad and from
this tablet, that Agamemnon had inherited a sceptre, the symbol of
some definite authority, from Atreus, who had been recognized by
the Hittite king as *koiranos*, perhaps the equivalent of *tyrannos*, or
tyrant, of the Achaeans. Other scholars remained unimpressed. There
are too many syllables in the Hittite names, they say, to make this con-
densation into the Greek forms likely. The layman would wistfully
like to believe that the identifiers have made an important discovery.

But Atreus is not the only personage who, having hitherto
existed only in the world of Greek poetry or legend, has been brought
into the sober air of history by recent archaeological discovery;
chiefly in the Mycenae-Hittite field of reference. Atreus of Mycenae
is the only one of these characters actually referred to in Homer, but
Farrer and others also identify in those same Hittite records the
names of Andreus and Eteocles, two figures from Archomenos,
another of Homer's "golden" cities. A more solid identification,
and the most recent, concerns a personage named "Mopsus". In
1946, a Turkish expedition investigated a site, now called Karatepe,
in Cilicia, in a wild part of the Taurus Mountains, where they found
a small citadel fortified by a wall and ornamented with lions in the
gateways.

"They excavated the gateways," writes R. D. Barnett, "and
found them to be flanked by sculptured slabs and inscriptions
partly in Phoenician, partly in Hittite hieroglyphs. A further
excavation on the summit of the hill found other inscriptions in
these two languages, which finally, when compared, proved to
be versions of the same text. The long-sought bilingual which
would interpret Hittite hieroglyphic script had been found.
Confirmation was now to be found of the slow and hesitant
interpretations of the hieroglyphs which had been interpreted
over ninety years."[3]*

From these reciprocally interpreting inscriptions it emerges that
he chieftain who thus places himself on record is one Azitawad, a
ord of the Danunim who here at Karatepe built his city. The

*For reference, see Bibliography, page 240.

Danunim are to be identified with the Greek Danaans who had long ago left Greece for Troy, left Troy for adventures further south in Asia Minor, and are on record as the Aegean Sea-Raiders of Egypt in the twelfth century B.C., wearing the same attire as the Philistines. Azitawad declares his descent from one Mopsus; and this is a good deal more dramatic than it sounds. For this Mopsus has hitherto existed only in terms of Greek legend. In those terms he was a celebrated seer, a son of Apollo by a daughter of Teiresias, that most famous seer of all classical legend (the same Teiresias whom Odysseus consulted in the Underworld). The legends further state that a year before the end of the Trojan War, Mopsus led a band of followers southward to Cilicia, this very region where the carved record of his name has been found. Here in Cilicia he married Pamphyle, daughter of Kabderos. "Kabderos can hardly be anything but a Grecised version of Kaftor," Barnett continues, "the Biblical name of Crete, the home of Minoan Cretans, the Keftiu of the Egyptians."

It emerges, in fact, that a Greek character hitherto considered mythological is now by archaeological cross-reference discovered to have had a documented historical existence. The cross-reference to Mopsus seems more positive than the connection between Atreus and Attarissyas, but it is probable that within the next few years the excavations will throw more light on these dim figures, hitherto illumined only by the spectral light of myth.

But Odysseus is my theme, and the luck of the wheel that spun some three thousand years ago, to get Attarissyas-Atreus, the father of Agamemnon, complete with his sceptre, recorded on a Hittite clay tablet. I regret that Laertes, the father of Odysseus, is on record only in the hexameters of Homer. But it is Homer who vouches for him as the son of a son of Zeus. It is Homer who made his son Odysseus a leading actor in one of the world's great poems, and the eponymous hero of another. Old Laertes did not do so badly for himself.

But as I stood on the summit of Hissarlik it was easy for me to believe that some day, soon or late, a stone will somewhere be unearthed which will give to Odysseus, if he needs it, the historic validity of an Atreus or a Mopsus. (An ancient stone actually bearing the name of Odysseus has, in fact, been disinterred; moreover, it was disinterred in Ithaca. But it was by about a thousand years too late. And it is a theological rather than a historical document. I wil' come to it in due place.)

Gazing down on the plain and the beach, I felt Odysseus to be a very living person without benefit of hieroglyph. I could tell myself I had caught up, as one might say, with my hero during the important Trojan phase of his career. He had come to this place with his peers to demand that Helen should be restored to the arms of Menelaus, her rightful lord. A good deal had happened to him before his marriage, and now he had left behind him in his native land a wife and a small son. His character had been formed. He was a mature man; palpably the same man in the Odyssey as the Iliad; on the one hand a fine talker, cunning, resourceful and prudent, on the other a warrior as brave as any of his fellows.

But that is not the Odysseus who took possession of my imagination when I was a small boy. It is true that as time went by, I realized there was, so to speak, a flesh-and-blood Odysseus, as real and vivid as the characters in the great prose works of fiction, and I identified with delight the lineaments of my hero which endow him with this notable actuality. But, of course, the Odysseus who enthralled me was the adventurer among perilous seas and faery islands forlorn, and the career of this Odysseus begins when the Trojan wars were over.

And over they were for both of us, as I descended the Hill of Troy. The ancient Citroën, which looked as if Schliemann had dug it up from one of his excavated cities, was waiting a few hundred yards away south and east of Hissarlik. Three or four miles away the blue-prowed ships of Odysseus were awaiting their captain.

For the Achaeans it was not plain sailing. As happens so frequently after a victory, a little trouble had arisen among the victors. Menelaus was for getting off without delay. Perhaps he thought that now he had retrieved Helen, the sooner he removed her from temptation the better, though she was not so young as she had been. Agamemnon was all for making ceremonial offerings to Athene. He stayed. Menelaus went, accompanied by Odysseus and some of the chief princes. But Odysseus got no further than the island of Tenedos close by, where he turned again to renew his allegiance to Agamemnon. That accomplished, he hoisted sail again. "Now, my lads!" he exclaimed to the sailors. "Now for Ithaca and our wives again!"

But as we well know, there was not one of all his ship's company, excepting himself, who ever saw Ithaca again. And that would be ten long years later. And there would be many adventures.

CHAPTER FIVE

Circe, Sirens, Lotus-eaters

I

FOR my own part I had already in days gone by visited a good many of the places associated with the adventures which now lay before Odysseus on leaving Troy. My narrative must, therefore, be retrospective for a time. I go back as far as the early twenties, the first war being over, my time in Oxford being over, and money so scarce in the foreseeable future that Ithaca is nothing more than a pipe-dream. However, I was young. I would get to Ithaca some day, I vowed, whether it took me five years or twenty-five. For the time being, I was well content to find myself in the Italian *mezzogiorno*, for I knew I was in Odyssean country again.

The present headquarters of the region is Naples, which, though a city founded by Greeks, had not been founded by the time the young Homer was in these parts, if he ever was, or Odysseus before him. What is much more likely, even certain, is the fact that in the first centuries following the composition of the Odyssey, the early colonists brought with them either the poems or the tales and myths out of which the poem was created; probably they brought both. How far northward along the Italian peninsula they carried this matter with them it is difficult to say, but certainly as far north as the present-day Monte Circei, rather more than half-way as the crow flies between Naples and Rome.

Now this Monte Circei, though a promontory, is the traditional site of Aaea, Circe's Island, and it may well have been an island even so recently as the Odyssean time, there is on its landward side so much silt of sand and ooze of marsh. So forth I fared by the slow, hot train southward from Rome to Terracina and thence found my way to the domain of Circe. It was all there, the narrow channel where the ships of Odysseus beached, the high place where he spied out the land, the murky woods where the creatures wandered whom Circe had bewitched, and over in the valley of San Benedetto some kilometres away the tumbled slabs of the temple of Feronia goddess of wild beasts, who has often been equated with the love-sick enchantress. I have since learned that even the magic herb, moly, which Hermes plucked and gave to Odysseus to make him

Chanakkale: Landing-place for Troy

Troy: a litter of ancient ruin

Capri: Island of the Sirens

immune from Circe's spell, is still to be gathered in that countryside, a plant which is pretty much as the poet describes it—with a black root and a milk-white flower . . . "an awkward plant to dig up, at any rate for a mere man; but the gods, after all, can do anything".

I did not find the herb, moly, but on the journey towards Naples I went to some pains in a *trattoria* in Terracina to order a meal as close as possible to the one Circe laid out for the hapless sailors, "cheese and barley meal, and yellow honey flavoured with Pramnian wine". The wine may not have been Pramnian, and the barley meal was maize, I think. But by the time I staggered into the train for Naples I was quite as drowsy as those old sailors were.

After liberating his companions and staying with Circe for a year, Odysseus begged for leave to depart, whether his conscience smote him, or because he was sick with longing for his wife and son, or because he had had enough of that Pramnian wine. The enchantress, it will be remembered, knowing that it was impossible to restrain him, compelled him to descend into Hades and consult the illustrious seer, Teiresias, who had lived several times the mortal span, but was dead now.

Now, according to the poet, Odysseus sailed westward for a day, to deep-flowing Ocean and to the entrance to the dark house of Hades. But if the topographical traditions are to be respected, he did not sail westward, but southward and a little east, to reach the dismal land. Westward from Naples, at a distance of some sixteen kilometres, is the Lago Averno, or Lake Avernus, which, according to many ancient writers and all present-day guides, is the site of the dark abyss where Odysseus made the descent that Circe had enjoined upon him, in the land where "the fog-bound Cimmerians live in the City of Perpetual Mist".

The countryside did not look like that when I got there, for the sun hissed and fumed like a molten ingot and the earth yawned with thirst at the entrance of the Sibylline Grotto they showed me, hollowed out in the pale tufa under Avernus. On the crater of the small volcano of Solfatara, where the sulphur-bubbles open and shut again like the single eye of Cyclops, the concourse of ghosts that had been invoked were very solid indeed, they were a troop of apple-green-jerkined German *Wandervögel* playing ball in formation. Perhaps it was not the region Homer had in mind. Certain Roman writers maintain he meant Spain, others the Crimea and elsewhere. Undoubtedly there was a historical people known by the name of Cimmerians, who were driven southward by the Scythians from their pastures in the region now called Southern Russia, and ultimately

F

reached Asia Minor, probably after Homer's day. It can hardly have been there he meant. Or was it that in this mephitic region, Bérard speculates, a race once dwelt who were keepers of an oracle of the dead? (For the tunnels in which such a people once lived, and kept the offerings of the faithful, are to be seen cut into the tufa to this day.)

But wherever the actual Cimmerians were when Homer composed the Odyssey, he treated them as a moon-people in a never-never land. He implies they were to the north somewhere, but in that land north is south and south north. He had possibly heard a tale from that old salt whom I invoked earlier, that there was a region somewhere where the day was very short and the night horribly long, and why should its inhabitants not be called Cimmerians? In fact, so early in my private Odyssey, I was well aware no place in the Odyssean voyages is incontestably anywhere. Excepting Troy and Ithaca. There could be little doubt of Troy and none at all of Ithaca. Schliemann, whose diggings were almost an Iliad in themselves, had established the site of Troy; and Ithaca, known as Ithaca from the earliest historical times, was self-evidently Ithaca. I had a dim notion even then that some scholar (it was in fact the renowned Herr Dörpfeld) had maintained that Ithaca was not really Ithaca but some island hard by. (I was to find out he meant the island of Leukas.) The idea made me rather angry then. Now, some thirty years later, it makes me just as angry.

So I left behind me the land of the Cimmerians—at least the Neapolitan Cimmerians—and set out for Capri, the Island of the Sirens, and the metropolis of Sirenland. If I identify Capri as the Siren Island *par excellence*, it is partly because that has been frequently done in the past, all the way back to Roman times, partly because there is no Caprese, permanent or temporary, who is not so convinced. The rocky ledge on which the Sirens sat was pointed out to me again and again along the whole perimeter of the island, sometimes with a note of anxious insistence when it was imagined I was a rich *forestiere* anxious to buy a rock to build a villa on. I once pointed out that the poe. explicitly states that the Sirens sang, not from a rock, but from the midst of a flowery meadow.

"And what's that yonder, *prego*?" the reply was on one occasion. My friend was pointing to a terrace about as big as a door-mat, with young wheat growing, and a blue tongue of lithospermum flickering here and there. It occurred to me that the island can hardly have been terraced yet in the time of the Sirens, but I did not pursue the subject, it seemed a little pedantic.

I loved the island, and love it still, though at the time of writing it has become so dizzily "smart". Perhaps it cannot long remain like that, and sooner or later the international "set" will take wing to something newer and smarter, and leave the island to its slightly scoundrelly natives, and the slightly crackpot writers, and the dim widows, and the painters of the Faraglioni, and to Edwin Cerio, sirenologue, island polymath, and one-time *sindaco*, who was born in the time of Tiberius (it has been mysteriously said) and has outlived Norman Douglas, and may outlive Gracie Fields.

II

Over on the adjoining *terra firma* of Sirenland, they have ideas of their own about the original Siren Island. Homer has made it clear that there was not one Siren but two. Why should there not be two, and even more, Siren Islands? And why shouldn't one or two of them have been headlands? For to the wandering mariner an island sometimes looks like a headland and a headland like an island.

It will always remain for me as delightful a memory as almost any in my own protracted Odyssey that it was with Norman Douglas himself, the archi-sirenologue, that I went hunting Sirens in Sirenland. In those springtimes of the early twenties, Douglas often spent a few weeks on the odorous plateau and in the entranced coves of the Sorrentine Peninsula. I had met him in Capri during this magical time and had told him of my Odyssean fantasy.

"Very well, young man," said he. "You're leaving soon? Join up with me in Sant' Agata. We'll go siren-hunting and see if we can't put a pinch or two of salt on their tails."

"What sort of tails?" I asked. "Fish-tails? Bird-tails?"

He put his finger to the side of his nose.

"One old writer, I forget who, called them centaur-destroying nightingales. They weren't. They were penguins." He grinned. "You didn't know that, did you?"

So I went siren-hunting with Douglas on the immortal mountain. Northward was Naples, once called Parthenope, after the lovely Siren whose body was washed ashore and buried there. In the time of Strabo they still showed her mausoleum there and held torch-races in her honour, because she was so chaste. " 'Chaste Parthenope!' they called her. *Chaste!*" Douglas repeated with that famous chuckle and the sudden magpie caw that topped it. He quoted the grisly lines from Homer . . . the meadow piled high with the mouldering skeletons of men, whose withered skin still hangs upon their bones. "Or turn this way! Look!" He pointed southward, where the mountains of Basilicata break down to the sea, and Leucosia, a sister-Siren, lies buried under the promontory of Licosa.

"Or there's the cliff of Pelorum at the entrance to the Straits of Messina," he said. "You can have your choice. My choice is the Galli Islands. You can't see them from here. They're inshore, just below us. You could spit on them, if your spit would travel that far. Three of them. Homer says two, but they probably mated. I've sometimes been in a small boat down there and a wind got up and I was on the rocks as near as dammit."

"Homer says the Sirens sat on a flowery meadow when they sang their songs," I reminded him. "Your rocks don't seem to have much room for flowery meadows."

"You'll see for yourself. On the Gallo Lungo there's a meadow big enough for a whole choir to sing a Handel oratorio."

"Shall we see penguins?" I asked.

"Perhaps, or we might see that dancer fellow. What's his name? Massine. He's just bought one of the islands."

If Massine danced on his new island, even without penguins (I thought) it would be a notable expedition. The Sirens did not sing and Massine did not dance, though, sure enough, there was a flowery meadow large enough for both on the Gallo Lungo. But the water chuckled from our oars in hexameters. A kestrel flew over the first island and the second. The odours of rock-vine and myrtle puffed hot and dry from between the boulders. Douglas suspended his wry and learned exegesis. "Siren" did not relate itself any more to *Sirius*, star of the dog days, the days when becalmed sailors became mad and hear the songs of maidens who are not maidens but keel-disembowelling rocks; nor to *Syrinx*, the pipe of the winds in the rigging which to sailors is enchantment and brings them death at length on desolate shores. "Siren" was exactly, literally, a singing maiden who at any moment might raise herself from among those tall stalks of asphodel, and, resting her body on her hands, sing the rest of that ditty on which Homer recorded too few verses.

III

From Sirenland, this time inshore and by train by way of Paestum, I went a second time to Scylla and Charybdis, and over by the ferry-train to Messina and Sicily. There were various reasons why I went to Sicily. Who would not journey to Sicily from much further afield, from anywhere at all, if the chance came to him—and I was already in Southern Italy? There was the landscape of Sicily; there were the remains of its noble civilizations all the way back to the Greeks and the pre-Greeks. There were the mosaics. I had already been spell-bound by mosaic in Salonica, Venice, Ravenna and elsewhere. There were the marionettes, of the same eloquent South Mediterranean race as had already captivated me in Naples. Then finally there was the Odyssey, and I knew that there has always been a considerable measure of agreement that if the episodes of the Odyssey are to be located anywhere on this side of the moon, then some must be located on Sicilian land and in Sicilian waters. I was aware that when Homer speaks of Sicania, it was held he probably meant Sicily, and that probably he meant Sicily again when he speaks of Thrinacria, a name close enough to "Trinacria", one of the island's undoubted names in antiquity. Still unaware of the incredible range and variety of Odyssean identifications, for me Sicily, Sicania, Thrinacria, Trinacria were all one . . . and still are.

There, in Sicily, according to Strabo and many others, I would find the land of the giant cannibals, the Cyclops, where Odysseus and his men underwent the first of their adventures after they had left behind them the Island of the Lotus-eaters. Sicily was also perhaps the land of the no less ferocious Laestrygonians, which he reached after he had been blown all the way back from Ithaca into these hazardous regions. The poet's description of the climate in the land of the Laestrygonians ("there might a sleepless man have earned a double wage, the one as neatherd, the other as shepherding white flocks; so near are the outgoings of the night and the day") reads a good deal more like the climate of Britain, or even Spitzbergen, than of a Mediterranean island. It reads also like the climate of the Cimmerians, who have been placed in regions far removed from Sicily. But one would not argue the matter with Strabo. According to the same ancient writers Sicily was also the island of Helios, also called Thrinacia. There, after surviving the frightful dangers of Scylla and Charybdis, Odysseus and his men were compelled by adverse winds to take shelter for a month, only to incur the wrath of the Sun-God, a more potent daemon, when the witless crew slaughtered the sacred cattle that pastured there.

Yes, there was Odyssey enough and to spare in Sicily. On that first visit, I saw more than one cavern in various regions where Odysseus had poked out the eye of the Cyclops, Polyphemus, with a stake of charred olive-wood. I saw more than one rock which Polyphemus in his pain and fury had sent hurtling after Odysseus and his ship. In the plain of Leontini north-west of Syracuse I made more than one excursion into Cyclopean and Laestrygonian land. But while I was engaged upon this canonical Odyssey (if the word is permissible in this context) I was brought for the first time into the traces of the Apocryphal Odyssey of Samuel Butler. By this I mean not that Samuel Butler produced another poem and said that that was Homer's Odyssey. He produced another author and said that he, or she, rather, was Homer. Her name was Nausicaa. She had, he said, produced a portrait of herself in the charming character of the Princess Nausicaa of Scheria, the young lady who was so helpful to Odysseus when he was washed up naked and solitary on the shore of her father's island. I have sometimes wondered whether Butler really started off by believing in the proposition he expounded in *The Authoress of the Odyssey* with so much ingenuity and bravura. I wondered whether it started off by being a provoking paradox, and ended up by becoming an article of faith only when he found people often his intellectual inferiors treating his ideas with contempt or, worse, totally ignoring them. Certainly, according to the biography written by Henry Festing Jones, he finally came to believe it with such passion that it made him quite ill. I did, in fact, discuss these matters with Festing Jones, in his house in Maida Vale, a few hundred yards away from the house where I write these words.

"Did it really start off as an absolutely serious theory," I asked, "or was it an exercise in paradox?"

Henry Festing Jones looked at me for a long time without saying a word, then at last he spoke:

"What do *you* think?" he asked.

What I thought then is what I think now. It's all rather too slick and easy. When a short time ago I put the same question to that distinguished Homerist, Sir Maurice Bowra, I received the identical words in reply: It's all rather too slick and easy. But it did not seem a tactful way to reply to Festing Jones three decades ago.

"It's all very convincing," I said hesitantly, "and very exciting."

"Very well then," said Festing Jones. An eyelid quivered. I could not decide whether he had winked at me, or whether the lid twitched in a Maida Vale draught. He turned the vast cylinder of his body round towards the mantelpiece. "Anyhow," he continued, without turning round, "he often used to say to me that it was much the most important thing he had done."

I felt that even that did not really prove anything, for Butler had this in common with Odysseus, one could never be certain whether he intended to be taken absolutely seriously.

As I say, I was not convinced even then, any more than the publishers, Murray, Bentley and Bell, who all rejected the manuscript as frivolous. I refused to throw the "canonical" Ithaca overboard, but the whole concept of an authoress for the Odyssey gave that extra stimulus and flavour to my travels in Sicily which have always been created for me by the association of landscape with a great personage or with great poetry. However stupendous the mountain scenery of the Rockies may be, however heart-searing the desolation of the Arabic tundras, in the absence of the elements I have spoken of I would soon find them stale and unprofitable.

So I explored the streets of Trapani, which Butler held to be not only Ithaca itself, but Nausicaa's Scheria, as well, and a good deal more. In fact, Butler's contention is that practically everything in the Odyssey began in Trapani, happened in and around Trapani, and ended in Trapani. He is not impressed by the fact that Thucydides, a writer considerably nearer in time to Homer than himself, gives as the view that "the inhabitants of Corfu were the descendants of the Phaeacians, and the rock into which their ship was turned as it was entering the harbour after having escorted Ulysses to Ithaca is still shewn at Corfu". Butler is well aware that Corfu was called Scheria in old times. But he is quite dogmatic about Corfu offering "no single point of correspondence with the description given in the Odyssey", a view in which he is in a very small minority. One feels that his claim to have visited every likely western shore of every likely Mediterranean island is probably excessive. Years later, on my final Odyssean adventure, the thought returned to me with emphasis when I visited Palaeokastritza in the north-western part of Corfu, which embodies every feature of Homer's account so exactly that you feel the poet must have been there only a day or two earlier and taken notes. Did Butler go to Palaeokastritza, I wonder? There is no indication that he did, in Festing Jones's *Life*. But Butler's *idée fixe* being as powerful as it was, would it have made any difference if he had?

What does it matter? He was good company as I walked the streets of Trapani, Nausicaa on my right hand, Butler on my left; and climbed the slopes of Monte San Giuliano, once called Eryx, to go visiting the Cyclops and the Laestrygonians and to explore the cave where Odysseus hid the treasure that Alcinous, Nausicaa's father, had given him. We were still together when I took the little

steam-ship westward to the Aegadean Islands which, according to
the theory, were the "demes" of Odysseus as listed by Homer in the
Catalogue of the Achaean forces in the Iliad, and later by Odysseus
himself when he told his story in Scheria, in the palace of Alcinous,
long after he had left Troy behind him.

It was not convincing, but it was all very intriguing. And picking
up Butler's book again only the other day, I found I was just as intrigued as I had been all those years ago by the master's delightful
non sequiturs.

IV

I come to another less debatable Odyssean scene I added to my
tally during those mid-twenty springtimes, with Trapani itself as the
point of departure. For finding that a boat from Naples and Palermo
stopped at Trapani to pick up passengers for Tunis, and knowing
that by way of Tunis you can reach the island of Djerba which lies
to the south, off the Gulf of Gabes, I packed my Odyssey in my ruck-
sack, and off I went.

For Djerba has been held to be the Island of the Lotophagi, the
Lotus-eaters, since classical times. Old Herodotus gives them a
footing in near-history, though not an absolutely clear one, by
locating them among the Libyan tribes who live westward from
Egypt, on a promontory jutting out into the sea from the country of
the Gindanes. But since there is only one promontory or peninsula
in the territory Herodotus is describing, and that is the Zarzis,
southward from the town we now call Tunis and at the north-east
corner of the Gulf of Gabes, Strabo places them offshore in the Island
of Meninx, now called Djerba, which may well have been connected
with the mainland at one time.

So forth I fared for Djerba, untroubled by the thought that
whereas, in the Odyssean sequence, the Lotus-eaters should have
followed straight on after my visit to the land of the Cicones in the
neighbourhood of Salonica, I had allowed a number of the Adventures to come between—Lipari or Stromboli for the Island of
Aeolus, Capri for the Siren Islands, Monte San Giuliano for the
land of the Laestrygonians. At all events, when I had paid my visit,
roughly, very roughly, to the land of the Cicones, I had behaved
rather more temperately in the Ciconian Salonica than my hero in
Ciconian Ismarus, where without compunction he had sacked the
place and murdered its inhabitants. The Ciconians, too, must have

Sicily: Laestrygonian landscape

Djerba: A land whe

always afternoon

Djerba : Island of
the Lotus - eaters

had their tutelary deities. They let him sail at ease as far as Cape Malea, the southernmost point of the Greek mainland; his sail was set fair for his native land. But then it was that a swell and a current arose, a fierce wind blew from the North, and all these combined drove him wildly off his course. "For six days," he complains, "I was chased by those accursed winds across the fish-infested seas." The s.s. *Ernest Simon*, the craft that, it may be remembered, bore *me* from the region of the Cicones evaded, at least while I was on her, the dangers that threatened her. So it happened that it was years later, not nine days, I fetched up among the Lotus-eaters.

Djerba is an island of such enchantment that it is impossible not to be sent a little crazy by it, with or without benefit of lotus. If Homer in his boyhood had been a ship's boy for a year or two, as I earlier allowed myself to speculate, perhaps his ship had been driven by a great gale as far as Djerba. Perhaps it was that old salt who told a tale or two as the ship waited for cargo in some foreign harbour. Or maybe the boy never got further than the quayside of Chios or Smyrna or whatever place he was born in, and there heard such tales of far places, as the youth Shakespeare heard in London taverns from the lips of bearded sailors discoursing of the still-vext Bermoothes. Today's traveller in Djerba will attribute part of his delight to the totally unpretentious and peculiarly lovely architecture of the place, the small white domes, the minarets, the arcades, the courtyards. But those are only an accident. The Lotus-eaters lived in houses and trafficked in market-places of a different style. The essence of the beauty of Djerba is something compounded of the colour of the sea about the yellow sands, the warmth of those sands, the light and shade of the groves they encompass, the taste of the containing air that lies like lotus in the hollow of the tongue. Yes, in Djerba, particularly by moonlight, one finds it easy to believe that a lotus-plant may once have grown there such as the poet describes, and that it may be growing there at this very day, if one knows where to look for it.

Where then to look for it, this "flowery food"? Was it eaten raw? Cooked? Or was it, is it, distilled, maybe? It is impossible, when one is in Djerba, not to think a lot about it, and in after days to look up the commentators, to see what they have to say on the matter. The sailors of Odysseus, Homer tells us, had disembarked to draw water on the island, and had eaten their midday meal on the beach. Three of them were then sent inland to find out what sort of human beings might be there. "It was not long before they were in touch with the

Lotus-eaters. Now it never entered the heads of these natives to kill my friends; what they did was to give them some lotus to taste, and as soon as each had eaten the honeyed fruit of the plant, all thoughts of reporting to us or escaping were banished from his mind."

In other words, Homer does not suggest the lotus was eaten any other way than straight off the stalk, as you might an apple or a strawberry. Herodotus is more precise. The Lotophagi "live entirely on the fruit of the lotus-tree". A tree, therefore. "The lotus fruit is about the size of the lentisk berry, and in sweetness resembles the date. The Lotophagi even succeed in obtaining from it a sort of wine." Polybius confirms this, saying that the lotus-berry is about the size of the olive, is purple when ripe, and tastes like figs or dates; but it is eaten for food as well as distilled for wine. Pliny hands us the *celthus*, a tree this time, known to us as the nettle-tree, the *celtus australis*. It grows small black cherries, such as some millenia later our British soldiery often ate in the Tripoli campaigns, without experiencing the Odyssean somnolence. Other commentators offer us the fruit of the date-palms, which we know from various sources to have been familiar to Greek sailors; and the fruit of the North African *zizyphus lotus*, commonly known as the jujube-tree, which bears a black and yellow berry. One need not consider the date seriously, for it looks neither like an olive nor a crab-apple. And one prefers to retain the utmost reserve regarding the fruit of the jujube-tree, for the unscientific and overwhelming reason that one cannot allow the lotus to have been the jujube.

What remains? A more recent writer, Rawlinson, editor of *Herodotus*, has very little doubt on the matter. "The lotus is evidently the *Rhamnus*, now called in Arabic *Sidr*, the fruit *Nebk*. It looks and tastes rather like a bad crab-apple. It has a single stone within it."

Let me add my confirmation, for what it is worth, to the assertion of Rawlinson. I have both eaten and drunk lotus *in situ*, that is to say in Djerba, the Island of the Lotus-eaters; and it was to the Jewish villages of Hara-Kebira and Hara Serira in Djerba that one had to go to eat and drink lotus. The French officials on the island knew nothing about it, and that is to be expected. The grape they know, to make wine and brandy. The apple they know, to make Calvados. But they are not likely to have much use for the *Nebk*, the fruit of the *Sidr*. The Muslims, too, refrain from distilling the *Nebk*; and that is not because the Prophet forbade them to drink fermented fruit-juice, for, indeed, they distil the peach to make *Boukha*, a potent liquor. No, it is the Jews of Djerba and the Jews only, who distil the

Nebk, to make wine and eat the fruit itself, preserved whole in that drowsy liquor.

It is the Jews, I told myself excitedly, who are to-day's Loto-phagi. (It should be remembered that those were serene days in the history of the relations between Jews and Muslims. At least they were serene compared with what they had been, and what they were to be two or three decades later. And I should add that many of those same Lotus-eaters whom I met in the mid-twenties have been roused from their millenial torpor, and have flown like their brethren from Tunisia, Morocco, Yemen, Irak, on the wings of an eagle to Israel. But some remain. At the hands of those same Djerban Jews it is still possible to drink lotus, and to eat it, preserved whole in the rich amber liquor of the *Sidr*.)

But it was still nineteen-twenty-six when my friend, Sidi Pinchas Sabban, Lotophagos, ushered me through the courtyard into the cool vaulted room which was his habitation, there in the ghetto of Houmt-Sûk. There he was, some minutes later, drawing forth a jar of lotus-wine from a niche in the wall alongside the deep recess where the folded rugs were, and pouring away the layer of olive-oil which protected it from the air, just as the wine of the Romans was protected two thousand years ago, and the wine of the peasant Italians is protected at this day. There was his wife beside him, a Jewess whose lineaments were purely Greek, broad chin, broad cheeks, full lips, the nose and forehead in one straight line.

I drank a glass. Sidi Pinchas Sabban pressed on me another and another. From a jar he extracted the fruit itself, the preserved crab-apple of the commentators. I must have another glass to wash it down. Once more the words of the poet swung through my brain like the shadow of wistaria swaying upon a wall. "And as soon as each had eaten the honeyed fruit of the plant all thoughts of report-ing to us or escaping were banished from his mind. All they now wished for was to stay where they were with the Lotus-eaters, to browse on the lotus and to forget they had a home to return to."

Let me get it straight now, I speculated drowsily. If the Jews of Djerba are to-day's Lotus-eaters, is it wholly impossible that they were Homer's Lotus-eaters, too? Can there have been Jews in Djerba at the time when Homer composed the poems, two or three cen-turies (let us say) after the beginning of the first millenium B.C.? What awareness of Jews did Homer shew? None at all. But he was well aware of the Semitic kinsmen of the Jews, the Phoenicians— the *Phoenikes,* he called them, the dark-crimson men, stained with the murex dye from which they derived their name; those famous

mariners who had already explored the Mediterranean and passed
through the Pillars of Hercules, and founded the towns of Gades,
or Cadiz, and Tartessus, or Tarshish, where in later centuries
Solomon was to pick up every third year his cargo of gold, silver,
ivory, apes and peacocks.

If Homer in Chios, or Smyrna, was aware of the Phoenicians,
then surely so were their kinsmen, the Jews, high on their Canaanitish
hill-tops. It is easy to believe that among the Jews there were from
generation to generation certain restless ones, as there have always
been, who looked down from their heights over the hostile plains
towards the sea, and thought they heard it whispering upon the
sands as they heard it whispering within the skull. At last they said to
themselves they had had enough of being fighting-men in the hot
dungeons of Jericho, enough of terracing the arid rock slopes of
Judaea in the sweat of their brows. So down they went towards the
sea, avoiding their enemies, the Philistines, and turning north-
westward towards their kinsmen, the Phoenicians, who lived in
Tyre on the seaboard of Syria, and spoke a language akin to their
own.

In course of time, they, or their sons, went to sea in Phoenician
bottoms, adventuring along the mythical shores. At some time
during those adventures a ship went aground on a far island off the
fabulous land of the troglodytes. They found a sort of crab-apple
tree and brewed from it a wine which stilled in them all heartache
for the busy docks of Tyre and the last dim memory they had of the
sacred city of Zion on the hills.

Then later a ship's captain named Odysseus, a Greek who had
been fighting far off in a place called Troy, and had been seeking to
get back to his native island, was blown off course by a great wind and
was grounded on the bright sands of Djerba. He had sent out
messengers to find out what sort of people the islanders were . . .

"One more glass, monsieur?" Sidi Pinchas Sabban was insisting.
"Yes, I have heard about this Greek. What do you say his name
was?"

"Odysseus. The Romans called him Ulysses."

"Yes, Ulysse. You do not think he was perhaps a Jew?"

"I think not."

"But they say the most Jewish of those Greeks?"

"That is not unlikely. Well, yes. Perhaps one more. . . ."

Odysseus had to use force to bring his men back to the ships.
But perhaps one or two stayed behind, and received in marriage the
hands of daughters of the Hebrew Lotus-eaters. And their seed did

not die out. And here was the wife of Sidi Pinchas Sabban, pure
Homeric Greek, standing in the doorway like Nausicaa newly-wed,
etched on an early Ionian vase.

V

It was 1926, and ten years since I had begun my voyages in the
wake of Odysseus. I was beginning to feel rather old. If I did not get
to Ithaca pretty soon now, I thought, I would probably never get
there.

So, being in Southern Italy once more, I set out for Ithaca in the
spring of that year. Naturally I chose Brindisi as my port of departure. And though I intended to wander about in Continental Greece,
as I had not been able to do in 1916, it was Ithaca I was making
for; at least Ithaca was to be my first port of call. In course of
time I would find myself in various places on the mainland where
Odysseus had been before me, and perhaps beyond the mainland,
in another Continent.

The grubby little shipping-office in Brindisi assured me that the
vessel I was going to sail in would stop two or three days in Corfu,
and I was happy about that; it would give me the opportunity of
seeing certain places on the north-west coast of the island which
many authorities were disposed to accept as Scheria, the homeland
of Nausicaa and her kind father, Alcinous, king of the Phaeacians.
It was from Scheria that Odysseus had made that last voyage which
had restored him to Ithaca at last, so it was a suitable order of
progress. I felt a little guilty still about the ghost of Samuel Butler,
with whom I had had such good times in Trapani, his own private
Scheria. But science came first, and off I went to Corfu.

In Corfu I realized that the Brindisi shipping-office hadn't really
known much about the boat's intentions, for we stopped there only
a day and a night, just time enough to unload the sacks of manganese
(I think it was) and to take on a colossal cargo of Paschal lambs,
which were to be slaughtered and eaten over in the mainland cities
during the Greek Eastertide, which was imminent.

But I was anything but depressed to be moving on to Ithaca a
couple of days sooner than it had been intended. I had been ten
years about it, as long as Odysseus himself, and in the epoch of the
steam-ship, too. So southward we sailed with the toothy mountains
of Epirus to port, and to starboard the silver olive-groves of Corfu,
punctuated with dark-green and indigo cypresses, like disinterred

statues of Herculaneum. The water about us was like lapis molten in a vast crucible, just faintly hissing. The multitude of lambs bleated with neither defiance nor hope. We were like a whole Sussex down-land floating, I thought, in these self-evidently Odyssean waters. (That morning, and forever, I said good-bye to the wilful ghost of Samuel Butler.)

There was an old man on board. He had been a watchmaker in Philadelphia, and was coming back to his wife after having been away from her for twenty years. "Twenty years," I said to myself. "It is, of course, a coincidence. But it's charming. He's been away from his old lady exactly as long as the other old wanderer had been away from Penelope."

"Twenty years?" I asked again casually.

The old man nodded. The creases folded on his neck like thick cloth bunched together.

I handed him an orange.

"My name's Lu-is," I said. "And yours?"

"Spiro," he told me. No, he did not say Odysseus. I breathed again. He was a watchmaker, after all, not a Greenwich Village artist-scholar making up a tale.

"And your wife's name?" I asked.

"Penelope," he said.

I did not believe it. And now I could not believe it was twenty years he had been away, either. He *was* cooking up a story. Yet he looked so exactly a watchmaker, an unlettered one, with that bristly chin, the tieless shirt, the grubby coat, the frayed and shapeless trousers.

Now, all these years later, I know better. The twenty years was neither this way nor that. It may be that, among the Greeks of the Islands, twenty is not a mathematical number, but a symbol meaning a long time. As for the wife's name, I have learned a woman is hard put to it, in Ithaca, not to have Penelope for her name. The first islander Schliemann met on his first visit to Ithaca was a blacksmith, he tells us, whose wife was named Penelope. His sons were named Odysseus and Telemachus. So is it still at this day.

We had left a long way behind us the small islands of Paxos and Antipaxos. A mountain, or a mountainous island, lay ahead. Was *that* Ithaca? No, not yet. It was Santa Mavra, some-one said. A peasant beside me retied his bundle. A lady, almost certainly no better than she should be, pursed her mouth and dabbed lipstick on it. A mountainous mass, this time certainly an island, hove up ahead. I looked at the map. There could be no question. That must be Cephalonia eastward and Ithaca westward, the royal domain of Prince Odysseus.

"Ithaca?" I asked the watchmaker.

"Thiaki!" he confirmed.

There it was. Ithaca, after all these years. There was a shifting forward of pulpy fibre suitcases among the few square feet of deck that was not a heave and a huddle of lambs. A ruck-sack was all I had of luggage. I switched it up on to my shoulders, but it was heavy and I let the straps fall. It would be a half-hour, maybe more, before we made our landfall in the tiny island harbour of Vathy.

The strait between the larger and the smaller islands was clear now. This high mountain was distinct Ithaca, not to be confused any more with its dependency. The lambs bleated. The engines coughed. Was it in that inlet there that Odysseus was put ashore by the Phaeacians? And if that were his landing-place, the Grotto of the Nymphs would be close by, just above sea-level, perhaps, the cave where, with Athene's aid, he stowed away the treasure those kindly Phaeacians had heaped upon him?

On the other hand, if Odysseus and his friends were coming from somewhere further west in the Mediterranean, wouldn't one have to look on the west coast for the landing-place? We ourselves were steaming south well over from the east coast. Surely we ought to be changing course soon and making westward towards the deep indentation where Vathy lies?

But we were doing no such thing. We were moving clear eastward, well away from the island. What was it all about? Were we not making for Ithaca at all? Or had a floating mine, or some wreckage, been reported in the vicinity?

"When, then, do we reach Ithaca?" I asked Spiro, the watchmaker.

He shrugged his shoulders.

"Who knows? When a boat leaves for Ithaca, we will go aboard."

"But we're *on* a boat for Ithaca, for God's sake, aren't we?"

"Patras, they said." Once again he shrugged his shoulders, disclaiming all responsibility for the vessel and the shipping-line it served.

A ship-hand interposed. He was an engineer, perhaps. He wore some sort of a peaked cap.

"Yes. We are for Patras. *Malista!*"

I was almost whimpering with vexation.

"But they told me in the office at Brindisi this boat stops at Ithaca."

He swivelled his palms round stiff on his wrists. The gesture seemed to indicate *he* wasn't going to be held responsible for the way the shipping-office in Brindisi conducted its business. He shoved off through the lambs, then turned again.

"We may stop at Ithaca, on the way back," he observed.

"When? How long do you stay in Patras?"

"Who knows? Perhaps we pick up cargo for Istanbul. *Then* maybe, we go back."

Ithaca was diminishing astern. The glow of the declining sun moved over towards it like a crowd of red-headed girls. My heavy heart was lightened a little by the thought that Odysseus, too, had been served this way. For after sailing from the island of Aeolus he, too, had got so near Ithaca as this; and then those blundering idiots had untied the leather bag, and let out the winds, and the business began all over again. In my case the blundering idiots, or petty crooks, I should say, were far off in Brindisi; I would get even with them some time.

Well, it's Patras, I said to myself. It's Patras, which is Greece. It might be an awful lot worse than that. What do I do when I get to Patras? I might take a boat back from Patras to Ithaca, and start again at the beginning. But I thought it likely I would not be able to afford that. I would go wandering through Greece, and might even get to Troy. Whatever happened, it would all *end* in Ithaca, anyhow. That is the glory of the Odyssey. Your beginning is the end, and the end is the beginning. If I'm careful, perhaps I can last out two months, even three, I thought. In three months, at most, I will be in Ithaca.

It took me a good deal longer than that. Thirty years in fact; all but four.

VI

I got off at Patras. It did not occur to me to camp out on the quayside and wait for the next boat for Ithaca. Besides, after my experience in Brindisi, there was no particular guarantee it would take me there. It might land me in Livorno or Oran.

It is true that Odysseus and the Odyssey were my major impulse. In certain places I might catch sight of the helmet of Odysseus gleaming far off, with its horsehair plume streaming like a combed cloud. But I looked forward also to other adventurers and adventures.

Sicilian landscape

Straits of Messina

There was Delphi and the unknown master in bronze who had made the Charioteer. There was Epidaurus, and certain other places where there was a theatre, and there were certain writers who had made plays to be performed there. There was Olympia, and certain athletes who had competed there and been immortalized by poets. There was Athens, again and always, and the ghosts of Pericles and Phaedias and Socrates.

Moreover (I had to remind myself) the Greece of the time of Odysseus was only one Greece, and the Greece of the time of Phaedias was only one more. There was the Greece of the Byzantines, too, and mediaeval Greece; and Byron's Greece; there was also contemporary Greece, of which I had caught a brief and exciting glimpse in 1916.

There was quite enough Greece to occupy both the time and the money I had at my disposal. There might be Troy, too. All in all, it would be better to keep Ithaca for later on.

So there in Greece I went wandering, in that mood alternating between exaltation and humility which the lovely land exacts from all who travel there, who receive in exchange an unequalled multiplicity of excitements and delights, confined in small space but free of great tracts of time. But through all my wanderings, I did not allow myself to forget Odysseus, though always and everywhere so many other notable ghosts appeared and beckoned and disappeared. When I went from Delphi climbing in the Parnassus region up those "steep and wooded heights", as the poet describes them, which remain steep but not wooded, I remembered that somewhere in the "windswept folds of the mountain" was that thick glade where, when Odysseus as a young man came to receive gifts from his grandfather Autolycus, the wild boar rushed out and gashed him above the knee. And many years later, when Odysseus, in the guise of a beggar, was back in Ithaca after all his wanderings, it was by the scar of that wound his old nurse, Eurycleia, was to recognize him, when she was washing his limbs.

That was in the Parnassus country. In Messene beyond the pronged ridges of Taygetus I remembered that Odysseus, still a young man, had been sent on a mission there by his father, Laertes, to demand reparation for the three hundred sheep a gang of Messenian raiders had carried off from Ithaca, sheep, shepherd, and all. There in Messene he was given the famous bow of Eurytas, so tough that none but Odysseus himself could draw it. He prized it so highly he never took it on board with him when he sailed to the wars, "but laid it up at home in memory of a treasured friend, though he did not use it on his own estate". And there it was when he got back there, as those insolent suitors were to learn to their cost.

In Corinth, where I kept myself by turning the handle of a resplendent barrel-organ, being a deputy for its owner who was down with malaria, I had time to learn from an old Professor in underpants, who was sitting by the water and sedulously hunting for fleas in the seams of his trousers, that Odysseus had been here, too, once. For Pallas Athene herself said (and the old man delivered himself of the pagan hexameters as if he were intoning a Byzantine chant) that Odysseus sailed to Ephyre to demand a poison for the bronze tips of his arrows, and it was refused him. "But where then is Ephyre?" the old man asked. "Some say it is over on the west coast. But it is not. It is here! Here!" he cried, slapping his hand down on the inside-out trousers. "Here, in Corinth, where the nymph Ephyraea was born, daughter of Oceanus!" He looked out over the shining waters as if he thought Odysseus in a black ship might come up from the west any moment and once again demand that Ephyrian poison for the tips of his arrows.

I went to Mycenae, too, not only for reasons connected with Odysseus. But the Prince of Ithaca can hardly have failed to pay a state visit to Agamemnon, the leading Prince of the Achaean world. And in Sparta, I recalled, there is an acceptable report that Odysseus went to woo Helen there, an undertaking which hardly any well-set up young man of that time can have failed to embark on.

I went to Tiryns, too, and naturally to Athens, which was certainly extant in the time of Odysseus, but not yet a city of stature. He cannot have failed to stop off there on his way to Aulis, the port of assembly for the grand Achaean fleet, for it is a long way round from Ithaca, and he would need to put in for provisions. This task discharged, he would proceed with his fleet of twelve ships through the Euboean narrows north-west to Aulis.

According to the poet the grand total of the Achaean fleet was one thousand bottoms, and it is difficult to see how so many ships were anchored in that small bay (they are two small bays, to be exact). But probably one thousand was a round poetic number, and doubtless many of the ships were drawn up on the beach, as they were most of the time over against Troy. Anyhow, it will be remembered that the fleet was becalmed in Aulis by Artemis, who wished thus to show her displeasure with Agamemnon. (He had been foolish enough to slay a hart in one of her sacred groves.)

The weeks went by, and still no wind blew. Then, as Odysseus himself recounts, while the chieftains were sacrificing to the gods on their altars near a spring "under a fine plane-tree, at the foot of which a sparkling stream gushed out", a momentous thing occurred. A snake, "with blood-red markings on its back", thrust from the undergrowth and devoured eight young sparrows and their mother, thus foreshadowing (as the seer Calchas explained) the nine years which the Trojan War would devour, for it was only in the tenth year that Troy would be laid low. Being present in Aulis, it is certain that Odysseus would not have forborne from being in the front row at the sacrifice of Iphigenia, Agamemnon's daughter, as prescribed by Calchas to allay the goddess's wrath. Indeed, according to certain accounts, when Agamemnon made difficulties over the harrowing sacrifice demanded from him, it was Odysseus who went off to Mycenae to persuade Clytemnaestra, the girl's mother, to let the child go. Whether or not he went to Mycenae on that occasion, it is impossible to conceive him absenting himself from the sacrifice of Iphigenia in Aulis. He was to show, twenty years later, in the courtyard of his own house in Ithaca, how little store he put on the sufferings of young ladies, however extreme their sufferings were.

It was from Athens I had gone to Aulis, then in the nineteen-twenties. From Aulis I went back to Athens again, hoping that I might find some cargo-boat which would take me to Istanbul for Troy, if I had money enough left. But when I reached the Poste Restante I found letters for me which made it imperative I should return to England at once. I would not have the time to go by way of the Corinth Canal to Ithaca, let alone to go eastward to Troy. There was nothing for it but to return by the first boat by Piraeus and Marseilles.

"Next year in Ithaca?" I asked myself hopefully, as each year most Jews for two thousand years had asked: "Next year in Jerusalem?"

For many reasons it was many years before I reached Ithaca; not till the late spring of 1953. And this time it was from Troy I set out for Ithaca, as I had dreamed of doing all those long years ago. But there were still certain adventures between Troy and the home island.

CHAPTER SIX

Island Diversions

I

THE adventures that for Odysseus lay between Troy and Ithaca were to transpire across ten years, though it must be admitted he was to spend seven of them in enforced dalliance with the nymph, Calypso, in the island of Ogygia.

After a false start, he left Troy a second time. But the wind would take him well out of his way northward to Ismarus, the city of the Cicones. He would, however, make the best of the diversion. He would sack the place, kill its men, and divide up its wives and rich plunder. No-one would go short, as he recorded with satisfaction. And, of course, he would have no compunction in the matter. In those days, people did not have compunction. The Cicones would have done the same thing to him in his own island, if the opportunity had presented itself. He had no compunction, I suppose, because Homer had none. It was still a cruel world, or so we of today would think it, in Homer's time. Even when they were people of your own race—if they lived in another land, that was what they were there for, the men to be killed, the women to be carried off as slaves. Such behaviour only produced heart-searchings if it offended against taboo. The Iliad begins with exactly such an offence, or, rather, with the account of its consequences. Following a raid on one of the coast towns, Agamemnon has carried off Chryseis, the daughter of the priest of Apollo. That was already impious enough, but when Agamemnon harshly rejects the father's plea that the girl should be restored to him, punishment is severe. Apollo ravages the whole host with plague. Day and night innumerable fires consume the dead.

Nothing so serious happened to Odysseus when he raided Ismarus. He killed the men and carried off the women, but he kept clear of the priest's daughter. (What he did with the women, in the small holds of his hollow ships, and how he disposes of them later, is not stated. They are not heard of again.) The idea now was, of course, Ithaca. But that was not to be. There was to be, instead, a terrible gale from the north, and the swell, and the current, and the North wind combined, so that, as he doubled Malea, he would be driven off course and sent drifting past Cythera. Then for nine days the winds would be chasing him across the fish-infested seas, and then at last, at last, it was to be the Island of the Lotus-eaters. From then on the best adventure-story in all the world is in full flow.

Well, I had started my own devoted Odyssey in the springtime of 1916, and I had been prevented from pursuing Odysseus along the straightforward routes, Ithaca to Troy, Troy to Ithaca— though "straightforward" is anything but an apt word. Now in 1953, with Troy behind me, my next objective should have been Ismarus. I had, however, already been as near as need be to Ismarus, during the first war. Starting out not from Ismarus-Salonica but from Trapani, in a way to delight the heart of Samuel Butler, I had some years later experienced in Djerba the second adventure, the Lotus-eaters. It had been a topsy-turvy Odyssey, one way and another, with bits and pieces lying about like a jig-saw puzzle. As the years had gone by, I had managed to fit a number of the pieces into the pattern, Aeolus and Laestrygonians, Sirens and Cimmerians. I had at last added Troy. There remained chiefly Ithaca. Odysseus had taken ten years about it, partly because his means of transport— the sailing-ship, the chariot—were limited and primitive. I would take advantage of the swifter and more complex means of transport open to me. I would reach Ithaca, now and at last, in a month or two.

A few days later the scene changes to Athens and it involves the Station Representative of the Air Line that carried us there. I must pause a moment to utter a word in praise of Air Station Representatives in foreign parts. I do not know when they came to occupy their present position in the field of foreign travel. Doubtless it has extended its importance as more and more people cover the long reaches of their journey by air. And certainly I have not had so frequent a necessity to throw myself on their good offices as of late. What men of energy, tact, intelligence, they are, as their positions require them to be! I will not say they have totally supplanted their predecessors, the consuls, the leaders of local society or local business, who may still be useful to the traveller in various directions. But how much fuller and gayer they can make life for you in their territories! They are at least as important as the "papers" I praised earlier. Blessings on them both!

So we duly arrived at Athens airport. The Station Representative was duly in attendance. (I shall refer to him as the S.R.) I had a note to him, which indicated my special interest in one Odysseus, a character in Homer's poems.

"Odysseus !" said the S.R. "Oh yes ! Of course !" One might have thought that Odysseus was regularly on the schedule of amenities supplied by the Air Line to favoured passengers. "The chappie who moved around quite a bit?"

"That's the fellow !" I agreed.

"We must do something about it ! I got one of these new Vauxhalls last week. A spanking job ! There she is ! Look at her ! Isn't she a honey ! She'll do sixty on top gear up the side of Lykabettus !"

"Yes. She looks lovely." Edward was already beside her, under her, exploring her points like a dog-fancier.

"Did that fellow—what's his name? Oh yes, Odysseus !—did he get to . . . let me see now . . ." he was thinking out the pleasant places to go to near Athens—"did he get to Sunium?"

"Sunium? He certainly mentions the place. I mean Homer mentions the place. Odysseus can't have failed to *see* Sunium, when he sailed north to Aulis."

"He should have gone by air," he reflected. "Perhaps we weren't organized yet. Well, let's go to Sunium. We'll have a look at it from the landward side. When can you make it?"

So we went to Sunium a day or two later. From a theological point of view Sunium is of interest to the Odyssean tale, for the temple on the headland, of which no gracious a ruin is still intact, was a shrine built in honour of the god, Poseidon, who pursued Odysseus so implacably after that unhappy business with his son, the Cyclops. Some five or six hundred yards away from Poseidon's temple are the formless ruins of a temple of that other deity, Athene, who so frequently helped Odysseus out of the tight corners where the malice of Poseidon had landed him. As Odysseus's little flotilla tacked round the headland, it was not these two buildings he will have descried from afar; but the site is one so radiantly beautiful, poised there between sky and sea, a site of the type that so imperatively imposed on the Greek mind the sense of the near presence of the gods, that one feels there must always have been temples here, since there were Greeks to build them. There was, we know, an earlier temple to Poseidon, which the Persians destroyed, on the site of the present one, erected in the time of Pericles. There may well have been one to Athene, too. Let us hope Odysseus made his due observances, as he passed by, northward to Aulis.

Another celebrated traveller came a good deal closer than that to Sunium. I mean Byron, of course, of whom the Odyssean traveller is so frequently reminded, and not merely by the picture of the noble lord in the fustanella. He came close enough to Sunium to carve his name on one of the pillars. That was evidently during the period when (as he wrote home in 1810) he had "topographised Attica, including, of course, Marathon and the Sunian promontory". The lettering is in the most pleasing early nineteenth-century style, and is as sharp as if it had been done last year. Indeed, one is tempted to think for a moment that it must be the work of a recent traveller, till one sees that the next signature carved above it is of one Louis Ravel, 1817. He had had some training in the art of carving his signature on the wooden desk-lids of Harrow, but at Sunium he must have gone to the trouble of picking up somewhere some really serious equipment. One is slightly chagrined to think of Byron sedulously tapping away there with hammer and chisel, but his attitude towards Greek antiquities was not so reverent as it might be. What was it he said to Hobhouse that he thought the Parthenon looked like? The Bank of England? The Mansion House? But then, of course, it sometimes does.

On a plateau near the temples there is a rather elegant café, with plate-glass and chromium and striped awnings, which is not surprising, for Sunium is a favourite excursion from Athens. It is solid as well as elegant, till you turn your head to the temple on the crest of the cliff, when suddenly it feels about as permanent as a meringue. One would have preferred it to be not there, but there it conveniently was, so we drank a little wine to toast our hero. We were about to arise, when it seemed good to us also to toast Penelope. It did not seem right to go off without raising a glass to the other ladies, Circe, Calypso, Nausicaa and to those others who may have been dropped out of Homer's narrative. We set off already in a happy mood, which had by no means worn off by the time we got to the restaurant of M. Michaelos Konakis, in the rich plain beneath the flanks of Mount Hymettus. The restaurant is not really a restaurant but a vineyard, an orchard, a garden. The last is the description that Michaelos approves, for that is how he describes it on a painted escutcheon lifted above the gate-posts: "Very Nice Garden." But if you are sponsored by a friend of Michaelos you do not enter the garden until you have spent a little time in the cellar. The cellar is not a cellar, either, it is a great barn, in which a number of large vats of wine are stored. The wine is all resinated, but there are various vintages, some more resinated, some less, some more delicate, some more potent. You are expected to taste all the vintages and pronounce judgment on them. The wine is drawn from the vat

into a large bronzey jug and then poured into measures, which you
knock back as you knock back vodka at parties at Russian Embassies.
Now it is Michaelos himself who draws the wine for you, now it is one
of his three sisters. Did you think *three* sisters? There are, in fact, four
sisters, five. The whole barn is full of sisters. They are very hurt if
you do not drain the measure each time it is filled, and when the
jug is empty it is promptly filled again at another vat. When you
have made up your mind which vat holds the vintage you most
approve, you chalk your name on it, in very distinguished company,
too.

For the Very Nice Garden has become fashionable. The élite
of Athens, both native and foreign, from the Embassies, the insti-
tutes of learning, the big commercial houses, drive out here of an
evening, to be welcomed by Michaelos and his sisters, and to chalk
their names on the preferred vat, if they have not done so already.

Despite all this success, Michaelos remains simple and unaffected.
He greets you tieless, in his shirt-sleeves, with a smile almost as large
as one of his own vats. In the dusky offing, you suddenly find that
his father, also in shirt-sleeves, stands beaming. Then hey presto,
in the arms of Michaelos, where there was nothing a moment before,
except perhaps a wine-jug, there is a baby. You must drink to the
baby's health. And have you already drunk to the health of the father,
the mother, the ranks of sisters? You have?—then it is about time
you drank again.

Processes by this time merge insensibly into each other. One
moment you are in the barn swigging *rezzinato*; the next moment you
are sitting at a table out in the garden, embowered in roses under a
pergola of vines, with a flask of wine before you, and glasses, and a
fork and knife and plates, because obviously you are going to eat
something soon. Michaelos is not in evidence. He has the tact of
every good restaurateur, the sense of knowing the moment at which
he should not be there any more. Here and there across the garden
are strings of coloured lights. But it is not they which illumine the
twilight. It is not the moon, and the stars have not yet risen. It is a
strange white light that is given off with their odours by the blossom
of lilac and orange and lemon; or perhaps it is diffused from the
limestone flanks of Hymettus. You are not alone in the garden. In
hidden arbours there are Greek families singing to the plucked
strings of guitars. Above the guitar-music, late birds are still twittering. Now there is food on your plate, and it was not there a moment
ago . . . it is *mezes*. And that means you are not having dinner.
You are eating *hors d'œuvres*, bits and pieces, for it is not to eat but

to drink you are there. Here, sizzling hot on skewers, are grilled
nuggets of lamb, and almonds hot from the pan, and cheese and
black olives, and salads and chipped potatoes, and walnuts steeped
in honey. These things may make you thirsty. But that does not
matter. The jug of wine is full to the brim again. . . .

So now we are in the car, though there is a memory of a last
visit to the wine-shed. The sisters now seem to be almost as numerous
as the Eleven Thousand Virgins of Cologne. The birds are still
twittering and the guitars twanging. Perhaps they are not outside
your head now, but inside.

The road seems a good deal rougher than it was on the way
here, with tree-roots reaching out and big stones lying around. Are
we going rather fast? I am rather sensitive to speed in cars, but that
doesn't seem to matter, even though we seem to wind our way now
and again through herds of goats and groups of belated peasants. It
does not seem credible, but here we are at last in the apartment of
our friend. It has been a very Greek evening, and we have been
drinking *rezzinato*, but it is pointed out we are, after all, English,
and the drink of the English is whisky. So we drink whisky. I
move over to the verandah, or at least I think I move over to the
verandah. I want to see what Ithaca looks like across the hissing
sea. But the lights in all the houses and ships go out. The sky and
sea are black. It is morning and I am in the hotel bedroom. It is
nine o'clock. It is as if time had been completely wiped out between
then and now. I am not feeling very well.

On the other hand, during that same time, Edward has had
an adventure here in Athens. He has been having adventures all
along, as I have, but his have usually been tied up with mechanisms.
When he saw that genuine Battle of Jutland cruiser in the Golden
Horn, with its shape like a housewife's flat iron, his eyes were like
a parched prospector's, who at last finds gold in the bottom of his
pan. When he saw a brand-new Bentley in Constitution Square, I
thought he would cry. The sudden screech in the air of the new
"Viscount" turbo-prop airliner as it hurtled in from London like a
thunderbolt, produced the reaction in him that the discovery of a
First Folio in a market stall might produce in me. When, on the
homeward journey from the Very Nice Garden, we sliced alongside
a racing bus, making a noise like a mammoth circular saw, his face
lit up like a small boy faced with ten ice-cream cones, all for himself.

Well, this last adventure, too, must have started off with some conveyance, presumably an automobile. But nothing certain is known. It might have been one a.m., or two, when he woke up next morning, aware that his head seemed to be split down the middle. He got up, hoping that the night-porter might arrange a cup of coffee. He could not. There might be coffee, he thought, at one of the kiosks in the square outside. Anyhow, the cool night air and the scent of the gardens might do him good. He went out of the hotel, then realized dimly that no kiosks are open at this hour, and in any case they do not serve coffee. He crossed the road and the pavement beyond the road, then descended a few marble steps, for the square is sunken like an enormous swimming-bath. There are metal chairs and tables down there, where you sit and drink at more reasonable hours. He sat down on the first chair, and closed his eyes.

When he opened them again, his head was still splitting, but not so badly as before. He was also aware that he was not sitting in a chair now, but on the ground, with a rough stone wall behind him. The air smelled strangely. It was not the air of a town, but of the country. There were no town sounds either, such as you hear however late or early it is—no motor-cars, no far-off train, no footsteps of belated or early workmen. Across the silence came only the voice of a dog, miles away it seemed, and an owl hooting. Where am I? he asked himself. He had not the dimmest idea. What time is it? It was so dark he could not have seen the time, even if he had his wrist-watch. But his wrist-watch was gone. His heart plunged the way it does on a flying boat. He felt for his wallet. It was not there. His fountain-pen. Not there. His pockets were empty.

A gust of anger buffeted him like a wave. He shook his fist in the blackness. "The dirty tykes!" he shouted at the top of his voice. But that did not greatly relieve his feelings. There was nothing to do now but find his way back to Athens, wherever that was. It must be in the direction of that faint glare in the sky. He set out, thinking bitter thoughts. For a long time he stumbled over rough ground, tree-roots, loose stones, narrow gullies. Several times he set off a frightful clamour of dogs, and expected any moment to get a dose of small-shot. Once it was a hen-house, and he found that hens could make even more noise than dogs. At last he stumbled upon a track, and after a time the track became some sort of a road. He continued along the road for some time, and then a taxi—there was light enough by this time to see it was a taxi—came up behind him, and stopped.

The driver said something, presumably: "Jump in!" Edward

turned his pockets inside-out, to show there was nothing there to pay for taxis.

"*Anglikos!*" the driver said, and again: "Jump in!"

So Edward jumped in, and got to Athens in time, to our hotel. "Wait!" he told the driver. He went up to his room, got some money, and then came down again. But there was no taxi there.

There was a silence when Edward finished the story.

"What do you think happened?" I asked at length.

"It's pretty obvious, isn't it?" The milk of kindness was lacking from his voice. "Some swine saw I was flat out in the square. So they called a prowling car or taxi that they're in league with. Then they took me miles out into the country and——" He stopped. "It's a good thing I didn't wake up before they ditched me!" he observed. I had been thinking that myself for some time. He would certainly have started flailing around, and there was no reason to believe the abductors would not have bashed in his skull.

"I wonder!" I said ruminatively. "I wonder!"

"You wonder what?"

"This isn't Marseilles, after all! It isn't Port Said! This is Athens! Athens is a law-abiding city. Such things don't happen in Athens, where the influences of the old gods still linger."

He did not seem impressed.

"Tell me!" I continued. "That taxi-driver you were talking about, that alleged taxi-driver. Was he wearing sandals with wings on?"

"He didn't get out, so I didn't see. And what would he be wearing wings on his sandals for?" He looked at me a little nervously.

"Perhaps he wasn't a taxi-driver at all. Perhaps he was Hermes, sent by the Immortals from Olympus to get you back safe and sound. Don't you *see*?"

"I don't *see*!" He looked behind his shoulder to see if the way to the door was open.

"It isn't really hard to recognize a god, when he's masquerading as a mortal. Homer tells you so himself somewhere. I know. In front of the ships, when Poseidon has got himself up to look like Calchas. You remember?"

"No."

"One Ajax is talking to another Ajax. He says all you've got to do is to look at the heels and the back of their knees. Did you look at this chap's heels and knees?"

"No."

"So he took you to the hotel, did he?" I went on. "You say he disappeared?"

"Yes."

"When you came down again, and you saw he wasn't there, was there a smell of ambrosia in the air?"

"There wasn't. A smell from his exhaust, that's all."

"Some people have all the luck!" I murmured.

"Luck! It was the finest watch I ever had. You could tell the day of the week, the month, and the year. I *loved* that watch!"

It seemed to me one ought to know what year it is, without looking up one's watch. But I did not pursue the point.

II

I was taken along to a party. The heat rose from the marble pavements, and surged against the walls of the apartment-house, and was flung back like the incoming tide from an embankment. It was all marble within the apartment-house, too, but cool as sea-weed. Inside there, we were like fish in an aquarium, nibbling at our cakes. Very nearly the whole of one wall was covered by a Victorian painting of Highland Cattle in a mist, that somehow looked like walruses.

On a low table supported by three marble tritons, there was a book of photographs of the Greek Islands, and one of the islands was Santorin. The name struck a familiar chord. There is a poem by Flecker called "Santorin, A Legend of the Aegean". I looked at the photographs again. But surely, I told myself, Flecker couldn't actually have been here. He would not have been inspired by *this* place to write a legend of the Aegean. Or perhaps these photographs have been sewn up by mistake in this volume? This is not the Aegean. There could be nothing less Greek, less classical than these contorted cliffs hanging over this profound harbour basin. It is some volcanic island in Polynesia. And what curious architecture is this, these houses standing on each other's heads? It looks like the crazy troglodyte houses of Medenine in Tunisia, which I saw the time I was *en route* for the Island of the Lotus-eaters, where the houses are like the piled-up top-hats of a comedian.

"Very strange!" I murmured. I spoke loud enough to attract the attention of the gentleman beside me. (I discovered shortly he was my host. He had white hair and twinkling eyes. He looked like a Banker, or a Shipowner, or a Cabinet Minister, and was, in fact, all three.)

"What is very strange, please?" he asked.

"This island." I pointed to the photographs.

"And beautiful!" he said firmly.

"Yes, of course. And beautiful!" But somehow I felt it was an inexact word. "One of our poets wrote a poem about it."

"Who was that? Can you remember the poem?"

I managed to recall a few verses:

> "*Who are you, Sea Lady,*
>   *And where in the seas are we?*
> *I have too long been steering*
>   *By the flashes in your eyes.*
> *Why drops the moonlight through my heart,*
>   *And why so quietly*
> *Go the great engines of my boat*
>   *As if their souls were free?*"

"So it is about the engines of a boat?" the Shipowner said.

"Well, not exactly."

"You should go to Santorin," he went on.

I looked down on the photographs.

"I should," I said. "But it's not in my plan."

"What is your plan?"

"I'm travelling in the places where the great Odysseus was before me."

"How do you know Odysseus did not go to Santorin? Santorin is one of the Cyclades. We know that he went to the Cyclades. He tells us so himself."

"Does he? I don't remember."

"You don't remember?" He looked surprised, and a little hurt. "He was in Delos. And if he was in Delos, why not Santorin? It is no great distance."

"Delos?" I asked again, knitting my brows.

"Look it up!" he requested me. The Shipowner wasn't really interested in Delos. He wanted to get back to Santorin. (I looked it up. He was right. Odysseus *had* been to Delos, or he *said* he had been. You never quite know with Odysseus when he recounts his adventures whether he is telling us what he thinks really happened to him, or whether he is romanticizing, to serve some purpose or other. He was giving an account of himself to Nausicaa after being washed up on the Phaeacian shore, and was trying to elicit the princess's sympathy, which he did with considerable success, in the process proving he could turn a pretty compliment to a lady, even when circumstances were very much against him.

"Never have I set eyes on such perfection in man or woman," he tells her. "I worship as I look. Only in Delos have I seen the like, a fresh young palm-tree shooting up by the altar of Apollo, when my travels took me there—with a fine army at my back that time, though the expedition was doomed to end so fatally for me.")

"As for Santorin," the Shipowner continued, "you should know it was the place where Odysseus went down to the lower world. Through the top of the volcano. Santorin was a great volcano in those days, as big as Etna."

It seemed as tenable as many other propositions regarding the itinerary of Odysseus.

"And do you know that Turkish coffee was not invented by the Turks at all? It was invented by the Greeks. Homer mentions that, too."

"Really? Where?"

"It is that juice of the seed for brides he talks of. Nymphokoro-soumon." (At least that is the way I remember it.) He returned to the piece about Santorin. "The poem says something about engines. What are those lines, please?"

I repeated them:

> "*And why so quietly*
> *Go the great engines of my boat*
> *As if their souls were free?*"

"I, too, have a boat," said the Shipowner. He looked up at the ormolu clock below the Highland cattle. "It leaves for Santorin in three hours."

"Three hours?" I repeated, a catch in my voice.

"It is a good boat," he affirmed. "Would you like to go?" But he had already risen from his chair and was over at the telephone in the hall. That is why he is not only a Shipowner and a Banker, but a Cabinet Minister. (Or he was, when I last read a Greek news-paper.)

So three hours later, minus a few minutes, we were climbing the gangway of the boat to Santorin. I knew it would be all right. In a flat in Brighton two or three years ago I had seen a painting

by Christopher Wood. It was a wedge of sea, and some sand, and a
pink café. "I am going to that place," I proclaimed. "What is its
name?" "Tréboul," my friends told me. "It's in Brittany."

I went to Tréboul. That time it had been a painting. This time
it was some photographs and some verses, and I went to Santorin.

Still, I was aware of a certain sense of guilt, even of frustration,
as I climbed that gangway. Up to three hours ago I had vaguely
thought that when I started moving among the islands, though I
would have liked it to be sailing-boats or caiques, it would at least be
steerage and sleeping on hatches, and striped rugs under and over
you, and the masts nodding to the stars and straightening up again.
Well, I was going to be a guest of honour, instead, thanks to my
impulsive and hospitable Shipowner. "Oh dear!" I said. But I soon
got reconciled. I corrected it to "Ah well!"

It is not a bad thing to be a guest of honour in Greece. I told
earlier how I was once a guest of honour in the guard's van of a
train going north from Mycenae, and how I met the most
distinguished barrel-organ in the world, and how I played it in
Corinth. This time I was a guest of honour in a ship going southward through Aegean waters towards the Cyclades. "He is a friend
of the Shipowner," people whispered, from the captain on his
bridge to the peasants in the hold and the donkey-boys in the
engine-room.

It was a good boat, as the Shipowner had said. He had a right
to be proud of it. Everybody on the quayside was proud of it, as
well as everybody on board. The Greeks have always had an eye
for a good boat, all the way back to Odysseus, and before. It was
an up-to-date Italian motor vessel, with modern interior decoration,
panelled walls, chromium fittings, beige leather furniture, flower-
decorated tables, and a cocktail-bar straight from Madison Avenue.
I had a pleasant cabin to myself, too, with hot and cold water and
cool sheets. But I soon felt lonely inside there. I was down on the
steerage deck aft in no time, where already the peasants were staking
out their claims for deck-space for the night, with a spread of goat-
hair rugs beneath them and lumps of luggage for pillows, tied up
in saddle-cloths. Tight-clasped under their arms, they carried the
new eikons they had bought in the big town, with paper flowers to
stick in vases in front of them. An old woman was gazing enraptured
on an eikon of Saint George. The main mass of the bodies of the
saint himself, the horse and the dragon, were worked in repoussé
tin foil, but special features were left visible through apertures—
the saint's head and the tip of his spear, the horse's head, the dragon's

acid-green eyes and fiery tongue. An old priest with a rook's-nest beard sat on the hatch eating his way through a bag of oranges. Somehow the long black caftan had worked its way up to the knee-caps so that the naked legs showed like a Boy Scout's. The musicians among the soldiers were already plucking their stringed instruments or blowing the crumbs out of their mouth-organs, and in a few minutes were tuning up tentatively like the first birds at sunrise.

I went outside to summon Edward to the music. He was leaning against the gunwale, following with absorption a sea-gull's flight around the foremast, the way it soared to mid-sky, turned on a wing-dip, hovered, glided, swooped, then soared again. For a long time he was unaware of me. I tapped at his sleeve. He spoke, but did not turn his head.

"Splendid, isn't it!" he breathed, then was silent for a time.

"Yes, isn't it!" I agreed reverently.

"Aerodynamically quite perfect!" he pronounced. "The gull probably has the best lift-drag co-efficient of any species of bird. You know what I mean?"

"In a way."

"Now you see why the glider's the purest type of aircraft. No problems of fitting engines and armchairs and undercarriages and things. Ah!" He caught his breath as the bird came down, skimmed the water, and soared again. Then once more he rose from his run-way into his private aerodynamic ether. All day long the creature was still there, floating, dipping, falling behind and above us in the glow of the ship's stern like a great moth, or a ghost.

III

It was before sunrise. We seemed to be suspended in a vacuum, like our own lost sea-gull, no water beneath us, no sky above, and nothing ahead but a grey bank of cloud. It could not be Santorin. It was an error of navigation. Then the right-hand section of the cloud-bank slid away, as one flat on a stage slides from another. There was open water there, and a narrow strait between two islands. The sun rose. The element beneath our keel liquefied, became separate from the other, more volatile, element above. The ship's siren blew, and just as the city of Jericho tumbled during the reverberations of the seven trumpet-blasts of Joshuah's priests, so, conversely, during the reverberations from those blasts of the ship's siren, a flank of the volcano of Santorin raised up its cliffs, heaping

Scylla

Circe's Mountain

perpendicularly grey-white layers of tufa on black layers of lava, confusions of saffron-red, rust-red, and veridian-green rock zig-zagged with streaks of sulphur, compacted blocks of shale and skeleton-dry pumice—till at length you saw strung out along the far sky-line the cupolas and bell-towers, roof-tops and chimneys of a pale-blue, sky-blue, rose-pink village that seemed at any moment likely to topple over into the vast harbour we had now entered, a cauldron of water red as port wine with the refracted sheen of risen sun and ruby rock.

When the reverberation from the last blast died away, a pro-found silence fell, unaffected by the drumming of the ship's engines, for this after a time ceases to be a sound audible outside the skull, becoming nothing more than a vibration within it. Then, as we moved inshore a soldier whistled thin and shrill across the void, and waved a handkerchief. A girl, hardly visible at that immense distance, waved back again. In an instant the island ceased to be merely a grandiose crucible of volcanic forces. It was a dwelling-place. Undiscouraged by the calamitous cliffs, the still-smoking islands in the centre of the harbour basin, the pressures that had visibly again and again seized the island like a huge fist that tightens upon a lump of dry clay—undiscouraged by all this, men and women lived in those houses, and worshipped at those altars. When, two or three times a week, the ship called in from Athens, for half-an-hour or so, they were part of the general scheme of things. Their small boats would come out with a sea-gull scuffle and babble. This morning, in the boat dedicated to Aghios Demetrios, they brought us in bow and stern a priest and a turkey, both robed in black, both with bright-red faces. In exchange we traded a goat and a harmonium which seemed curiously at odds with itself, all that way from Merthyr Tydfil. Then we were on our way again, our course drawn like a bow-string across a profound indentation on our left. Now another cliff-top village became visible. Phera, they said it was, though some said Thera. From a narrow quayside carved out of the base of the cliff, a stairway of seven hundred hewn steps zig-zagged steeply up the mountain, past lava blocks and banks of red scorciae, dusted over with a faint breath of grass wherever the slopes were off the perpendicular. On the quayside was a narrow cluster of domed sheds and dwelling-houses and an arcaded building which seemed to be at once a shipping-office, a Customs bureau, and a café. Under the arcades was gathered a synod of priests sipping coffee through their enormous beards. What were they doing there? They were not tourists. They seemed far too many to minister to the spiritual needs

H

of the island's small population. Had they combined to make an evangelical onslaught on the decaying faith of the islanders? But Greek priests do not make evangelical onslaughts. They did not leave by the boat that had brought us. I did not see them again.

Alongside the arcaded building, in evident response to a fiat issued by the Shipowner, a delegation of the island dignitaries was gathered, who included two Shipowner brothers, as well as the doctor, the miller, and a guide, Nikolaos by name, a tall sad man, who wrote poetry and hoped to see it published some day. There was also a platoon of donkey-owners, very well-behaved this morning, though they are normally a vociferous group of men. Beside them their donkeys drooped, mourning, rubbing flank against skinny flank, only now and again raising their heads to discharge against the cliffs salvos of melancholy sound that ricochetted like stone cannon-balls.

Soon we were mounted and ascending the dizzy stairway, now scraping our legs against the spiny rocks, now suspended over the blue gulf, hardly assured by the low walls that revetted the angles. Caves, some of them still inhabited, pock-marked the whole slope. On one hand was the blank white side of a domed church, apparently inaccessible to anyone but a sea-gull; against the top of the mountain was a buff-fronted sky-blue-domed church, with a Venetian-style campanile that hinted at one of the chapters in the island's immensely diverse history.

At length we debouched upon the narrow shade of the main street, and we were in the new Thera, which looks old enough, though in fact it dates from so recently as the middle nineteenth century, when the Therans thought it wise to move over from the near-by village of Merovigli, finding it was sliding into the sea from under their doorsteps. But I thought of the new Thera that it looked neither new nor old, that its arches and buttresses, barrel-vaults and belfries, stairways and cupolas, were of an aspect so primitive that they seemed to have been less designed by men than to have happened in nature.

According to Greek legend the island grew from a clod of earth which was presented to the Argonauts by Triton, the rather fearsome divinity who was a son of Poseidon and Amphitrite, and had green hair and eyes, breathing organs below his ears, hands rough as the outer rind of a sea-shell, and a dolphin's tail. The Argonauts planted the clod of earth in the sea, Triton blew upon his wreathèd horn, and the island rose from the depths. It was a very beautiful island, and a round one, for its earliest names were "Kalliste" and

"Strongylé", and though the Argonauts had other things to do than settle in Santorin, it was still settled before the dawn of history, for prehistoric sherds, well before the Mycenaean epoch, have been excavated from several places, including the village of Akrotiri, in the southern horn of the main island, and in Thirasia, the second largest island in the group.

At last history dawned. In those same neolithic settlements, Mycenaean sherds have been found, mixed with a certain amount of ceramic and bronze wear from Crete, not far off to the south. It is tempting to speculate whether these same Mycenaeans, or Achaeans, as some scholars permit us to call them, may have been flotsam and jetsam of the broken fleets returning from the sack of Troy, representative of the layer of Greek legend that succeeds upon the generation of the Argonauts. Perhaps even Odysseus himself, refreshing himself too liberally after a hot day, had dropped a cruse of wine on the ground, of which the broken pieces were to be there for a thousand years, and again two thousand, until some archaeologist's spade uncovered them and his skill assembled them again.

But, alas, we must put this fancy out of mind. For the clod of earth which Triton had originally presented to the Argonauts, had the seeds of chaos in it. Kalliste, in fact, was a huge volcano, and in about the year 2000 B.C. (that is to say several centuries, at least, before any possible date for the Trojan War) raging Poseidon sucked down a great deal of the island's cone to the sea's depths, and with it whatever settlements those early Mycenaeans had had time to establish on the lava, which by this time lay thick and hard on the primal marble of the island's base. It may be that in the depths of that blue cauldron, notable treasures of bronze and marble lie buried for all time, unless perhaps a cataclysm as immense as that which engulfed them, should some day spew them forth again.

At all events, after that hubbub, it probably took a long time before a new race of adventurers set a timid foot on the alarming island. The first there is any mention of is the Phoenicians.

"For Cadmus," writes Herodotus, "when he was sailing in search of Europé, made a landing on this island; and either because the country pleased him, or because he had a purpose in so doing, left there a number of Phoenicians."

The purpose, it has been speculated, was the collection of the murex-shell, out of which the Phoenicians made their famous purple dye, and of which few evidences have been since discovered on the island. Anyhow, eight generations of Phoenicians succeeded each other until at last, some time in the eighth century, a certain Lacedaemonian named Theras crossed the sea, built a new city high on the sun-whipped plateau, and gave both island and city his name.

Thera the island remained, all through those long centuries before the Christian epoch, and for several centuries after; during the Hellenic time, the Ptolemaic, the Roman, until at length, after the Fourth Crusade, the Latins partitioned the Byzantine Empire, made Thera part of the Duchy of Naxos, and to the shades of Theras, the Lacedaemonian, Santa Eirene succeeded as the island's tutelary genius. For Santorin is a corruption of the saint's name, and she still palely inhabits the place, though it is a long time since the Turks planted the Crescent here, and a long time, too, since the Turks left, and the Byzantines took over again.

The island of Santorin produces a wine famous throughout the Aegean. It seemed to me a good thing, before we repaired to our hotel, to sip a glass of Santorin wine at a café where we could sit looking out over that unparalleled panorama. So we followed Nikolaos, our guide, down a narrow lane to the left, and entered a shadowy café where they were already at that early hour playing dominoes with sombre absorption; then we stepped out to a terrace hung out over the blue chasm, and ate black bread, and lumps of cheese, and drank our wine, like melted amber to look at, aromatic in the nostrils, sweet and heady to taste, hitting the head, like that other pumice-bedded wine, the wine of Lipari.

And there it all lay stretched out to right and left of us, below and before us. North to south ran an eighteen-mile arc of cliff, curving westward its southern horn. This was Santorin itself, the chief island. Beyond the northern point a broad channel separated Santorin from the island of Thirasia. Still further round, Aspronisi, another much smaller island, stood up out of the steel-blue water.

Once, maybe for some centuries, or maybe only for some years, all those islands were linked together in the multicoloured vallance of rock that enclosed the lagoon, until once again the sunken crust of earth heaved, and the excluded sea breached the glaring dykes, to presage an epoch, which has not ceased yet, of such planetary high jinks as Poseidon has rarely indulged in; for before long in the depths of the sea-floor the sunken volcano got to work again, throwing up island upon island, which in a day or two disappeared or remained smouldering for centuries, as one island still smoulders at this day. The Kaymeni, or Burnt Islands, they are called, and to-morrow or next week one of them, or more than one, may disappear again, amid such frightful flame-spoutings out of the convulsed water as Strabo described only yesterday, and the ashen-hued survivor of some Conducted Hellenic Tour may be describing only to-morrow.

There it lay then, that fantastic phantasmagoria, the least classical landscape in all the classical world; Polynesian rather than classical, as the cliff-top villages are less Greek than troglodyte African. Beautiful? one asks oneself. It is, of course, beautiful, set in such waters and topped by such skies. And the Greeks who lived here once, did *they* find it beautiful? "As to the beauty of the fearful and magnificent in Nature which, as here in Thera, we find so exciting," pronounced Hiller von Gärtringen, its excavator, "it had no meaning for the Greeks; even to Goethe on the way to Chamonix it was still an unfamiliar sentiment." And, I suppose, even to us it is not the quality of beauty in Santorin which catches the breath, so much as a strangeness, a hauntedness, a non-tellurian terror, such as I have known only in two or three other places, Petra, Akaba, the Grand Canyon of the Colorado.

I wondered, as I sat there sipping my sweet wine, whether the most fanatical word-weaver can get much further in describing such places than to compare them with each other, and whether the most purple of his passages can ever be more adequate than those virulent postcards are, that portray camels and palm-trees and pyramids by the Nile at sunset.

IV

It was now time to be on our way. Proceeding along shaded alleys paved with squares and lozenges of marble cobblestones worn down to the smoothness of ivory, and flanked with the shining porticoes of wealthy islanders who had built villas and endowed churches here, then returned to their more comfortable mainland apartments, before long we presented ourselves at the Evanghelios, the only hotel the island for the moment possesses. There we were greeted by an old lady wrapped round in an esquimo thickness of shawls and sweaters and underskirts and overskirts. With a great puffing and blowing she led us by steep steps to a burning-white roof terrace, then up into the boudoir, as she mysteriously called it, a stone-paved room almost as bare as the terrace, apart from a table and two chairs and, strange to say, another harmonium, an instrument to which, I gathered, the island had an especial addiction.

Above the harmonium was an oleograph of Lord Byron triumphant over a heap of Turkish corpses.

Two or three doors led off the *salone* into, presumably, the bedrooms. The old lady pointed to the door nearest to the exterior wall.

"Et voila, messieurs, votre appartement!" she regally declared, as if there were thick carpets beyond that door, and concealed lighting, and deep armchairs, and beyond the private sitting-room was the private bedroom with its private bath. There were no such things, of course. There was a bare floor, two iron bedsteads, a rusty basin on a washstand under a minute water-container hanging on a nail. With great ceremony a ewer of cold water and one small towel were shortly produced.

"Je ne suis pas d'ici," the old lady was at pains to inform us while we washed ourselves. She was obviously very lonely, and was always loth to leave us, even on those occasions when the most gregarious prefer complete privacy. She was always there before us, or coming up just after us, shuffling in her outsize felt slippers, with that puffing and blowing as of leaky bellows. Madame lost no time in informing us she was not from Santorin. There was nothing insular, or even provincial, about Madame. She was, in fact, from Constantinople. *"Moi, j'ai l'âme internationale,"* she announced. She thought of writing her life-story. She did not intend to spend much more time in Santorin. She thought Athens was perhaps a little Levantine; she would prefer Paris, or Rome.

She had been a great beauty, it was to be gathered, in her young days in Constantinople, the daughter of a Prussian Junker family. There she had met her husband, a distinguished engineer, who had been summoned to the Turkish capital (as it was then) in connection with a project of international importance. He had been born in Santorin, a scion of one of the old Venetian families that had once owned the island, but he had studied in Athens and built bridges in South America.

The gay Lothario of the Greek Islands, in the teeth of all his competitors he had swooped down and captured her. For a time he had continued with his undertakings, but had found it more and more difficult to let her out of his sight for even five minutes. He was ravaged with jealousy, and at last determined to confound her rivals by carrying off the beautiful young woman to the eagle crag of Santorin. Things had not gone well with them here. Certain families had intrigued against them and ousted them from the position they had occupied for centuries, but the less said about certain families the better. They had finally been reduced to taking on this hostelry as a temporary occupation. They were waiting from day to day for news which might alter the situation. Patience. One must have patience.

That was the picture as I built it up from the somewhat muffled conversation of Madame herself. But I heard several conflicting accounts of their origins before I left the island. Some said Monsieur was not a decayed Venetian nobleman, nor even a Greek islander. He had been a horse-tamer in the Argentine. As for Madame, she was not Prussian, she was German-Jewish. She was not German-Jewish, she was Russian-Jewish, insisted the White Russian lady who, with her husband, was staying at the Evanghelios. Madame Land-lady, she announced, was a ritual slaughterer's daughter and came from Slutsk. That strata of legend in Santorin seemed almost as contorted as the geological strata.

"And perhaps the two gentlemen will have a cup of coffee with Monsieur and myself in our own suite?" asked Madame. Whatever the country of their origin, they were both devoted to our great country, and above all to Lord Byron, the greatest of our country-men. She made the ghost of a curtsey to the picture of the poet waving his blood-stained scimitar.

So in the course of time we were summoned downstairs to coffee. The *salone* was dark, and well below ground level, hewn out of the solid rock, as so many of the island habitations are, so that often you see nothing emerging but their chimneys. You found your way down by devious staircases, and there in his shirt-sleeves sat the husband, a beret on his head and a huge scarf round his neck. We gathered later that he could be not only voluble, but explosive. But he was in a taciturn mood that day, and did not address a word to us, not even on the subject of his passion, Lord Byron. He did no more than move towards us the registration forms for our signatures. Perhaps he was grieving for the old frivolities of Constantinople, or the vanished splendours of his own family. Perhaps he disapproved of our sponsors. The coffee was weak and cold and chiefly watered goat's milk. In the presence of the silent husband, Madame fell completely silent, too. It all felt like a session of early Christians in catacombs. In course of time we rose to our own bare room and flung the shutters wide-open. Immediately sunshine filled it like a glittering, chrystal chandelier. There was hardly room to stir with all that sunshine. Hung like pictures in the two window-frames were the smoking islands and the blinding sea. Van Gogh would have been sorry stuff in the wall-space between such canvasses.

.   .   .   .   .

We were not the only guests in the hostelry, as I have said.
There was also a rich Danish business-man and his wife, the White
Russian lady. The husband was obviously out of his element, in
that comfortless eccentric establishment. He was one for the Hotels
Ritz of this world, and for holidays in opulent watering-places,
with ballrooms and casinos and champagne of the best years. He
was very knowledgeable on solo flying and racing-cars, and had
himself raced at Monte Carlo. He soon discovered that Edward was
a kindred spirit. Whenever the White Russian lady and I seemed to
be preoccupied with amphorae, as in the little museum along the
main street, or with the ruins of some god's temple, as up in the
ancient town of Thera on the high hill-top, the other two would
get into an excited huddle like two schoolboys, comparing the merits
of the Disco-Volante Alfa-Romeo with the 300 S.L. Mercedes-
Benz, and whether the steering-column gear-change is a boon or an
affliction, till the stern voice of the White Russian lady recalled the
truant husband to his responsibilities towards his wife and classical
archaeology. She considered herself a classical scholar, and may have
been one. But I maintained a certain reserve regarding that large
omniscient bottom, tightly encased in its navy-blue slacks, bouncing
ahead purposefully, and that clipped voice more authoritative
than Porson, Jebb and Verrall rolled into one.

We took a station wagon part of the way to old Thera next day.
A station wagon sounds very modern, but the petrol age has begun
in Santorin, for there is not only a station wagon, but two jeeps,
three transport autos, and even an omnibus. There is not very much
length of road for them to cover. But there they move from time to
time, with or without passengers, just to show the flag, as it were.
As we drove along to the village of Pyrgos, it occurred to me that
Santorin is at present at the stage where Capri was when I was first
there in the early twenties. Santorin has a few motor vehicles and
a few strips of road. Capri had no motor vehicles, but it had a
funicular. True, it also had a luxury hotel. But Santorin is trying
hard to build one, though it doesn't seem to get much further than
the foundations, for water is very scarce on the island, scarcer than
wine, in fact. And the masons and carpenters who might be building
the hotel are steadily leaving the island. A race is on, between the
forces that might keep Santorin what it is, despite the station wagon,
and has been for many centuries, and the forces that will introduce
a casino and striped umbrellas and Tom Collinses and *homard à
l'américaine.*

And what Santorin is (I realized on that same road to Pyrgos) is very different on the inward side, with which I was already familiar, the side that drops sheer and swift as a plummet, and the outward side, which slopes in terraces of tufa and pumice gradually to the open sea, putty-grey except for the tomato-plants, the vivid young vines from which the islanders grow that notable wine, and the occasional fig-tree and palm and cactus. It is a powdery, gritty landscape on that side, and the absence of water along with the clouds of hot dust that move about whenever a slight breeze rises, has always meant a considerable incidence of eye-disease among the islanders. For part of the way we carried with us in our station wagon the devoted little doctor we had met earlier whose sole job it is to treat the eyes of the island children; and it was reassuring to know that among them, at least, the situation improves yearly.

The road was punctuated with a series of those circular dome-topped windmills, of a style exclusively Greek, I fancy, with their six triangular canvas sails fixed to wooden spokes, these in turn joined by wire at their extremities. An odd sight they made, particularly when the sails were furled, and each windmill seemed a giant spider's web. At length we reached the strange twisted labyrinthine village of Pyrgos, where buttresses suddenly thrust out at you that support no wall, and doorways suddenly open into nowhere. There, hearing the voices of children reading aloud in the village school, it occurred to me that I would like to find out what these Greek children were doing for their morning lesson. The White Russian lady was rather cross about it. Her interest in the island products did not extend beyond the Hellenistic period, or even as far, and she much preferred potsherds and marble to vulgar flesh and blood. But I insisted, and the lady stayed outside saying *"Tiens! Tiens!"*

Even up in Pyrgos my fame had gone before me, this Englishman who was the friend of the illustrious Shipowner. I was ushered into the schoolroom with great cordiality, and exchanged courtesies with the schoolmaster, the schoolmistress, and a company of village dignitaries who, in various stages of dress and undress, appeared from nowhere in no time in order to be in on the interesting occasion. The walls of the room were placarded with portraits of the heroes of the Greek War of Independence—this admiral, that general, that doughty priest. But suddenly I realized that the portrait of one hero, of special interest to myself, was absent. Where was Lordos Byron, the Turk-slayer, the waver of the blood-stained scimitar?

I ventured to ask the schoolmistress how came it that Byron was not in that company. Almost in tears, she admitted the oversight. Some clerk in some dusty office in the Ministry of Education in Athens had been criminally remiss. The Lordos Byron would have his due meed of honour, she assured me, when I came round to Santorin again. As she spoke, I glanced at the schoolbook that lay before the small schoolboy at the desk nearest me. It was open at a picture of Lord Byron waving the scimitar.

I raised the book and showed it to the class, who had been sitting shy and silent all this time. "Who is this gentleman?" I asked. Immediately the whole class launched into an account of the poet's devotion to Greece, his incredible valour in battle, and his noble death in Missolonghi facing fearful odds. It was not the strictly historic version, but it was detailed and enthusiastic. They rendered it with shining eyes at the tops of their voices, like a lot of trains with all their windows lit letting off steam in a railway station. Their arms rotated like the fantastic windmills of their own island. I felt *amour-propre* was more than vindicated as I rejoined my companions to set out once more on the journey to Thera.

The traveller in Santorin does not go directly to and from new to old Thera, which would already be quite a strenuous journey. First he climbs to the highest point in the island, by an ankle-twisting stairway of harsh rock which gives place at length to steep banks of slithery pumice where every few yards the foot slips and sends up clouds of hot dust. Up on the top there, alienated from even such lugubrious frivolities as might be found in the villages below, a monastery has been erected to the Holy Elijah, who is often thus honoured in high places throughout the Orthodox Greek world, and very appropriately, for the Prophet-Saint was himself the hero of a celebrated Ascension.

It is a stiff climb up to the monastery, and it is good to know there that for a short while climbing is over. It is also good to see that though the monks themselves eschew the dissipations of the lower places, those dominoes, those harmoniums, they are not averse to a little of it, in this mild form, coming up to them. Their greeting is formal, courteous, almost impersonal, yet curiously wistful. They summon you into the sitting-room, where first a glass of ice-cold water is brought out of the roof-top cistern; then, while coffee is being prepared, you look round upon ranked photographs of bearded deacons long since dead and gone; and indeed, if not for the beards on those faces you must pinch yourself to make sure you are not miraculously transported into the parlour of some boarding-house in Bognor Regis, with this horsehair sofa you are sitting on, and these plush chairs, and this table with its velvet cloth and its embroidered linen table-centre. But soon the coffee comes, and a plate of *loukoumi* and a glass of the potent liqueur the monks themselves have brewed. Then they will lead you into the Chapel, where the eikons smoulder under their thick accretions of candle-smoke; and from the chapel the way is to the small cemetery, where only a week or two ago, Johannos, one of the monks, was laid to rest in quicklime, and only a week before that the bones of Nikodemos, another monk, were dug up to be stored in the ossuary, for three years is more than the time a body needs before quicklime eats through to the undevourable bone, and Nikodemos had already had his time as a complete skeleton. He had had a cat and was devoted to it. The cat disappeared the day old Nikodemos died and has not been seen again.

After that we climbed out upon the bone-white roofs, and looked southward across the water to the far shadow which is the coast of Crete. At least so we might have done, but not that morning, for the top of Elijah's mountain was scarfed with cloud, and there was no Crete to be seen, only, far down below, when the cloud-banks shifted and before they fused again, the rippled ink-blue sea.

V

The grinding journey to old Thera began again, first precipitously descending, then as precipitously ascending, by those shifting slopes of pumice where, the more energy you expended, the more you seemed to be standing still. There was no cloud now. It was as if cloud were the proper element of that Christian shrine we had left behind us. We were ascending towards an early Greek city through withering hot air, crystal-clear as soon as the pumice-dust eddies we raised settled again.

"But what's this?" I asked myself. For it was not only nuggets of pumice we were dislodging. "And this? And this, too?" I saw that the whole hillside was scattered with antique sherds, some on the surface, many just below it, easily revealed by thrust of heel or toe. We were still on the downward slope. There was a long upward slope to climb before we reached Thera. But already the evidences of old civilizations, extending over many centuries, were scattered everywhere—fragments of bowl rims, of handles, of pedestal bases, Roman, Ptolemaic, Hellenic, here a fragment of a Boeotian amphora, there of an Attic oil-lamp, there of a Cypriot-geometric wine-jar, all identified by our White Russian companion, with uncompromising decision and (so far as my knowledge went) frequent accuracy.

At last we reached the Sellada pass, a region of rock-hewn tombs where the Therans laid their dead during the centuries that lay between the Dorian foundation of the city and the time when the Romans, and, later, the Byzantine priests, abandoned it. Here four tracks meet, if anything can be called a track in so muted and muffled a landscape, the track which we had just descended from Mount Elijah, the two tracks which lead down left and right to the honey-blonde bays of Kamari and Perissa, and the track by which we now began the climb to the wind-scoured plateau of Mesavouno, where the ruins of Thera lie, high-lifted from the dribble and dust of the rolling pumice.

A recent writer on the Aegean islands, and one by no means lacking in enthusiasm for them, speaks of the ruins of Thera as a "muddled ensemble", and finds "the archaeological interest of the site much greater than its beauty".[4]* I do not like to believe that his faculty of appreciation was blunted a little by the discomfort of the climb. But it seems to me that the beauty of Greek sites has no necessary relation either with their muddledness or their orderliness. For my part, though I consider that the efforts which learned societies and governments sometimes make to arrange the tumbled and broken fragments into some sort of order are very laudable, I usually find these arrangements less aesthetically than academically interesting. In terms of time it is true that the ensemble of Thera is "muddled", though it is immensely less "muddled" than the ruins of Hissarlik, and these, too, I did not find unbeautiful. The ruins of Thera are less muddled than the ruins of Athens and Rome and many another renowned site, if only because they are not imbedded in the clutter which two thousand years of subsequent inhabitation have deposited upon them. How shall there be no muddle, and why deplore it, in the ruins of an ancient city founded by Dorian Greeks, taken over some centuries later by the Egyptian Ptolemies to be a citadel for a naval base, a city subsequently colonized by Roman soldiers, and prayed in by Byzantine priests? Yes, in a sense there is "muddle", I suppose. But there is a delicate order, too, imposed by a tracery of asphodel and grape-hyacinth, purple mallow and coppery dandelion, by root of wild fig and branch of wild olive; in the prostrate stones of that scheme the static pattern of lichen abides, the fleeting pattern of the hawk's wing goes in a flash, lizard twinkles, butterfly hovers, coney is seen and is gone; where hot blue sky is over-

*For reference, see R. Liddell, Bibliography, page 239.

head, and on all sides the mountain thrusts down to the hare-bell sea.

Yes, I found Thera beautiful enough, and as I wandered on that aery platform from shrine to altar-stone, from temple to theatre, I found myself wondering whether the Dorian founders of the city chose that site primarily because of its beauty or its defensibility. There are no traces on the hill-top earlier than theirs. Their predecessors on the island lived by the sea's edge, for the sea that encompasses an island is its most reliable bastion, as the ancient Minoans knew in Crete and we in the British Islands have known, ever since the success of that first and only Conquest.

What possessed old Theras to choose a site so difficult of access? Was it because he knew it would prove an impregnable bastion, with those two steep tracks up from the sea round the flanks of Mesavouno not any less unsure then than now with the slithering pumice? Did he want to get away from those Phoenicians? Herodotus tells us explicitly the sentiments of Theras were friendly. "Far from intending to drive out the former inhabitants, he regarded them as his near kin, and meant to settle among them." But in fact he did not. Perhaps the sentiments of his followers were less friendly, those Dorian desperadoes. They preferred to show their mettle by toiling up that strenuous mountain, to a place so high and lonely that it would give especial delight to their deity, the Carneian Apollo. Or was the reason, perhaps, none other than that the place was so peerlessly beautiful?

There is a theatre here on the plateau of Thera. The ancients almost always contrived to build a theatre, however exiguous the space might be, finding a theatre a more imperative necessity than modern cities do fifty and a hundred times their size. It is certain that the sense of beauty in landscape controlled the sites of their theatres. They always sought the convenience of a natural arena, but it went further than that; they lost no opportunity of using the most enchanting spectacles in the Mediterranean world to serve as the backcloth of their drama, thus interpreting, and being interpreted by, the depth and splendour of sky and sea. If, then, their theatres were sited for aesthetic reasons, why not, whenever possible, their citadels and their altars? Clearly the creators of that matchless beauty in poetry, sculpture, and architecture, had a sense of beauty in landscape at least the equal of ours. It is not surprising that even with the changes the millenia have brought, we are so enslaved by the classic ruins, even when they are encompassed by coca-cola and hot dog stands, and when the waiting cars are packed close by, flank to flank. Is it because their background, with its constituent elements

of sea and sky, rock and vegetation, is as beautiful as anything we
know on earth; because the material, the limestone, the marble,
out of which the ruins are mostly built, were shaped with such
taste and love that, however incoherent, they always have beauty?
Above all, is it because of the power of these "muddled" ruins to
evoke in even the unlearned, like myself, the sort of buildings those
ruins were when they stood foursquare in the blue day, and the sort
of people who built them, who maintained them, who worshipped
there, who lived in those small houses, and were buried in those
empty tombs?

So beautiful as this I for my part found the old city of Thera,
as evocative in its way as Hissarlik itself. In Hissarlik the mind's
duty was to give substance to the images of Homer. In Thera, which
no Homer sang, the mind could write its own poems if only by
reciting the names aloud as you moved between one antiquity and
another, from Byzantine to Hellenistic, from Dorian to Roman, now
with the eyes open, gazing on what survived of the old awe and the
old beauty, now with the eyes shut, while the associations they
invoked took shape behind the eyes. Here was the Chapel of Haghios
Stephanos, and a candle burning on the forlorn altar, and no-one
had been seen to enter and light it. Here was the Temenos of
Artemidoros. Who was Artemidoros? There were a dozen, two dozen
Artemidoroses, of Ephesos and Ascalon, of Parion, and Tarsos. But
what are any of these Artemidoroses doing in Thera? Anyhow,
here is his Temenos, this is the Precinct he can still repair to, whenever he is so minded. Move over the ridge, and you find yourself
at the Barracks and the Gymnasium of the Ptolemaic Garrison.
What uniforms did they wear? Did they look like the male choruses
from *Aida*? What exercises were they put through in the Gymnasium,
those old-time Guardsmen who were the same sort of breed, after
all, as our own Guardsmen in Knightsbridge? Knees Bend, was it,
Arms Upward Stretch? What games did they play, sprawling on
their palliasses, yawning through the hot afternoons, trying to put
out of their minds the girls they had left behind them in Alexandria?
Did they play the wrist-and-elbow game? Were they great dicers?
Oh yes, there were dice in Thera, for those earlier exiles, the
Achaeans, had played dice, too, as long ago as the Trojan War.
(So we learn in a fragment of Sophocles, who even gives us the name
of their inventor, Palamedes, who dedicated a set of dice on the
altar of the temple of Fortune, so that his other sets of dice should
bring him luck.)

Move some yards further now, and here is the terrace of the

Temple of Dionysos. Ah, what vine-leaves in the hair! What swiggings from the brimful wine-pitchers! This is the Agora here, where the citizens came up from these narrow streets and met and slapped each other's backs and talked the whole clock round.

And not far off . . . there is something rather special not far off, to judge from the demeanour of our friend, Nikolaos, the guide. "This way!" he breathes behind his hand, hoping that the White Russian lady's attention is totally absorbed by the temple of Isis, Serapis and Anubis, with whom she is so familiar they might have been her first cousins. We, the men of the party, move off quietly after him. The White Russian lady is obviously quite furious. As if there was anything about the excavations in Thera she did not know. As if she had not digested the three enormous black tomes of Hiller von Gärtringen.

But they did her no good. While the gentlemen were taken off by Nikolaos and moved off behind one old wall and another, the lady, almost visibly torn apart by the conflicting emotions of her propriety as a high-born lady and her passion as an *archéologue*, remained with Isis, Serapis and Anubis. And there was the secret thing, a large phallus in high-relief dedicated by some anonymous gentleman to his friends, some lecherous old toper, I do not doubt. What induced him to carve the thing there? Did he make a bet when he was in his cups, and his friends held him to it, and there the old Silenus's indecency has persisted for not much less than three thousand years? I don't suppose his wicked old ghost minds. It probably cackles its head off, when it comes walking this way.

The ridge is narrowing now. Here is what survives of the temple of the deity to whom in its beginning this city was dedicated, Apollo Carneios, the deity that the conquering forbears of the Dorian Theras bore with them from the north to Lacedaemon, and Theras himself carried from Lacedaemon to this island across the sea. He was Carneios, the Horned One, with horns transferred to his forehead from the heads of the animals sacrificed in his honour, the ram and the goat. During nine days in August, the high heat of the year, the Therans celebrated the Carneia, their god's chief festival, here within these precincts worn smooth with the feet of long-dead worshippers, and slumbrous now with pink thickets of asphodel. Not many yards away, buttressed by a stout wall on the extremity of the ridge, are the ruins of the Gymnasium of Apollo's Ephoboi, leaning over the gulf of blue air. Here, at the gymnopaedia devised in the god's honour, for eight days the naked youths danced and fought in the prescribed rituals, and on the ninth day awaited the climax of it all, when the priest, decked with garlands, sprang away from his altar and went running down the mountain-side, running, running, till at a signal the lads sprang after him, bearing vine-clusters in their hands; running down the slopes, over the vineyards, seeking to touch the priest-god, to fill themselves with his virtue, so that they might in turn give virtue to the ripening vines with the grape-clusters thus magically beatified.

And I wonder whether it was during the intervals of waiting for the return of these lads to the shrine on the hill-top, that their love-lorn friends carved their names on the rocks through all the long bee-buzzing hours, telling all time to come that Arasimandros is grand, and if ever there was a good-looking boy it is young Tharres, and Eumelos is the best dancer? I muse, too, on the odd fate that makes of these pederastic *grafitti* the first instances known of specimens of a Greek script; and whether the Dorians up on the hill impounded a few of the surviving Phoenicians from their dwindling settlements by the sea's edge to teach them this new craft which (as is well known) the Phoenicians were the first to teach their kinsmen over in the mainland?

It may have been so. Or can one from now on believe that the Dorians may have brought some sort of script with them? Is that one of the inferences which may be drawn from the recent discoveries at Pylos and Mycenae which suggest that a form of written Greek speech existed in the region from which these Dorians came some half a millenium earlier?

I did not dwell long on such arid speculations as I pondered on those love-lorn carvings at Thera, not one of which presents a woman's name. I was more concerned with the thought that, after all, they were the handiwork of Dorians, the strong-arm men of the Greek world. Does that indicate that the aberration in those melancholy imperishable messages has no necessary connection with the phase in a people's history known as its "decadence", such a decadence as in the over-ripeness of time had befallen the classical world when Strato of Sardis, in the second century A.D., compiled his *Mousa Paidiké*? If anybody can be conceived as tough and virile, it must be these adventurous Therans of the dour Spartan blood, settlers in this remote outpost, dwellers upon this awkward and narrow fastness. (Commenting on all this, Hiller von Gärtringen is surely reversing the accepted view of the order in which these processes develop in a people, when he says of the inscriptions that they show the "rawness" of the Dorian invaders, along with a lack of modesty and a sensitiveness sharply opposed to that which is to prevail later among their descendants.)

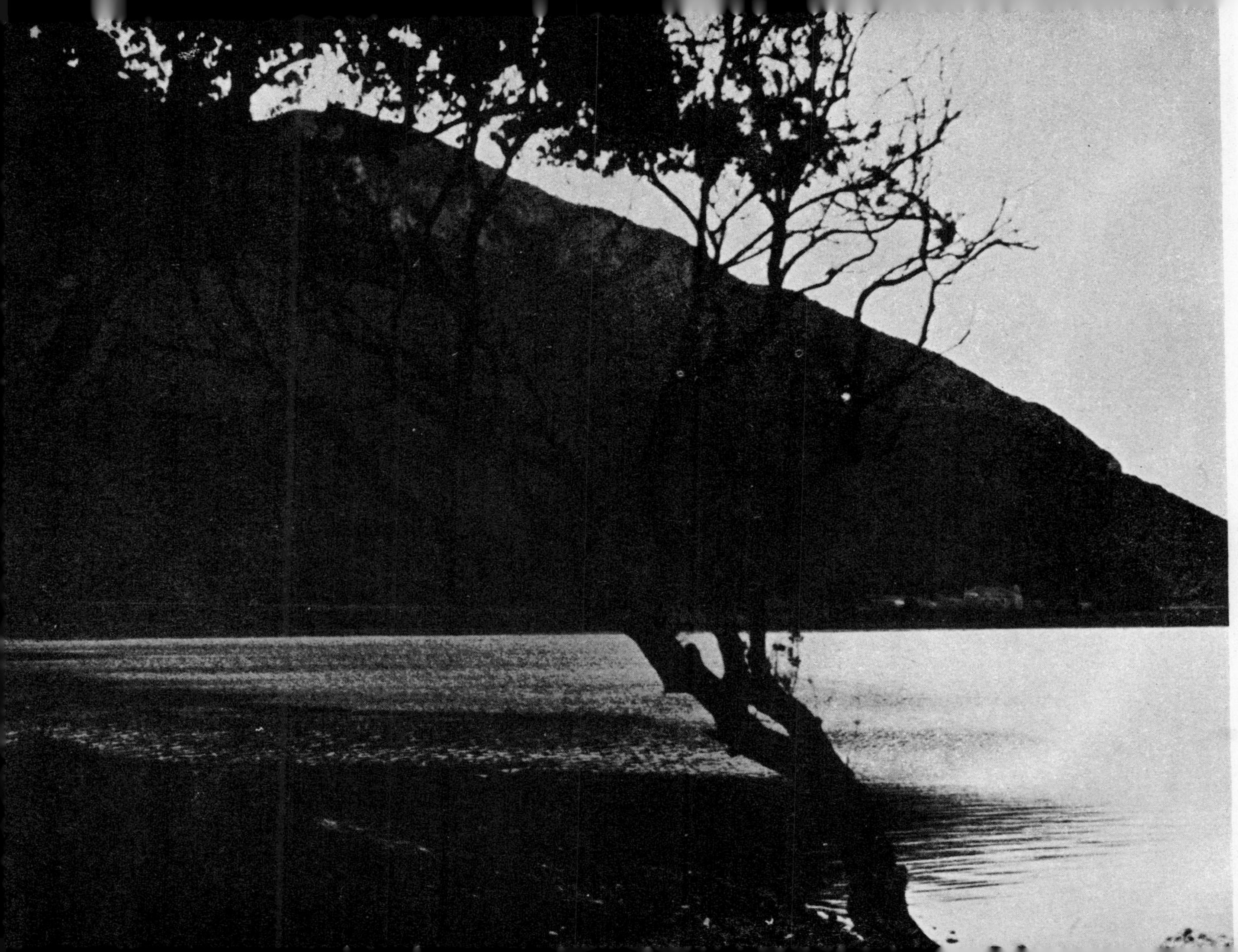

Circean landscape

As the mind moves around and across the brief circuit of Thera, from the barracks of the Ptolemaic garrison to the dancing-place of the Dorian youths, one begins to wonder whether females were as rigidly excluded from the male fortress as they are at this day from the monasteries of Mount Athos. Alike on the altars of the Greek divinities and in the caverns consecrated to the Byzantine saints, there is no trace of female divinity on Thera, no Hera, no Panaghia.

I confided this speculation to my friend, the learned White Russian lady. She turned pale, then blushed furiously, and made off down the ridge, where the blue seat of her trousers switched on and off like a harbour-light among the clouds of pumice-dust she raised.

VI

It was good-bye to Santorin a morning or two later. One of the donkeys preceded us with our luggage down the Skala. We ourselves were going down on foot. A considerable distance below us we saw a radiant vision, a young man and woman clad in the most impeccable white beach suiting I have seen outside Florida. They were on donkeys. The vision came closer and became more radiant, the headgear, the shoewear, the man's Sulka tie and socks, the woman's Dior scarf and sheer silk stockings. They were good-looking and obviously rich. She was too blonde to be English, he was too dark. Their jaws were set. They were doing all they knew not to have the white beach suiting scratched against the rock.

We went on our way down to the narrow platform from which the skiffs go out to the steamers. There was a lot of excitement down there, and we thought no more of the radiant couple. On board we had some coffee, wrote a few notes, and went forrard, among the peasant-women and the priests and the goats and the chickens and the service-men going back from leave. It was, therefore, some time before we were on the top deck, with Santorin behind us, and ahead of us Sikinos on the left hand, Ios on the right. A man and a woman in a bad temper and white beach suiting were pacing the deck, round the wheel-house, over amidships, back to the wheel-house again. They were good-looking and well-dressed, wore the most expensive footwear and so on, the man was dark, the woman was blonde. In fact they looked exactly like the couple we had seen an hour or so ago riding up to Thera, but they could not possibly be. It was odd. The couples looked identical. Perhaps one pair was ghosts. I turned to Edward.

I

"Do you see what I see?" I asked. He was not sure. There was only one thing to do. I went up to them.

"Excuse me," I said. "It *was* you we saw, wasn't it, riding up the stairway at Santorin, just an hour or so ago?"

"Filthy place!" said the dark man.

"Disgusting!" said the blonde woman.

They both spoke English with a sort of Antibes accent.

"But you can't have been there half an hour all told," I objected. "If that!"

"Too long!" cried the man.

"That foul staircase!" cried the woman.

"Couldn't they sweep it? It was knee-deep in muck!" said the man. He used a nastier word.

"Donkeys are donkeys!" I murmured. "Did you have time to see anything over in Santorin?"

"We didn't get any further than that hotel," said the woman. "I never saw anything more horrible in all my life."

"A bit primitive," I admitted. "Excuse me. What on earth did you expect in so out-of-the-way a place?"

"That disgusting old woman," the woman went on. "Crawling in your hair, she was, like a bat!"

"And that filthy husband of hers!" said the man. "If he *is* her husband!"

"Did you have time to meet him?" I asked.

"Time to meet him? He said if the place wasn't good enough we could go somewhere else! I told him if he didn't shut his mouth I'd throw him into the sea!"

"So he opened up," I said. "I found him rather a silent old man."

"They're still yelling their heads off, both of them, up in that pig-sty."

"So you didn't like Santorin?" I summed up.

"Disgusting place!" said the dark man.

"Filthy!" said the blonde woman.

Well, there it was. They hadn't liked Santorin. I shall never give up wondering what it was they had expected to find when they got there.

All day long it was a dazzle of islands, coming up from the sea like so many Venuses with the sunlight dripping on their shoulders. Santorin was behind us, where Odysseus, according to the Ship-owner, had climbed to the top of a volcano in order to descend into the Cimmerian darkness. At the centre of the islands was holy Delos, where Odysseus had seen a fresh young palm-tree shooting up by the altar of Apollo. Ios was the first port of call, although if I do not consult the map it is hard to remember in what order the islands came. Yes, it was Ios first, with the gaily-coloured kites, like captive birds, struggling to break free over the flat white roofs. And it was Ios where the slightly lunar philanthropist came aboard, who was *en route* for the Piraeus where he was to meet two French artificial-flower-makers. He had imported the artificial-flower-makers from Chartres, and was going to settle them in Ios so that they might teach the islanders how to make artificial flowers. It all seemed a little strange. Who would want artificial flowers in an island of the Cyclades, with all those anemones of its own, and all those crocuses, those orchids, and roses, and poppies, and sunflowers? But the philanthropist looked not only kind, but intelligent, and doubtless he knew what he was up to.

Then the day was Naxos climbing up the slopes of its rocky hill, and the marble portico of a temple said to be of Dionysos, on a minute island at the extremity of the harbour, and it was so beautiful you wondered whether the temple had ever been more complete than that. It was in the harbour of Naxos, I think, that a fisher-boy leapt with the grace of a swallow from the bowsprit of one schooner to the ratlines of another, and hovered a moment in mid-air, I say again, hovered a moment in mid-air, as Nijinski did making the last exit in the *Spectre de la Rose*. Was it Naxos? Perhaps it was Paros. For these islands are cyclical, they are the Cyclades, with Delos at their centre, and I am hard put to it to evoke the impression of that day excepting in a cyclical order, or no order at all.

Was it still Naxos where the octopus sprawling across a sack was swung aboard by the ship's crane? And the deck-hand let it droop from the rigging, separating its tentacles before he left it to dry in the sun? And then he smiled to himself darkly, and wiped the back of his hand across his mouth, thinking how succulent his supper would be. And under the gangway as we went ashore, there was a jet-black school of fish darting and dazzling over a screen of brilliant white sand like the dots and dashes that made up the images of the early cinema.

Was it Paros where the small girl stood inside an antique marble doorway carved with fruit and leaves, and she seemed grave and timeless as any archaic image carved from the marble seams of that same island? Was it on the waterfront at Syra where the crowd listened with rapt faces to the broadcast of a Greco-Italian football match in Athens, while the salmon-pink, cornflower-blue, grass-green, apricot-yellow caiques stood off in the harbour and the lime-green hills of another island were painted cardboard in a play and the water in between was like a city at twilight with an infinite switching on and off of lights from a hundred thousand switch-boards?

In the square of what island was the line of down-at-heel taxis drawn up, those mid-nineteen-twenty American touring cars, the Chrysler, the Dodge, the Essex, the Buick? And that solitary Maybach of the type the S.S. had used once, did the islanders deliberately avoid it because of some unsavoury collaborationist history during the Occupation? And was it in that square the photo-graphers were doing a roaring trade, seating their subjects on wicker chairs against the dusty palm-trees, those affianced couples whose eyes stared so rigidly you thought they would drop at any moment out of their sockets?

But all day long, round the circle of the Cyclades, there was music, not only from the individual instrumentalists, but from the loud-speakers relayed all over the ship. Sometimes it was radio, but more often it was gramophone-records, and most often Bing Crosby wanting to know how long is the journey from here to a star. All day, too, there was a moving and bleating from the sheep and lambs already packed in the stern. One old ram that was being pulled along by his horns made it clear, with a cough, a splutter, a kick of the trotters, that he was not used to such unceremonious treatment. One huge black goat with clear intelligent brandy-ball eyes managed to butt a space clear where he could fold his legs under himself and sit cool in the stern's shadow. So it went on all day long till at the end of it the stern was as choc-a-bloc as the hold of Odysseus's ship must have been when he carried off all that booty from Ismarus, at the outset of his travels. And still Mr. Crosby wanted to know how long is the journey from here to a star, and still no-one told him. The Cyclades were well behind us now. The stars were so close above our mast-head they seemed to be hanging like plump pale-green apples in an orchard.

VII

When we put our gangway down at the Piraeus, there was another ship with its gangway down along the quayside. This one had not just come in, it was just going out. There was the usual excitement.

"Where is that one going?" I casually asked the steward by my side.

"She go to my island," said the steward. "She go to Chios." The note of proprietary pride was familiar, and endearing. It was exactly the accent in which the Shipowner had spoken of Santorin, *his* island.

"Oh yes, Chios," I repeated. I had played once or twice with the idea of going to Chios, as I looked through my maps and lists of sailings, chiefly because Chios (as I have said earlier) is a strong favourite for being the place where Homer was born. But Smyrna is another strong favourite, and I had suppressed the temptation to go to Smyrna. After all, my scheme, my pattern, was Odysseus. Old Odysseus had thrown his net far enough and wide enough.

"You no been to Chios?" the steward was asking.

"As a matter of fact, I haven't."

"You no been to Chios?" the steward repeated. "Where the Homeeros teach boetry?" He really sounded quite hurt. I felt a barb lodge in me. Homer had not only been born in Chios, as some have held. Apparently he had taught poetry there too.

"Where?" I asked. "Who says so?"

"Everyone know," he looked at me scornfully. "Near Basha Fountain. I have uncle is fisherman there." Basha was Pasha. There was some reminiscence here of the Turkish occupation. "The stone where the Homeeros teach boetry is near Basha Fountain. Is a long time ago now." He put up both hands, and raised them again and again, to show how long ago it was. "Very old boetry, very good, like wine," insisted the devoted Homerist. "Is a great shame you shall not go to Chios."

The siren of the Chios boat hooted. The excitement by the gangway quickened like the crowd at a première outside a movie theatre when a star steps from a motor-car.

"If we hurry we can make it!" proclaimed Edward suddenly. He knew my defences were practically down. The steward had taken charge now. Was this our luggage? It was. A porter came charging towards us from the gangway. "Hi, you!" With a thumb he successively indicated the luggage, ourselves and the Chios boat.

A last flicker of resistance awoke in me. I knew a day or two's rest at the hotel would be helpful. There would probably be some mail to attend to.

"There'll be another boat in two or three days," I ventured to point out.

"Is plenty time to catch this boat," said the steward firmly. "If you no catch this boat——" He shrugged his shoulders.

He was right. It was either Chios now, or Chios never. Things happen like this in an Odyssey.

"We're going to Chios, Edward!" I announced, as if the idea had come from me in the first place. "How lucky there's a boat in!"

There *was* plenty of time, as the steward had said, despite the hooting, time enough, anyhow, for a few *ouzos* at the "Uncle Sam Bar".

We sat down at a table on a pavement. The American ties flickered to and fro, like peacocks and mocking-birds and cockatoos. Then a lady sat down at our table, a charming lady. She wore a smart navy-blue costume with a white-frilled blue blouse. In one hand she carried an expensive crocodile leather hand-bag, in the other a string-bag containing a chicken with its neck sticking out through the string-mesh and the neck-feathers puffed out like an Elizabethan ruff. Overhead an incoming plane glittered like a mackerel as it turned in the blue waters of the sky.

The lady pressed her thigh against mine. It seemed discourteous not to press mine against hers.

"We will go to nice night-club?" she asked.

"I am sorry. We are leaving by the boat to Chios."

She shrugged her shoulders.

"*Koniak!*" she told the waiter. She drained it, rose from the table, and continued along the quayside.

The sun was setting behind Salamis. On the mainland the three southward-thrusting promontories were repeated in the three peaks at the extremity of the central promontory, like three notes of music. A small breeze sent up a flurry over all the ink-blue water, then it died down again and the sea was glass, except for the trouble at bow and stern. The thrust of the bow created a short first ridge, then a much longer second ridge, with the snarled lace of both almost instantaneously unravelling. The sun's reflection was a broad milk-white path all the way between Salamis and the ship's rails.

The company of sea-gulls that had been following us from the Piraeus had now whittled itself down to a devoted equipage, or avipage, of three birds at most. One sea-gull flying far off did not flap its wings. It was, in fact, an aeroplane, skimming in towards Athens airport. Another, nearer, planed down to water's level, the wings fluttered for some moments in protest, then agreed to accept the water.

Now came Aegina, range beyond range, the furthest away just mist. Then suddenly, all in one moment, the most delicate colours were everywhere. Was it a trick of my own eye, or could any watching eye attest that the hithermost ridge of Aegina was grass-green and the next anemone-purple, and the water under them deepening down from turquoise-blue through a hueless interval into a warm lilac?

How sweet it all was, marrow-meltingly sweet! A young man sat down a few yards along the passage-way, took a mandolin out of a case, and put it into music. The words were Greek, the tunes American. I had hoped he would play some melodies of the Greek Islands, if these now exist. Perhaps they do not any more. The tunes were vaguely familiar. I realized at length they were the tunes of the celebrated American "team", The Ink Spots, which hitherto have always provoked me to banshee madness. But the young man handled the instrument and the voice with skill. The romantic sounds were exactly that turquoise-blue and warm lilac. His shoes were flaming sunflower.

Half an hour passed. The water was cross-hatched with infinite lozenges which fitted over each other like a lizard's scales. Over Aegina a cloud was teased into a flung flux of tenuous hair, or a length of gauze torn apart by too rough a touch. I put on my dark glasses to see their effect on all this. The sun emerged whole and round from a nimbus which made it invisible to ordinary sight. The clouds, low and parallel with the horizon, lost all their nuances of colour, but were now charged with electricity, the whole air was now lurid with volcanic dust. The sun was terribly aggrandized. It might have been Santorin, on the direful day of the cataclysm. I removed the dark glasses with relief.

A yellow-gold moon shone over Sunium. Where the water was still, the moon's reflection was no more than a dropped handful of silver pennies. Where a breeze rose and troubled it, the sea was like a capital city *en fête*. A cloud came from nowhere and cut off the moon's halo, so that the moon now looked like the helmet of an Achaean warrior on an early Attic vase.

A hand touched me on the shoulder. A Greek eye winked in the moonlight. It was the mandolin-player. The sunflower shoes were now dull copper.

"You play games like in Monte Carlo?" the young man asked. His voice was honey-sweet like his playing.

"Why not?" I rather liked the suggestion.

He put his mandolin in the case.

"Come!"

He had a suitcase in the saloon from which he drew a roulette-board of a type new to me. Instead of deciding the issue with a running pebble, you throw a dart at the number you fancy. Soon everybody was playing and losing nicely. I lost the equivalent of fourteen shillings, but, I did not think it had been an ill-spent day and night.

I was awakened a minute or two after I laid my head on the pillow, or so it seemed. It was five-thirty and we were at Chios. I sprang out of my berth, and into my clothes. And then I remembered. One could take it easy. The boat went on to Lesbos, or Mytilene, as it is more frequently called to-day, after its chief city—since the Middle Ages, in fact.

But there was no getting back into the berth again, in Chios harbour, and the sun just rising. And exquisite that sunrise was, delicate and astringent as opposed to that Ink Spot sweetness of the turquoise and blue sunset, a palest sky of topaz brushed with clouds of daffodil and briar rose, the silhouettes of two steel-plate harbour moles between which the rigging of a hundred caiques made a black tracery against smoky blue hills, beyond the sea-walls, a cardboard cut-out of a fisherman standing up motionless in his boat, returning after all night at sea.

Then the sun rose and in a moment flushed the whole world with primary colour, plumped it with a third dimension, the blue and yellow and red ships, the red roofs, the green wooded hills.

"Good?" asked the mandolin-player, his waxed moustache looking a bit bedraggled. He had not left his roulette-table since we saw him last, three or four hours ago. Through the windows of the saloon you could still see the *aficionados* throwing darts.

"Fine!" We raised our thumbs.

"Fine? Maybe yes, maybe no!"

The nostrils curled. We had not taken the cue correctly. "You go to Mytilene?" We nodded. His expression changed. "Ah, Mytilene!" He touched his lips with his fingers and blew a kiss towards Mytilene. "Wait till you shall see. Like Switzerland!"

The Greek islanders have the same feeling for their islands as the British for their football-teams. For my part it is not only because Mytilene is like Switzerland that I was happy the Chios boat went on there and spent a few hours before turning for Chios again.

For I was on my route once more, as I had realized a few hours ago. Yes, Odysseus had been to Lesbos, and had spent an exciting hour or two there. Or was it Lemnos? I took out my Odyssey and thumbed the pages. He must have been to both, but Lesbos is specifically mentioned, our authority is King Menelaus, the fellow-hero of Odysseus, which makes the episode more credible than if we had learned it from the lips of Odysseus himself, who sometimes tells the truth, sometimes not. The occasion is the visit that Odysseus's son, Telemachus, pays to Menelaus to find out if he has news to give him of his absent father. As is to be expected, Telemachus tells his host all about those dreadful Suitors who were devouring his mother's substance back in Ithaca.

"For shame!" Menelaus breaks in. "So the cowards want to creep into the brave man's bed? Once in the pleasant isle of Lesbos I saw Odysseus stand up to Philoeleides in a wrestling-match and bring him down with a terrific throw which delighted all. By Father Zeus, Athene, and Apollo, that's the Odysseus I should like to see these Suitors meet! A swift death and a sorry wedding there would be for all!"

So Odysseus and Menelaus and the others had been to Lesbos and found it a pleasant isle. The Achaeans were *en route* for Troy, and were taking it by easy stages, for we get a vivid account of the good time they gave themselves on the next and presumably the final stage of the voyage, the Isle of Lemnos. And of course, Odysseus must have been there too. This time we learn of the episode on the life of Agamemnon, and the occasion is a good deal more dramatic. Things are turning out very black for the Achaeans, it looks as if Hector is going to set the whole Achaean fleet alight, when Agamemnon climbs on the bulging black hull of Odysseus's ship and thunders:

"For shame, Argives, contemptible creatures, splendid only on parade! What has become of our assurance that we were the finest force on earth? What of the idle boasts you made that time in Lemnos as you gorged yourself on the beef of straight-horned cattle and drank from bowls brimful of wine?"

I should imagine that they did very much the same thing in Lesbos, after Odysseus's magnificent performance in the wrestling-ring. I think, too, that is a very sensible spirit to go to war in. A soldier is as liable as not to be absent from the merry-making when the war is over.

It was, of course, not the spirit they came back in, not from that war, at least; and there were many that went who never came back again. There they were, back again in Lesbos. (This is the only other reference to the island in Homer.) So old Nestor tells us, or so he told Telemachus, the time he was on his way to question Menelaus. A handful of the princes were there in Lesbos and late in their wake Menelaus followed, too. They were debating what route they should take to get back home again,

"whether to choose the long passage outside the ragged coast of Chios and by way of Psyria, keeping that island on our left, or to sail inside Chios past the windy heights of Mimas." They did neither. "Heaven made it clear that we should cut straight across the open sea to Euboea to get out of harm's way as quickly as possible."

As for Odysseus, he was at that moment sacking Ismarus, the city of the Cicones, or perhaps the winds were already blowing him on his way to the Lotus-eaters, the first of the sea-adventures.

Yes, to this day Lesbos is a pleasant island, as it was when Odysseus and Menelaus went there on the way to the Trojan War, and all the world was young. If Homer lived in Chios, he can hardly have failed to have gone to Lesbos some time to find out for himself how pleasant the island was. And it was in this island that a poet was born some two centuries later who alone among the poets of antiquity rivalled Homer in fame; I mean Sappho, who was held to be "the Poetess" as he was the "Poet", Sappho, the Miracle, as they called her, the Flower of the Graces, the Tenth Muse. She was the "violet-crowned, the pure, the sweetly smiling". So the poet, Alcaeus, sang of her, and he must have known more about her than her subsequent detractors, for he was her contemporary, and lived in Lesbos, too. I hardly hoped the islanders would be able to point out the field in which Odysseus threw Philoeleides in the wrestling-match, for the reference to the episode in the Odyssey is very cursory, and, after all, Homer is not *their* poet. But Sappho is the glory of the island. I hoped for some luck with Sappho.

We landed in the usual parrot-bright shrillness of light and colour. There was a good deal of merchandise loading and un-loading, jars of olive oil and casks of wine, cases of soap, hampers of fruit and vegetables, and, of course, droves of sheep. I wondered why the islanders do not agree among themselves to let all the sheep stay on in the islands they were born in. There would be less excitement on the quaysides, but everybody would eat exactly the same amount of mutton. We inquired for the Mayor, and were taken along to a somewhat bare carpetless office not far off. The man we met might not have been the Mayor himself, but he was obviously a person of some importance, for there were a good many people in the office, and he shouted at them all, and nobody answered back. It did not seem to derogate from his dignity that he wore neither tie nor waist-coat and had not shaved for some time. However, as soon as he realized two Englishmen were attending on him, he gave us his courteous attention. I told him we were interested in Sappho, the famous lady poet who had once lived on his island. He looked a little puzzled and went into a huddle with the other people in the office. No-one had heard of the lady. Was she, perhaps, one of the early Christian martyrs? No, I said. There was a further consulta-tion, and it was finally decided to send for Dimitrios, who had a taxi, and talked English, for he had lived in Australia. With Dimi-trios we struck oil. He said that he knew all about Sappho, and near the church of the Haghios Theophanos there were the ruins of Sappho's School where she used to teach the small children of the island and had then been eaten by a lion. We went along to the ruins, which looked rather Roman than Aeolian, and per-haps there is some confusion between two ladies of the same name.

I then asked Dimitrios if he knew anything about the Leucadian rock, from which the first Sappho, the pagan one, had jumped to her death when she was spurned in love by a young man named Phaon. I told him that in the island of Leukas they claimed the rock was there, because of the name. They were always making extravagant claims in Leukas. Nowadays they were claiming that they were really Ithaca, the island of Odysseus. For my part, I preferred to believe the Leucadian rock was in Lesbos. Probably Dimitrios could point it out for us. If we were interested in rocks, said Dimitrios, he could show us as many as we had time for, for there were a great many in the island.

Before long, under the flanks of still another Mount Elijah, we were driving along the island roads at a speed which I personally considered excessive, through rich vineyards and ancient olive-groves and woods of that shady Vallona oak we had met in the country round Troy, the oak whose acorns are so fruitful in their yield of tannin. If we went left, we reached the shining waters of the Gulf of Kallioni; if we went right, we reached them again, for the Gulf almost cuts the island in two, thrusting south-west to north-east. Now and again Dimitrios remembered we were looking for some sort of a rock, though it was clear we had not conveyed to him the sort of rock it was.

"Do you have picture of rock, maybe?" Dimitrios asked. Alas, no, we did not. Might it be that one? He pointed out a fallen boulder. We thought it unlikely. A gleam came into his eyes. He had, after all, been to Australia, and had heard tales. "You mean, maybe, you look for gold in rock?" It was not that, either. We tried once more to explain to him it was the rock from which a lady poet named Sappho had jumped into the sea.

He looked rather helpless, then he perceived an old peasant napping at the edge of an olive-grove while his goat grazed beside him on a tether. He had a sack drawn over his shoulders to protect him from the sun. Dimitrios hooted his horn repeatedly, till at last the peasant woke, and came out from under his sack.

"Hi, you!" Dimitrios called. "Do you know anything about a rock? A lady jumped from it!"

The peasant was very cross about this nonsense. He knew nothing about ladies jumping from rocks, pulled the sack firmly round his shoulders again, and disappeared.

On our way back to Mytilene, we learned that Dimitrios kept not only a taxi but a restaurant also. He opened his restaurant, we gathered, just as he drove his taxi, whenever there was a demand for it.

"You would perhaps like me to open restaurant? I make you nice Australian dinner? I learn in Australia, where I have restaurant. I make much money in Australia, a thousand pounds. I come back with thousand pounds, one wife, two children. Under occupation is no good, the drachma. Is finish." He removed his hands from the wheel and rubbed the palm of one hand against the palm of the other, to show how finished the thousand pounds were. "You would like nice Australian meal? I make Irish Stew, Lancashire Hot-Pot." His pronunciation was eccentric, but we finally decided these were the dishes he meant. It did not seem proper to come to the Isle of Lesbos in order to eat Irish Stew or Lancashire Hot-Pot.

"We don't think we have time, Dimitrios. But, perhaps, when we come again—do you think you could turn out something a little more, how shall I say, of your own country?"

He looked rather crestfallen for some moments. Then a thought came to him. In that disturbing manner he had of removing his hand from the wheel to illustrate his ideas, he had one hand stroking his stomach and the other lifted to the sky, thumb rubbing against forefinger.

"Bird!" he said. "Bird! Tcha! Tcha! I forget the name! He travel plenty. He come from Rumania! Fat like this, in the cheek, in the neck! He eat plenty corn in Rumania, but is thin like this when he go to Egypt." He showed his little finger.

"Quail?"

"Ah, quail! Yes, yes! Quail!" He turned and embraced me warmly. The taxi drove itself round a sharp corner, with a fifty-foot drop under the road. It knew Dimitrios as well as the back of its own axle, and could probably have driven itself to its own garage if Dimitrios had fallen asleep at the wheel.

"Next time you come to Mytilene," begged Dimitrios with shining eyes, "come when quail is coming from Rumania. Yes? I will roast you, with rice and currants and honey! Will be marvellous "

It seemed to me that would be as pleasant a reason as any to return to Mytilene, to eat a dish of Dimitrios's roast quail; for it was unlikely we should ever find the Leucadian rock, and certain we should never see a bevy of maiden poets gathered round their principal, violet-crowned, sweetly-smiling, while she taught them to pluck the harpstrings in the Mixolydian mode.

Lesbos and Sappho were a detour from a detour. Chios was also a detour, but it had Homer in it. Back then to Chios, to "rocky" Chios as the poet calls it (Ithaca, too, is "rocky" Ithaca. There are few islands in the Greek archipelago to which the adjective is not applicable. Anyhow, the word for "rocky"—*paipaloessa*—slides sweetly into the hexameter).

The association of Chios, as I have said, is not with Odysseus himself but with his creator, Chios and Smyrna having been the two principal claimants to the honour of having been Homer's birthplace. The reasons given for these claims have been tenuous enough, and are for the most part connected with post-Homeric Epigrams and Hymns falsely attributed to Homer, and with the fabrications called "Lives", which were concocted in the first or second centuries under the inspiration of these same Epigrams and Hymns. The fourth Epigram, for instance, tells us of a blind poet, born in Smyrna, on the banks of the sacred Meles. The idea is then taken up in the *Life of Homer* attributed to Herodotus, in which we are told quite simply that this "son of the Meles" was Homer. From then on Smyrna becomes the birthplace of Homer. So do certain other places, for similar and even more fragile reasons.

The case is not quite the same with Chios, the reasons are less fragile. Far removed from the time of Homer though Strabo may be, his pronouncement has weight. "The Chiotes lay claim to Homer," he declares, "advancing a powerful testimony, namely his family, called the Homeridae." An older testimony is that of Thucydides, who quotes a passage from a hymn to the Delian Apollo (which a recent authority accepts as, at least, "not impossibly" the work of Homer himself). The hymn was recited at a famous festival in Delos. At the conclusion of the festival the poet would address himself thus to the Delian maidens:

> *Remember ; when perhaps some traveller*
> *Coming to Delos puts this question to you :*
> *Maidens, which of the poets like you most*
> *Who come to Delos ? Who's your favourite ?*
> *Then think of me, and answer, all of you*
> *"A blind man, and he lives in rocky Chios."*[5]*

And it is Homer, declares Thucydides, none other than Homer, who was this blind man, the dweller in rocky Chios.

I will quote one final speculation regarding the birthplace of the poet of the Iliad and the Odyssey. It is this: That he had two birth-places, one in Smyrna, and one in Chios, for there were two poets, one, a mainlander, who knew the Troad country well, and he might well have been born in Smyrna. This one wrote the Iliad. There was also an island poet born in Chios. He, who knew the sea and islands, and loved them well, wrote the Odyssey.

At least that was a speculation I permitted myself to entertain before I went to Chios. I found it an unnecessary refinement when I got there. I found that an inhabitant of Chios lives so close to the mainland that he can feel himself mainlander as well as islander, like the inhabitant of the Isle of Wight or Manhattan.

So the blind poet could have written both poems. I was happy to take to my heart again my two-in-one Homer.

Are these Greek Islands as beautiful as we remember them, almost in as many different ways as there are islands? Does one particular moment of experience with one or the other senses seize on our imagination, so that henceforth we recall each island in terms of that particular sense? I, for instance, recall the beauty of Santorin

* For reference, see Acknowledgements, page 237.

as the red fire of its cliffs hot upon the cheeks; the beauty of Corfu is above all, visual, the silver-grey sheen of olives, the bronzy sheen of cypresses. The beauty of Ithaca was in the nostrils, the tingle of the smell of dry myrtle and juniper. And the beauty of Chios was light, the unearthly pure light of morning, the thudding waves of light at mid-day, and by moonlight a surf creeping and crinkling along the sands of darkness.

The name, Chios, was derived by certain fanciful commentators in antiquity from the word *"chion"*, snow. It was stated that snow fell on the island at the birth of one of the sons of Poseidon, who was therefore called "Chios". As etymology this is nonsense. But one feels the fantasy has something to it, if one thinks of snow as light, white light, the element which seems to ride upon the narrow channel between Chios and the mainland of Asia, and course through the streets of the villages, and sit upon the hill-tops, a light which does not annul colour, but integrates and harmonizes it.

Perhaps my association of white light with Chios derived from the spectacle of a great yacht that was lying at the further end of the quayside, immediately opposite the Hotel Pelinaion, to which we were making our way. There was a whole flotilla of coloured caiques in the harbour, but the hull of the yacht subdued them in its mysterious whiteness. There it hovered, like a sea-gull that is at once only a few yards away and immensely far off, folded up in its secrecy. The yacht bore no name either on its stern or its life-belts. We were soon to learn that its present owner is a rich Turk who lives in a villa over in Asia, only a mile or two across the narrows; he kept the yacht in Chios harbour, for maintenance dues are much less in Greece than in his own country. A Turkish man and boy were in charge of it, but they were rarely visible, and when they were they had little to say to each other. There was even less speech with the islanders, which is not surprising, for the memory of the Turkish massacres of 1822, following the abortive rising which a body of headstrong Samians had engineered, is as fresh in the island as to-day's weather. Where had the yacht come from? Edward thought it might be the celebrated *Britannia*, which had once belonged to King George the Fifth; it was certainly one of that fabulous class that was built and raced in the twenties, by the Sopwiths, the Liptons, and their kind.

I myself would not have found it impossible to believe that, though it was not the standard shape of the galleys of the old time, it had once belonged to Chion, the son of Poseidon, who was born when snow fell. I would not have been surprised if one morning we had seen its milk-white sails hoisted, though no crewmen hauled at the yards; and then the wind filled the sails, and the thing was gone like a sea-gull into the white light from which it came.

"Welcome, gentlemen, welcome!" a voice cried. We turned to a broad smile and a pair of outstretched arms. "I am Vanya. I own hotel. I will tell you all about the Homeeros." We must have looked a bit startled. "*Tipote!*" he requested. "Nothing at all. The man tell me from ship. Come in, please!"

"How do you do?" we said, feeling like Enoch Arden, and other returners after long absences. We entered. "These papers will explain, perhaps——"

"Thank you. Your room also is waiting. You would like wash first? Then you have dinner? Yes. Come in, please!"

We entered. The dining-room seemed almost as spacious as a railway-station. In a corner a man was sitting at a typewriter which at that distance looked like a match-box. Far off was a cooking-range, with things simmering in copper pans.

"You like fish, yes? Maybe meat?" Vanya removed a lid. From the depths of the saucepan the heads of three lambs gazed towards each other with profound melancholy. We thought we like fish.

"Now you go up, then you come down. Is plenty we shall talk about," he promised.

We went upstairs. The rooms were on the same scale, each as large as a branch of Barclay's Bank. We washed, came down, and dined. The fish was good, spiny, but hot and well-fried in the good Chian oil. The wine was worthy of the repute it has enjoyed since ancient times. There was a lemon-flower jam called "anthos", special to Chios, which smells like hair-oil and tastes like ambrosia. During the course of the meal a group of gentlemen, all of substance one would say, assembled at the adjoining table; the gentleman came over from the remote typewriter. Then Vanya emerged from the cavern behind the range, and announced that the gentlemen wished us to drink coffee and eat a preserved cherry with them. He himself and the dactylographist, who was the island's chief Shipping Agent, would interpret. Our new friends were the Leading Lawyer of the island, the Chief Librarian, and the Assistant Prefect. We were introduced, and compliments were exchanged. In their official capacities, they had perused our papers, and the conversation at once turned upon the question of the island's connection with Homer. It was apparent that these Chiotes were as convinced that Homer was born in Chios as the Corsicans are convinced that

Evening in Santorin

Santorin: Cupolas and bell-towers of New Thera

Old Thera

Napoleon was born in Corsica. It was very pleasing after the total unawareness of Sappho in the Mayor's parlour in Lesbos. I wondered if a panel of Smyrna aldermen would have pronounced the Smyrna claim to Homer with such promptness and verve. I felt somehow not.

"For of course, Homer himself says he was a man of Chios," pronounced one of the worthies, I think the Assistant Prefect. "Do the gentlemen know?"

I said I knew about the line in the Hymn to the Delian Apollo. But it wasn't quite established that Homer himself had written the line. Some thought it perhaps one of the Homeridae, who came after him.

"It was Homer," pronounced the Assistant Prefect, and was silent after that for some time.

"There is no doubt at all the Homeridae came from Chios," said the Chief Librarian. "Did they come from Samos? No. From Paxos? No. Cyprus? No. So why shouldn't their ancestor have been a man of Chios, too?"

"They went on making songs here till quite recently," continued the Shipping Agent. "The people still sing them, just as they still use the same plough and spin on the same wheel, and call them by the same names as in the olden times."

It was the Homeridae who interested me. "Till how recently were they making songs here?"

The worthies consulted with each other. It was hard to say, they decided. Perhaps when the Turks seized the island during the sixteenth century, they put the last of them to death. (They have, of course, been ready to believe any unkindness of the Turks, since that horrible massacre. The fact that the Greeks themselves behaved in a rather similar fashion in Turkish Asia Minor after the First World War just a century later, has not dimmed the memory.)

The line taken by Vanya was psychological rather than historical.

"The people of Chios, they are many sailors, yes? Yes. Always they have been many sailors? Yes? The Homeeros was a sailor? Yes? Well?" He waited for me to draw the inevitable inference.

"I feel it probable Homer was a sailor," I admitted. "That is very much my own line of thought. Sailors go away and have adventures, then they come back and talk about them. He wrote them down." It really was rather simpler than one had thought.

"Then there is comic," said Vanya. I did not quite get that. He explained his meaning to the Shipping Agent, whose English was

K

good, and who could make up what it lacked in two or three other languages.

"He means the sense of humour," expounded the Shipping Agent. "The people of Chios have always been known through all Greece for their sense of humour. Homer had a sense of humour, too. He says that proves also that Homer was a man of Chios."

It seemed to me an interesting argument, and I told the company that a famous English writer, namely Samuel Butler, had written a long essay on that very subject: "The Humour of Homer." In fact, it had first been a lecture which he had delivered to British working-men, which showed that everybody in Britain was interested in Homer, just as in Chios; Vanya was delighted. I saw no point in adding that Butler praised the sense of humour in Homer not to prove that his poems, or, at least, the Odyssey, were written by a male inhabitant of Chios, but by a female inhabitant of Trapani far off in Sicily.

I asked Vanya what particular specimens of Homer's humour he was thinking of. For a busy hotel-keeper it can be said that Vanya had a creditable knowledge of the poet. He recalled the episode of how Ares and Aphrodite were caught in bed together, and how Hephaestus, the husband of the Goddess, threw a net over them. Is that funny, yes, no? I said yes, I supposed it was; anyhow all the other gods split their sides laughing. The same happened, I reminded him, when they saw Hephaestus hobbling around the floor of heaven, after Zeus had dropped him from the top of Olympus and lamed him. The more you come to think of it, I agreed, the more you see how funny Homer was. There was Ithaca, for instance. I hadn't been there yet, but I was going to find out for myself quite soon. Well, Homer had described a number of places on the island—the cave with the two entrances, the plateau where Eumaeus herded his swine, and so on. And his picture was so exact, it seemed, you could identify the places to this day. Then he had added a topographical detail, about Ithaca being the furthest island up in the darkling west, when as a matter of fact it isn't, for it is almost completely shut off from the darkling west by the island of Cephalonia. I now realized he had introduced that detail as a joke, to provoke to madness all his commentators in the times to come. My friends were interested, but they didn't like to switch the limelight from Chios to another island. The Shipping Agent asked if I knew that the narrow water where old-time mariners would come up against Scylla and Charybdis, was the straight we were looking at through this very window, between Chios and the Turkish mainland? I did not. And that it was here, in Chios harbour, the big fleet was assembled before it sailed for Troy? No, I objected. No.

"*Malista!*" They were quite firm.

The Assistant Prefect, who had been silent for some time, spoke again. There were places all over the island, he said, which had had a traditional connection with Homer from the earliest times. Some of the associations might be merely old wives' tales, but did you ever have smoke without fire? For instance, there was the School of Homer, declared the Chief Librarian, near the Pasha's Fountain. They called it the Daskalopetra. It was no distance away, just northward along the harbour. We could catch a bus there. (This was evidently the place referred to by my friend the Chiote steward, in Piraeus harbour.) There was a stone there where Homer used to sit with his pupils around him. If we looked in the guide-book, we would find it said that the Daskalopetra had been an altar-stone to some old god. Could they prove it? They could not. Could they prove that it was *not* the School of Homer? They could not. He shrugged his shoulders.

Further it had always been said the poet had been born in a village called Pytios, and had died in Kardamyla, a village up in the north there. At the mention of Kardamyla, Vanya chuckled loudly. The others grinned, too. There was obviously some association with Kardamyla more comic than the fact that Homer had died there. The place seemed to have a funny ring in a Chiote's ear, like Wigan to an Englishman, Kirkintilloch to a Scotsman, and Oshkosh, Wisconsin, across the Atlantic.

"You know about men from Kardamyla?" asked Vanya. "I tell you." But the others seemed to consider Kardamyla irrelevant to the conversation. We moved on to a place called "Meeros", which was obviously a shortening of "Homeeros", and they used to show Homer's tomb here, as well as at Kardamyla. There were also the Aipos hills, added the Shipping Agent. Homer was once being chased by his enemies, and he came to these hills which are so high that the poet cried out "*Ai, pos?*" meaning, "Alas, how?" About that same time, he went on, the poet was resting on a hillside under a fir-tree, when a pine-cone fell on his head. "*Phila oré!*" he called out. "Dear mountains! Are you after me now, too?" So ever since the place had been called Phlori. Vanya now came in with a story about a place called Kolosyrtis, over on the flank of the island's own Mountain of St. Elijah. "Is fine place," said Vanya, "and you shall go if is time. And one day the Homeeros is walk there, and is very wet, so he slip down. Bo! Like that! So is call that place Kolosyrtis. See?"

"Well, not really," I admitted. "What does the word mean?"

Vanya hesitated a moment, then he explained.

"It mean fall down." (I felt this was inadequate, and recalling that brief hesitation, I later consulted Argenti's erudite pages and discovered that the word means: "slipping on one's behind".) It was a pleasing touch of decorum. It was altogether a decorous little gathering, the worthies of Chios, and the two earnest inquirers from England, solemnly establishing for all time the question of the birth-place of the first and greatest of epic poets.

The concluding and most irresistible argument came from the lips of the Assistant Prefect.

"Gentlemen," said he, "go into our countryside, go into our valleys and into our woods. Stand on a hill-top and look out on our sea. You will know there that the old man, he was not from Smyrna, not from Cyprus, not from Crete, he was from here, from our island, Chios."

With that he rose, and his friends rose with him. "Good-night," we said. "Good-night." Soon we too went out and walked along the waterfront. The lunar logic of these speculations seemed to have an irrefragable validity in that milk-pale air. The white flanks of the yacht's hull lay against each other like folded hands.

It had been more or less admitted by our friends that the association with Homer of places like Phlori and Kolosyrtis is tenuous. But the Daskalopetra, near the Pasha's Fountain, is something you can see and touch. You can get there by bus, and a bus is not an argument you can contradict. So off we went next day into the square to catch the bus, past the waterfront shops which sell the celebrated mastic of Chios in miniature two-handled clay vessels of a pleasingly antique style. The square is shut off from the sea, and was very hot and dusty. Among the trunks of palm and pepper trees the hot white light ran about in streams like steel ingots on the floor of a foundry. The bus had that air of the Early Iron Age which all public vehicles have in the Greek Islands. Homer himself, or at least the Homeridae, might have travelled in it. Rarely had we heard such rumblings and galumphings. Rarely were louder pro-tests uttered by donkeys braying, geese quacking, dogs barking. Rarely in travellers' nostrils were the odours sweeter of thyme and rock-rose and myrtle in the hills, of sprawling roses and lop-eared lavender in the tangled little roadside gardens between the hills and the sliding white-metal sea.

And when we got there, we found it was some sort of a festival day when children are taken from their schools to go on outings. The air twittered with swallows, the small green Dorset-combe hills heaved with children. Up hill, down dale we went to find the Pasha's Fountain, but that had temporarily dried up. However, there was Homer's Stone sure enough, on the top of a small knoll, asprawl with purple mallow and white rock-rose and a bell-shaped flower I did not know, yellow, with glabrous leaves. The stone is some three feet high, roughly semicircular, hollowed out on the right and left flanks, so that one can easily sit there, and rest one's feet in the hollows. It faces a sort of carved stone bench a few yards away about one foot high, with a back projecting almost as high again. Scholars have little doubt that this is the relic of some ancient altar to Cybele, one of the least gracious of the goddesses, and that human sacrifices may well have been performed there. But the Chiotes themselves know better than that, as our friends the night before had insisted. When we reached the Stone, a tall angular spectacled schoolmaster was telling tales to a clan of youngsters who sat with their eyes goggling, clustered like barnacles on the long stone bench in front of him. He would have looked more like Homer without that big scarlet handkerchief and the green rolled-up umbrella; but not the Homeridae themselves could have listened more breathlessly.

We made an excursion over the hills next day to the ancient monastery of Nea Moni, built during the middle years of the eleventh century to house a miraculous eikon which was discovered near by. We went partly because the excursion would give us an idea of the country which, according to the somewhat transcendental argument of the Assistant Prefect, was the most convincing proof of the birth of Homer in Chios; and partly because we heard there were some fine Byzantine mosaics in the monastery. Or they had been fine once; the Turks had hacked them about with their rifle-butts and whatever weapons they happened to have about them, in that frenzy of 1821.

The monastery lies some seven or eight kilometres away as the crow flies, but it is a good deal further than that by the time you have taken the rocky road as far as a car can travel along it, and have then continued for some two or three hours on foot and by donkey.

We were pleased to have the company of Vanya as far as the car went, both going out and going back. He was anxious to drive home the arguments the company had laid before us on our first evening, by proving to us that, just like Homer, the people of Chios were great story-tellers, and they had his sense of humour. One was to think of Homer, in fact, as a sort of P. G. Wodehouse of the early Mediterranean world, a new and slightly disturbing conception.

During the course of the day he told us a whole series of delightful stories. I am not folk-lorist enough to know which of them are to be met with elsewhere in Greece and the Greek Islands, and I find that Mr. Argenti has versions of some, at least, in his *Folk-Lore of Chios*. But the versions are not identical; and certainly by the time Vanya's stories had passed through the mills of Vanya's mind and vocal organs, they had a quality quite their own. It is likely that the conditions in which he narrated them added a special flavour, the chug-chug of the labouring engine, the conviction from time to time that we were going to hurtle down a precipice, the occasional interruption by meandering herds of sheep and goats, and the breathless beauty of the landscape.

There was, for instance, a story he told soon after we left the town, about Orion, the huntsman, which was in several important details different from the version given by any of his predecessors, who include Homer, and Horace. All agree on placing Orion in Chios at some time before his elevation to the night sky. According to Vanya, Orion at one time came to Chios to kill all serpents. So he kill all serpents, so is hungry now, and wants to have good dinner. So he kill beautiful deer, but deer belong to Artemis. So Artemis opens ground, and out comes dragon and kill Orion. Orion goes up to heaven, and he is waiter to gods, but instead of wine, ha-ha, he gives urine to gods, so in Chios is called always Urion.

"I see," I said. "He had practically become a naturalized Chian."

"How you mean?"

"That Chios sense of humour. Tell me now, what happened in Kardamyla."

"Kardamyla!" He roared with laughter. "I tell you what happen in Kardamyla." It was like this. A group of peasants from Kardamyla were walking through the fields and it was moonlight. Then do you know what happened? Suddenly the moon disappeared, it had fallen down into a big hole. They went up to the hole and there it was, sure enough. It was really a big rock, of course. What shall we do without our moon, they said. So next day they got ropes and hooks and tied it round the rock, and there on the edge of the hole they pulled and pulled for hours, till finally with a great heave they dislodged the rock. In doing so they fell flat on their backs, and found themselves gazing into the sky. "Look!" they cried. "Isn't it fine? We have sent our moon back into the sky again!"

I agreed it was a very funny story. By this time we had reached a village called Karies, and I asked whether there were any funny stories about Karies, too. He was not very kind about Karies. He wouldn't say a word against the present inhabitants, but in former times they were well-known as thieves and robbers all over the island. They were descended from the workmen who had built the monastery of Nea Moni for the Emperor of that time. They had, however, plotted against the Emperor, so he had condemned them all to death. But he was a kind Emperor, so he cancelled the death-sentence and instead had the wicked workmen transported to this shelf on the mountain, where they had built the village of Karies long ago. Vanya thought there was nothing much wrong with them nowadays, but the funny people of Chios always said if ever a bishop visited the village of Karies, he never got away without having his saddle stolen from under him.

Vanya was glad to leave Karies behind him, for he at once changed the subject to the village of Kalamoti, further south. He had a story to tell about a man and his wife. The man went to market and there he met another man who was selling a big green water-melon. What do you want for that water-melon? asked the first man. It is not a water-melon, it is a mare in foal. I want a gold Turkish pound. So the first man gave the gold Turkish pound to the second man, and carried off the green water-melon. On his way home, he dropped the water-melon in a ditch, and at that moment a big rabbit jumped out of the ditch. He picked up the pieces of the water-melon, reached home, and his wife asked, what are you doing there with that water-melon? It is not a water-melon, said the man. It is a mare, and she has just foaled. What a pity the mare is all in bits and pieces, said the wife, for I could have ridden her when I went out into the village. What, you great fat thing! cried the man. You would put your weight on the back of my poor mare! So he took of his belt and said Take that! And that! And beat her till she was black and blue.

The road was getting rougher and steeper, the car more clamorous, the scenery more lyrical. It was not easy any more to disentangle the thread of Vanya's stories from the threads of pine-wood and limestone cliff and hawk-shadow with which it was interwoven. But the tale of the three men of Chios remains with me because Vanya showed me exactly where it happened. We had been climbing along a steep valley for some time, when we reached an ancient aqueduct spanning a vigorous stream that came crashing down from boulder to boulder.

"Stop!" cried Vanya. The driver stopped. Vanya opened the car door, and we went out. He pointed to a pool below. "Is here! Is here!" He went on to tell the story with such fervour it all might have happened yesterday, though it belongs to the time of that Turkish misery. Well, there were three men of Chios, and they had come up into the hills here along the banks of this stream to take refuge from the Turks who, as everybody knows, were killing everybody all over the place. And then they saw a single Turk all on his own up here on the bridge, and they made up their minds to kill him. But no, they told each other. It is better not, for the Turks are all counted, and he will be missed. So they continued further along the stream, and the Turk happened to see one of them. Hello, said the Turk, who are you? The first man of Chios thought he would be clever, so he made a noise like a frog to make him think he was a frog. Well, then, if you are a frog why are you so big? asked the Turk. Because I am last year's frog, said the man. But, unfortunately, he was wearing a very nice hat, and the Turk wanted it, so the Turk killed him. When the Turk reached for the hat, the wind blew it away and the Turk ran after it, till at last it came to rest in the bushes higher up, and the Turk started hunting round for it. As it happened, the second man of Chios was hiding in the bushes, and, being afraid that the Turk would come upon him if he went on searching, he handed the hat up to the Turk, saying: Here it is. On which the Turk killed the second man then and there. Now the third man of Chios, who was standing on the top of the bank, thought it was very silly of the first two men to have opened their mouths and given their whereabouts to the Turk. Unfortunately, he said so, too. Said he: So now you see why I didn't say a word. So the Turk went up and killed him, too. And that was the end of the third man of Chios.

And that was the end of Vanya's story. He turned and came back towards the car. Then a thought struck him. He stopped, and held up his hand.

"You hear?"

We could hear the sound of the water, and the air moving in the pine-branches. A bird was chattering somewhere. That was about all.

"You hear?" asked Vanya again. "Frogs, no?" Yes, from some invisible pool came a faint croak of frogs. "Like I just tell you," he announced. "Back in car now." He must have been suggesting that the fact that there were frogs around gave a certain plausibility to the story; perhaps three of the frogs we could hear housed the souls

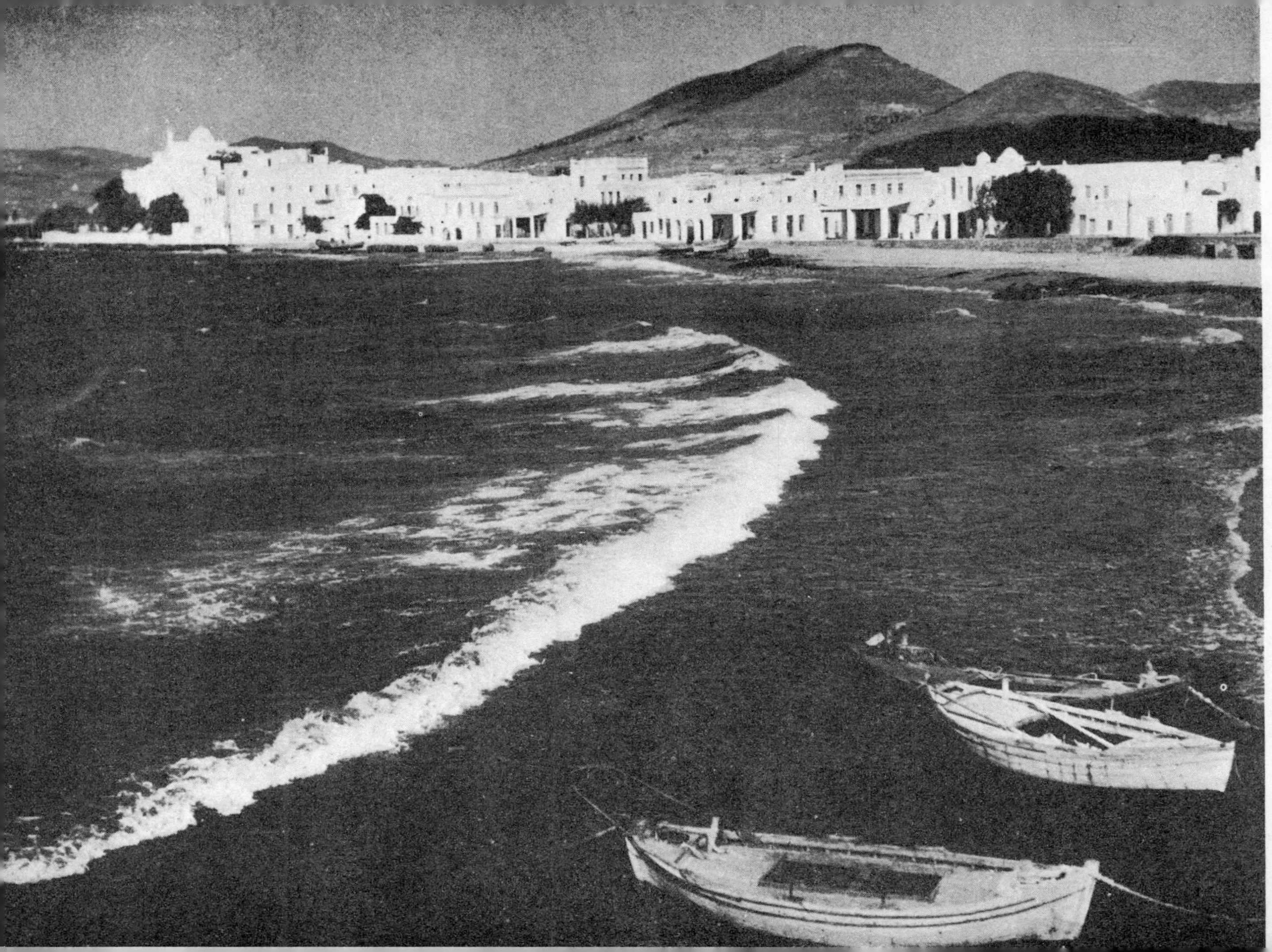

Island of Paros

Naxos: Temple Ruin

Chios: School of Homer

Chios: Monastery of Nea Moni

Corfu town

of the three men of Chios. Or perhaps the remark was still another example of Chios humour.

A mile or so further on, the road petered out, there were only goat-tracks, of which one led sooner or later to the monastery. The hillside swooped down south towards the bed of the invisible stream, and then the further hills rose, white with the afternoon sun. On our right, to the north, the hills were steeper and shaggy with tracts of wood and a scrub of arbutus and ilex and wild olive.

"I go fetch your guide, sheep-man," said Vanya, and strode off to a small cottage that clung precariously to the hillside some three or four hundred yards away. A woman appeared, a small parcel of blue and scarlet under the slim bare chestnut poles of the vine-trellis in front of her door.

Vanya returned. "He come soon! He come with donkeys! Monastery is high up and long way. Is better you shall have donkeys."

We sat down and smoked cigarettes, the smoke curling up between the steeples of asphodel and evening primrose. Half an hour passed, and there was still no sheep-man. The driver was getting impatient. He had work to do in Chios before coming back for us. Vanya rose, and put his hand to his mouth, and called out "*Bastora!*" again and again. There was no answer. The shepherd was much further off than his wife had thought. We assured Vanya we could find our way to Nea Moni on foot. Perhaps later the shepherd would be back and his wife could send him after us with the animals.

"Is good. Shall see you later," said Vanya. The car drove off, the explosions dwindling and at length dying away. At last, at last, silence was all about us, a silence not fretted but deepened by the sounds contained in it, as the sky is enlarged by the clouds that float in it. So birds called and bees buzzed and sheep bleated and far off somewhere a donkey brayed, somewhere nearer a dog barked. A shepherd somewhere called to his flock, a sound of goat bells lifted in the still air. No, I said to myself, the Assistant Prefect knows his island better than I do, but if Chios is Homer by the edge of the sea, here in the heart of the island, Chios is Theocritus.

So off we went along the goat-track, over the hot and arid hill, and into a deep green hollow the stream had made. In a bower of ash and willows there were three small pools in which we bathed, stepping down from one to the next, as long, long ago (I remembered in a flash that fused the intervening four decades into one moment of cool time) I had bathed in three pools on a flank of the Langdales.

Then, as now, small birds flashed from boulder to boulder, flicking their bright tails, and uttering syllables short and sharp as pebbles. Insects darted above the water in sequences of dot and dash like morse signals. Then as now from beyond the edge of the streamside wood loud and clear a cuckoo called. Not Homer, I said, not Theocritus. For as long as that cuckoo calls, Chios is Wordsworth.

Then a new bird-sound thrilled upon the air, a single brassy note repeated three times, piercing and staccato. Again and again the bird called, if it was a bird, and what else could it have been?

"Vaughan Williams," murmured Edward dreamily. "Do you remember?"

"No. Where?"

"That menacing insistent trumpet in the Sixth Symphony; the slow movement."

His hand jerked for a moment or two as if there was a baton in in. For a time he was in the Festival Hall, I in the Langdales. Then the Vaughan Williams trumpet and the Wordsworth cuckoo were silent. We were back again in Chios among the pools under the willows. At last a mournful sound came to us from far off, *ai-é!* *ai-é*, like a messenger in a Greek tragedy, approaching with woeful tidings. It was the shepherd at last leading his two donkeys. So we emerged from the three pools and the cool thicket and mounted the animals and went further on our way. Soon the stream and the flanking woods were well below us, for the track was all uphill now, with the sun hot and chalk-white. It was very quiet—no sound now but the shepherd's wail from time to time when the donkeys' hooves clicked as they stumbled among the loose stones. Now at last the monastery of Nea Moni came into sight, standing on a plateau within a circuit of four walls, its central dome and its campanile flanked by coal-black cypresses, and a small olive-grove muffling the roofs of the out-buildings. In the dip of land under the plateau were bare walls and unrelated arches, where perhaps a small community of peasants had once lived to work the monastery lands; or they may have been the lay brothers and novices of the foundation. The terraces they had carved out of the hillside survived, and a few olives and fruit-trees that had gone to waste. Perhaps the earthquake of 1881 was responsible for the ruin, perhaps the Turks some decades earlier. One could not tell.

A tense hush held the atmosphere. No leaf moved. No bird crossed the sky. As we entered the monastery gate, a dog howled but did not show himself. The fabric of the church was in fair shape; it must have been put to rights lately. It could be assumed that monks still lived there, and tended these altars. But none made their appearance.

"Is everybody dead?" we asked the peasant. "Can't you find somebody?" We managed to make him understand, for he went off. He was away for so long we wondered whether he, too, had fallen into a spell, like the monks who must be around somewhere, inert and enchanted. The main door was open, and we entered. There was little light in the church, and the mortally injured mosaics only slowly revealed themselves. So, in a battlefield at evening it might take some time to realize that the soldiers lying around are not resting, but dead or dying, and that the extremities have been lopped off, and the bone pokes through envelopes of cloth and skin. I have seen slashed canvases and statues hacked like firewood. But I found a more fearful horror in the violence done these mosaics, which more than all other achievements in plastic art are associated with dignity, severity and a millenial calm. There was a mosaic of Jesus at prayer in the Garden of Gethsemane where, because of the desecration, the loneliness and the anguish were as poignant as anything I have ever known, as if both Jesus Himself and the nameless makers of the mosaic had foreseen the day and the night of the terror to come. Michael and Gabriel were not archangels but martyrs with no end to their martyrdom, the Madonna looked down with grief upon the Child crucified in her arms.

So we moved from scene to scene, from the Crucifixion to the Descent to Limbo, from Limbo to the Ascension, from a world too wicked to save. Then there was a moment at which we were aware of a tugging at the sleeve, and, turning, we saw an old woman, so old, so shabby and emaciated, you had the feeling she had just managed to work her way out from under a heap of corpses somewhere in the monastery precincts that had not yet been shoved out of sight. She wanted to make sure we paid our respects to an oleograph Madonna peeping out behind a tin-foil shield, with paper roses stuck into her frame and a wick burning before her in a broken salt-cellar. Was it her notion that those older eikons had been desecrated and had therefore lost all their potency, and her own eikon, worth only a few drachmas, was inviolate and therefore commanded all the talents of Heaven? Or was it merely that it was bright and new, and therefore delighted her dim old eye as a baby's ear is delighted with the sound of a rattle? I looked round for her to see if I could extract a word which might illuminate the matter, but she was gone.

A minute or two later a small boy appeared at our side, just as silently and mysteriously as the old woman had come and gone again. It was evident that there was another sight he wished us to see, and we followed him. Are there no monks any more in the monastery? I asked myself. They are usually so hospitable, what keeps them from receiving us? There can hardly be so many visitors to Nea Moni that they are tired of them. Are they some distance away in one of their fields? Have they vowed to keep themselves to themselves in their cells? Or since those Turkish visitors came howling up the valley have they forsworn all strangers, these old men in whose memory a century is a day and a day a century?

We had by this time reached the first of the two barn-shaped buildings outside among the olive-trees. The boy stood at the door, unlocked it, and waited for us to enter. We crossed the threshold. There were no windows. Once again it took several moments before the eye accustomed itself to the darkness. Then slowly a phantasmagoria of skulls and thigh-bones and leg-bones sprouted, as it were, before our eyes, took shape and texture like a submarine vegetation, till at last the whole place was filled with it. They were, of course, relics of the victims of the massacre, the men and women and children who had fled into the interior from the blood-dripping Mamelukes, and had thought to find sanctuary within the precincts of these ancient hallows.

We turned to leave the place. The small boy was standing half-turned on the threshold, not a shadow of expression on his face. He took hold of my wrist as if to take me over to the other building which clearly was an ossuary, too. But skulls are like skulls and thigh-bones are like thigh-bones. I shook my head. He shrugged his shoulders, but it was almost an imperceptible movement; then he reached out his hand, laid a finger on the dome of a skull, and withdrew it. The gestures were all extremely delicate, like his hands, and his unsmiling face. I fumbled for a note and placed it in his hand. A moment later he, too, was gone, like the old woman, or like a lizard into the crannies of a wall.

It was all very strange and very silent. The monks, if there were any about, remained where they were. We mounted our animals and rode off, down to the whispering boughs and the running water. The car and Vanya were both waiting for us, those two eloquent exponents of the Chios sense of humour. The noises the car made and the tales Vanya told were very comforting as we went sputtering down from the hills. But it was exhilarating to have the sea in sight again, Homer's sea, swinging easy and noble like his hexameters.

CHAPTER SEVEN

Corfu

I

A DAY or two later we returned to Athens, where I met a friend with a car who suggested we should join him on a journey to Salonica. He remembered my devotion to Byzantine mosaic. Later that day I met a friend with a ruck-sack who said he was going on a walking-tour to the country around Olympus, and why not join him. That night in a bar I met a man who expected to acquire a sailing-boat in a day or two and make for Crete; for a small payment down he would have room for us.

My suspicions would not have been aroused if I had been presented with only one of these three enchanting propositions. But the coincidence of three was clearly the work of my private Poseidon, who was determined to put every obstacle in my way to prevent me getting to Ithaca. He had already intervened with a Santorin and a Chios, taking on the shape of a Shipowner and a Steward.

Thank you, and no, I told them, all three. No, no, I told myself. I must be on my way to the Western Islands and the principality of Odysseus.

The boat did not leave for the Ionian Islands till the day after the next day. I went to bed, rose next morning, and stole off stealthily to immure myself from temptation in the museum. And there, shut off from the Athenian sunshine, from the warm hills and the lively streets, I spent all the day hiding from the Old Man of the Sea, I who have fought shy of half an hour in a museum, though there was nowhere else to go, and it was raining cats and dogs, and it was Birmingham. It was a whole day in a museum, under a roof, between walls, in Athens. And the museum for the time being was not displaying its most sensational exhibit, the Golden Treasury of Mycenae. Yet, as I look back across the intervening months, I recall that tabulated, documented, indoor day, with a pleasure as intense as almost any I recall during these wanderings. The collocation of their marbles and bronzes, their amphoras and steles, gave perspective to, and illuminated, the Greek experiences which had been dispersed for me over many years and much of the classical world. I had

seen some of the actual objects and had been additionally familiar
with them as photographs or in facsimile before; yet I felt myself
seeing them that day for the first time, as sometimes one reads a
familiar poem and knows one has never read it before. There were
also a number of objects new to me, which have been discovered
more recently. Not a few were as magnificent as anything in this or
any other museum, and have only not attained the same celebrity
because they have had only a few years, rather than a good many
centuries, for their fame to spread. It is certain that a great many
objects as magnificent as these are likely to be disinterred, or brought
up from the sea's bed, in the decades now ahead of us. In particular
the technique or the discovery of objects lost at sea by ship-wreck or
land-subsidence is only in its infancy. Alas, alas (I said to myself, as I
wandered through the rooms of the museum), whilst I admit there
are several reasons why I am happy to think that in two or three
decades from now I am not likely any longer to behold the light of
day, there are a few reasons why I am sad about it. And one of these
is the thought of the many new riches that will be by then housed
in the enlarged galleries of this museum in Athens here. I envy you
those things, oh you later travellers, as much as I envy you your
nightingales and your hard sweet apples and the melancholy pink
faces of your bull-terriers.

During that day's haunting of the quiet galleries I noted down a
few objects which especially seized my eye and heart. I have no
photographs of them, but as I enumerate them I see them as vividly
as if they were ranged about me now, on shelves or pedestals, in the
room where I write.

The bronze statue of a Boy Jockey found in the sea by Cape
Artemision, off Euboea. His hollow eyes, his thonged sandals. The
youngster takes the breath by his staggering vitality. You can almost
hear the lash of his whip.

A post-geometric amphora from an Attic workshop from the
end of the eighth century. So a Greek potter presented to his imagination and presents now to mine his dream of the warriors of Homer.
So were their beards dressed, this was the cock of the plumes on their
helmets, so they carried their shields and spears.

A painting on a wooden slab in a lovely bright blue and a warm
terra-cotta. How then preserved so well and so long? A lamb, led by
a small boy, is being dedicated for sacrifice. There is music from a
gold-filleted boy in blue with a lyre and a man in red with pipes at
his lips. A woman, a priestess, I suppose, pours a libation from a one-
handled wine-flask.

On a votive stele from Sunium, a youth crowns his own head with
a wreath of wild olive, a smile of the utmost delicacy and sadness on
his lips. On another a mother brings to her baby boy just dead the
rabbit he was playing with hardly any time ago. On a third is
presented a funeral bouquet. An old man sitting on a bench offers
a plate to his wife. A boy on the left pours wine into a mixing-bowl
below. On the right a servant awaits orders. Near by, a dog is
chewing a bone. On a fourth a boy mourns his dead friend, and the
dog he has had to leave behind him lifts its head and howls with
grief.

The water-jar from Vari in Attica that presents the Sappho I had
found no trace of in her native island. She is seated in a chair reading
from her poems, and one of her disciples accompanies her on a
stringed instrument. Another has her hand gently on her shoulder,
another raises her hand in salutation.

The superb bronze statue of Poseidon drawn up from the sea
not very long ago, the formalized beard, the classic hair-clusters on
his forehead. If he was Poseidon, he held in his hand a trident no
longer there. Or perhaps he was Zeus, and he held a thunderbolt.

The large stele commemorating the dead young huntsman. The
mourning father, heavily bearded, stands hard by, contemplating
his dead son. He leans upon his staff. On the left, a chubby small
brother, worn out with weeping, is asleep at last. The long-snouted
hunting-dog lies on his paws, dreadfully dejected. Is there any
product of any art so moving, of a simplicity so exquisite, as the
funeral stele of the Greeks?

The lovely hetairae of the Attic wine-cooler, painted by a certain
Euphronios. One raises a wine-cup to her companions, one soothes
them with the strains of the two-fold pipe. What elegant dalliances
long ago on those striped rugs, what erudite conversations between a
kiss and a kiss!

The attendants are looking a little restive. It is time to leave these
gentle ghosts. Good-bye, Agathocles, whose name catches my eye as
I turn to leave. How well that dog of yours loved you, who barks so
inconsolably because you have left him! Good-bye, Agathocles!

II

If any direction is certain in the whole of the Odyssey it is the
direction the hero took when he left the nymph, Calypso, behind him
in the Island of Ogygia, and set sail for Ithaca. It will be remembered

he had been held by the amorous nymph for seven years, and that it was only after the interposition of Athene with the gods that she was induced to let him go. Once having steeled herself to the loss of her handsome guest she was very co-operative. "I do promise," she vowed, "with good grace and unreservedly to give him such directions as will bring him safe and sound to Ithaca." So she gave him tools and shewed him where to get the best timber to build himself a boat, and off he sailed, with careful instructions that, as he made across the sea, he was always to keep the Great Bear on his left hand. And there he was sailing happily homeward, when that old sea-god espied him. "Ho, ho!" said he to himself. "I had only to go to Ethiopia for the gods to change their minds about Odysseus! And there he is, close to the Phaeacian land, where he is destined to bring his long ordeal to an end. Nevertheless I mean to let him have his bellyful of trouble yet!"

So Poseidon went to it, bringing down all the winds of Heaven on poor Odysseus; and it was only the intervention of another nymph, Ino of the slim ankles, who saved him from a watery grave. Have no more truck with that boat, said the lady, it will not get you anywhere. First throw off your clothes, then take this veil, wrap it round your middle and swim for it. It will be hard going, but in course of time you will finish up on the shore of the Phaeacian land, and there, for the time being at least, your troubles will be at an end. Remember one thing. The moment your feet touch land, throw my veil back into the sea, and keep your eyes averted while doing it, according to the convention that rules in these matters. Having said this, the nymph handed him the veil, and then like a sea-mew, dived back into the turbulent sea and the dark waters swallowed her up.

And this was the state of Odysseus, prince of Ithaca, as he swam out for the land of the Phaeacians, stark-naked, with nothing but the veil of Ino to preserve him from the tremendous malice of Poseidon and the sea. But of course we are not so anxious as we might have been. For we know in advance the intention of the gods regarding our weary way-worn wanderer.

Odysseus was requested always to keep the Great Bear, that is to say the north, on his left hand as he made for the land of the Phaeacians. In other words, he was to sail east. How those Homeric geographers who place the adventure on the Black Sea reconcile these instructions with their ideas defeats me, for to return to Ithaca from the Black Sea he would be sailing west. But the Homeric

Capo Santa Caterina

PALACE OF
ALCINOUS

PHAEACIAN
GAMES

KERKYRA
(corfu)

Palaeocastritsa

Ermoni

Canoni

Odysseus washed ashore

NAUSICAA

SCHERIA

The Land of the Phaeacians

(Corfu)

Punto Levkimo

Edward Thorpe

Capo Bianco

to Ithaca →

L

geographers are broad-minded. Apart from the most frequent identification, which is with Malta, Ogygia has been placed in the Aegean and North Seas, in the Canary and Madeira Islands, and in a number of other places, including both North and South Poles. A certain Herr Krichenbauer believes that Odysseus did not voyage at the mercy of wind and tide, but followed a definite plan; so he starts him off from Egypt, takes him by the Red Sea and the Gulf of Aden to the Indian Ocean. Then he continues southward via the Antarctic and the South Pole, till he finally returns through the Atlantic to the Straits of Gibraltar and the Mediterranean Sea. However, with respect to the two Poles, this, at least, can be said that in those regions, whether north or south, a lost sailor from the early Greek world would certainly have seen any number of Wandering Rocks and Clashing Rocks . . . of icebergs, in fact. And it is just possible that it was the rumour of these objects that first put into the minds of the myth-makers the idea of the foot-loose Planktae, to be called Symplegades later, which first the Argonauts and, later, Odysseus, encountered, in the dreadful hollow between the cave of the yelping Scylla and the thrashing vortex of Charybdis.

Well, I would have found it impracticable to visit the North and South Poles to try and establish whether one or the other was the original world where the Planktae wandered, and I had contented myself long ago with accepting Malta as my Ogygia, for at all events no other island in the Mediterranean so clearly fits Homer's description of it as the "navel of the sea". Moreover there is a *Grotta di Calipso* on the north coast of Malta complete with a spring of water, which is pointed out to this day. It is true that in the enchanting description of the grotto, Odysseus recounts that just near its mouth from four separate but neighbouring springs four crystal rivulets were trained to run this way and that. But it is easy to believe that with the passage of time three of the springs may have passed out of the picture. I should add that there is also a grotto in Gozo, the smaller Maltese island, likewise, identified with Calypso. I had seen Gozo. I had been to Malta. That was in 1916. I had to be content with that.

It took Odysseus some twenty days and nights of hard sailing and hard swimming to reach Scheria, the land of the Phaeacians, where presently he landed on the east coast, for we read nothing about his being carried round the north or south tip of the island, wherever it was. It took me longer than twenty days and nights, in fact, it took me ten years, to get from Malta-Ogygia to Corfu, which the inhabitants themselves (who are, of course, prejudiced) as well as many writers, ancient and modern, have accepted without question for well over two thousand years as the Odyssean Scheria, domain of Alcinous, King of the Phaeacians. As I have described earlier, it was not given me on that occasion, in 1926, to spend more than a short time in Corfu, and to see more than very little of the delectable island. This time, in the springtime of 1953, I would see a good deal more.

I was coming up from the east, of course, not from the west. I was not swimming, and I wore more than a white veil round my middle. But the air was almost as full of sea-drenched wind and lopped-off wave-tops as it had been for Odysseus approaching the sea-coast. My mind was full of Odyssean images and when I saw a wrecked ship red and rusty wedged upon the rocks just outside the harbour-mouth, I told myself proudly that here was all that was left of the vessel Odysseus had built for himself under the instructions of the devoted Calypso. He had had to abandon it, as we know, when Poseidon smashed it to smithereens, and here it was, brought hither and thither by tide and wind under the sea-wall of Corfu city.

An islander who was standing beside me gave a grimmer account of the ship-wreck. It had happened a lot more recently, but it already had acquired the aura of myth. The ship had been a requisitioned Greek tramp steamer of some thousand or more tons which the enemy had impounded. Later it had hastily been converted into a troop-carrier when the Allies got a foothold in the Mediterranean. Orders came through that Corfu was to be evacuated, or perhaps the garrison was to be strengthened, it was not known which. The ship was bombed just outside the harbour, with four hundred troops on board. All were lost. The burning vessel was washed up against the rocks there. There it lay, and would lie for a long time to come, the stern half and the midship submerged, the forrard half and the bridge sticking up at a grotesque angle, the fo'c'sle gun a mass of twisted and rusted wreckage. The seaweed-covered iron rails protected no-one and nothing. There was a great hole in her flank, where the rocks had gored her. Or it had been the bomb, perhaps.

She looked a haunted and lonely thing, with the water washing over her. It was good to get inside the harbour, where, through the close rods of rain, you could make out a flotilla of caiques anchored at right-angles to the quayside; all pitch-black, as Homer so frequently describes the galleys of his mariners, all flank by flank, like a herd of black horses. Beyond were the customs-buildings and an

archipelago of rain-puddles in the harbour square, and a proliferation of umbrellas like a colony of black toadstools in a damp wood-
land. How different it all was from that earlier landfall long ago, of
which the memory was so vivid that, if I shut my eyes to that
Manchester rain, I could see it again not sensibly obscured by the
passage of three decades, as one sees a stage-set behind scrims of
gauze which the stage-hands are soon to raise to the flies. I could see
the crowds thronging the harbour-front as gaily coloured as a border
of mixed tulips. Beyond the crowds the tall Italianate houses jostled
against each other like trees crowding for the best of the sun. And lo,
as we waited there for formalities to be discharged, there was a
sudden clangour of instruments, and a procession like an explosion
of fireworks appeared from one of the side streets. We had arrived
on one of the four days in the year when San Spiridion, the revered
island saint, is carried about the city in his crystal casket, with his
hands folded over his breast and his silver-brocaded shoes tidy
upon his feet, and before him bands blaring and over him banners
streaming and all round him enormous candles like groves of
saplings all ablaze. There, then, we stood on deck, like an audience
in a theatre, and the procession passed across the stage and into the
wings, as if some super-Reinhardtesque producer had contrived it
all for us. But the defile moved so slowly we had time to land and
intercept it before it entered San Spiridion to lay down the saint's
casket. And of all that pomp of vestments and images and hieratic
peasant women with enormous coils of false hair piled under silken
kerchiefs and earrings cascading towards their shoulders and
brocade skirts stiff as boards—of all that pomp I recalled most
clearly that wet forenoon years later a banner inscribed in gold
letters and crimson thread with the non-sectarian legend: "Lord
Mayor of London's Fund." Some-one told me, I think, that the Fund
in question had been raised to help the victims of the bombardment
that had some time earlier been ordered by Mussolini, in one of
his earliest fits of megalomaniac self-assertion; but what was to
be expected from Mussolini, who was, after all, a Mussulman, as his
name proved? For my part I did not think it likely that so dignified
and discreet a gentleman as the Lord Mayor of London always is had
sent his cheque along wrapped up in a silk banner. I wondered
whether it might be a carefully-preserved relic of that halcyon
period in the island's history, between 1815 and 1864, when Corfu
was the headquarters of the British Protectorate of the Ionian
Islands. (Not that the islanders themselves thought it a halcyon
time while the British were actually in occupation, any more than,

say, the Cypriotes do to-day. But that is the way the islanders have
come to think of it since it ended, and that perhaps is the way the
Cypriotes will think of it to-morrow.) But I decided from the style
and the lettering of the banner that it probably was not a relic of the
Georgian or Victorian epochs. Perhaps some islander had acquired
it during a term of employment in a Soho café, and had brought it
home to lodge it in Spiridion's treasury. However, there it was that
day, wherever it had come from, floating high and splendid among
banners of a more saintly sort.

We landed and paddled our way through the puddles and the
umbrellas, and observed with distress that the façade of tall houses
had been smashed up a good deal, and doubtless the damage in the
town itself had not been less severe. A young man held us up at a
barrier, seal-black with oilskins from head to foot. I waved a paper
at him, he flashed a smile white as rock-salt and proclaimed: *"ego
Christus!"*, he was Christ. Perceiving my bewilderment, which he may
have encountered in others before, he continued to explain that that
was the name by which he had so literally been christened, and opening up his oilskins he revealed the very British-looking naval uniform
of the Greek Customs Department. *"Kalo!"* he said. *"Kalo!"* we
replied. "Whisky? Girls?" he asked. "When it stops raining," we
said. We went over to the Hotel Astir which faces the waterfront, and
is as comfortable, I suppose, as any hostelry in the Greek Islands; for
already one is beginning to look over from the regions where a hotel
is a *khan*, a place to spend the night under cover, towards the regions
where a hotel may be, sometimes is, an aesthetic proposition, like
a picture or a piece of music. On emerging from the hotel we found
that the mood had switched from Manchester to Dover. The toothed
mountains of Albania beyond the channel were still invisible, as
Calais is from Dover, but there was a grey castle up on the hill, here
as there, and the air was full of driven Dover mist. To heighten the
illusion, there was even an "English" bar, "Dirty Dick's", though the
celebrated original is, I believe, by Liverpool Street Station. As we
passed the door Christos, now off duty, came rushing out towards
us, as if we had known each other for years, and insisted that we
have a drink or two together. The place was full of melancholy
young men recalling the great days of the bar when American sailors
with money to burn, drained every bottle dry, and the British sailors
on pay-day set out, as their phrase is, "to fill their boots". The walls
were decorated with photographs of *décolletée* Edwardian ladies
recommending cigarettes that people have long ceased to manu-
facture, and the cracked gramophone-records repeated the songs of

the early jazz age. The young men were seamen, they said. They were waiting for jobs, but were not very hopeful about it, for there are thousands of unemployed seamen all over Greece and the Islands.

"What you drink?" the bright eye of Christos demanded.

"What about that whisky?"

He was embarrassed about that. He hadn't really got any whisky. He hadn't any girls for that matter. It was just a line of talk, to establish contact. He put his finger to his mouth, whispered Hush, then took something furtively out of his pocket, and allowed us to see it in the shadow under the edge of the table. It glowed and glimmered there. It was an English gold sovereign. Had we, he asked hopefully, for we were English, any gold sovereigns to sell? Alas, it was a long time since either of us, though English, had seen a gold sovereign. He recovered from his disappointment. Would we care to *buy* a gold sovereign? Christos asked. It didn't really matter which it was, so long as there was buying and selling going on. We pointed out that in our country gold coins were not current any more. But this is a *man* sovereign, Christos insisted, not a woman sovereign. Look! We peered closer. The coin bore the image of King Edward. It was to be gathered it would have been less valuable if it had borne the image of King Edward's mother. But no, we could not sell, and did not wish to acquire. Christos sighed, and accepted with dignity a packet of English cigarettes.

By evening the clouds were all dispersed and the wind had died down. Manchester and Dover were both of them quite gone now, and it might have been Brighton, or Hove, rather, with that great square by the sea, flanked on the north by the exquisite Regency building built the year after Waterloo to be his residence by the first High Commissioner. It is built of white Maltese limestone, large in its actual dimensions but maintained in decorum by the admirable proportions of its flanking wings, its long ground-floor portico, and its upper-floor pediment. I should imagine that no Regency building outside England, and possibly inside England, too, is more charming and distinguished, but the guide-books (least of all Hachette, which never gets hoarse with enthusiasm over the products of English taste) waste no asterisks over it. I imagine that the feeling for English Regency has not spread widely among European con-noisseurs, for it was late enough in establishing itself among our own. However, it is a good thing that you should not have all the *Sehens-würdigkeiten* of your wanderings sedulously asterisked in advance, though I confess to some irritation when I remember the dullness or feebleness of many a European artifact which Baedeker in particular, when he was the chest-protected arbiter of Europe's taste, ringed round with stars like a rash of pimples.

With regard to his Residence, Sir Thomas Maitland, the first Resident, knew he had a grave responsibility. He had the reputation of being a somewhat starchy old gentleman, but he was a Homerist. He knew that he was building a pavilion for himself in an island where a previous governor, King Alcinous, had a palace of the greatest distinction.

"A kind of radiance like that of the sun or moon, lit up the high-roofed halls of the great king. Walls of bronze, topped with blue enamel tiles, ran round to left or right from the threshold to the back of the court."

So Homer described it. Sir Thomas did not quite rise to that, but he did well. It is gratifying that his effigy survived the Fascist-Nazi wrath, and that further down the Esplanade, embowered in deep trees in a demure Ionic rotunda, his effigy still stands, every inch a proconsul, a scholar, and a gentleman.

A more recent resident in the island of the Phaeacians has studied the poem with such devotion that he has come to a disturbing conclusion regarding its merits.

"The Odyssey is a bore," he writes, "badly constructed and shapeless, dignified by poetry everywhere degenerating into self-pity and rhetoric; the characters are stylized to the point of irritation, and their conventionalized drama serves simply as a decorative frame for the descriptive gift of the author, which is a formidable piece of equipment."[3]*

A formidable piece of criticism. The Odyssey goes the way of *Paradise Lost*, which it was for some time fashionable to describe in similar language. There remains the *Divine Comedy*, that desert of propagandist clap-trap, and *King Lear*, or perhaps it will be *Hamlet*, those jejune comic-strip melodramas. I should say, I actually picked up in Santorin a translation of *Hamlet* into the comic-strip formula, which had been executed in Broadway, and in Athens translated into the demotic. But if the Odyssey is a bore, I suppose the comic-strip makers will ignore it, though the concluding episodes of the *Slaughter of the Suitors*, surely, would provide perfect material.

We were sitting that evening, or the next, out on the edge of the pavement against the handsome colonnades which shelter the shops

* For reference see L. Durrell, p. 238.

and cafés, looking out on the flowering acacias and the high-bosomed chestnut-trees and the old leather-carapaced *carozzas* clop-clopping to and fro. Here and there the boys walked in groups, the little finger of one lad around the little finger of his neighbour. At a discreet distance the girls walked giggling and tittering, arms around waists. Far down the perspective the large electric globes bloomed, the shape of peonies, the colour of wistaria. We were feeling well at ease. In the admirable Rex restaurant we had eaten well, a local fish called *Vallanida* fried with rice, and a dish of *Dolmades*, which is mutton, I think, stewed in vine leaves, and a large heap of wild strawberries, all washed down by a bottle of the white wine from Theotoki. And sitting there by the pavement's edge, at peace with all the world, suddenly a projectile whistled towards us. Edward ducked left, I ducked right, and so it missed us. A small boy appeared, retrieved the ball, and ran back into the square again. Then I saw with incredulity that he was aiming the ball with a fine overhand action in the direction of three sticks, which were in fact wickets, and that these same wickets were being defended by a bat held in the hand of another small boy, with his shoulders squared as firm as any Bedser Twin.

"Cricket!" we were both constrained to cry out, for we had not yet heard of its association with the island. We turned our heads at once to the Residency of the High Commissioners. It was clear they had left as a legacy to the island, as well as that very English building, the most English of games. It was a touching thought, the garrison run-stealers flickering to and fro all those many decades ago across Corfu cricket-pitches under the hot Ionian sun, far from their own land. We were both very thoughtful, for cricket in foreign parts has a unique faculty to fill the English head and heart with nostalgia. Though I can describe myself only as a first-generation cricketer, my eye misted over, and it was only partly the white wine from Theotoki. I recalled the cricket I played when I, too, was a small boy, like these in the square. It was in Hightown, in Manchester. The wickets were a lamp-post on the pavement in front of our house. I was allowed to bat, but only rarely—for the other boys were bigger than I—and I batted briefly. Above the geraniums in the window-box of a first-floor room opposite, a fierce old lady in a bonnet wagged her finger. "I'll tell the High Master!" she cried. "Out!" called Hymie, the demon bowler. Out I was. Tell she did.

Such were the memories that wandered through my mind as I sat sipping my coffee on a metal chair by the colonnades. Edward's eye was thoughtful, too, as he recalled his school cricket-pitch, the Chapel beyond the elms, the cawing rooks, the small boys on the bank keeping the score, and the Dundee cake that had arrived from Mummy in that morning's hamper and was to be cut up that night in the dorm. after Lights Out.

And, at that moment, "Lights Out!" went a bugle, from the old Castle on the promontory eastward beyond the old Residency. Now it can be safely said that of the infinite orchestra of earth's melodies few, if any, are as moving as the tune of "Lights Out!" blown on a bugle at evening anywhere, even across a cinder-tip in the Five Towns. Edward furtively wiped away a tear. "Aldershot," he murmured, under his breath. I had never before heard him refer to the place excepting with extreme dislike. "Ah, Aldershot!" Everyone throughout the vast square stood to attention while the silver notes thrilled out on the snow-pure air. The small cricketers straightened up. The old horses drew up in their traces. The napkins drooped like carved drapery over the arms of the waiters. The notes died at length. The clop-clop of the horses' hooves started up again. The boys and girls, a distance of never less than ten yards separating them, resumed their parade, pretending to be unaware of each other's existence. But the bugle-call was still ringing in my ears.

"Tell me!" I said. "That was the *British* Lights Out?" Edward was sure it was. "But they're Greek soldiers in the fort there, not British! How do the Greek soldiers come to play a British bugle-call?" It was a little mystifying, for, obviously, military bugle-calls can hardly be common currency among armies without leading to considerable confusion in times of action. Perhaps the Greek garrison had picked up the call from the British ships in the harbour. Or was it possible that it was one more legacy from the time of the British Occupation?

The small boys were back at their cricket again. A ball flew through the air. A wicket fell. "*Owza!*" cried the small boy. The words sounded like a corruption of "How's that?" And they were. But it meant quite simply: "Out!" The other small boy, after a fierce argument, surrendered his bat. We rose from the café-table and took a stroll under the colonnades. Not many yards further away, a painted escutcheon nailed on a door attracted our attention. The coat-of-arms consisted of two cricket-bats crossed, with a ball gules in chief. The legend read: "Lord Byron Cricket Club". It was evident that the game was one of the abiding legacies of the British Occupation, along with the Regency palace and, perhaps, the bugle-calls of the present garrison, but I could not help wondering whether the Cricket Club was called after Lord Byron because he was the paramount British poet of the Greek world, or because it was considered he was a talented and enthusiastic cricketer. As far as I know, he was not. In a letter written while he was still at Harrow, he reports: "We have played the Eton and were most confoundedly beat; however it was some comfort to me that I got 11 notches the 1st Innings and 7 the 2nd, which was more than any of our side except Brockman and Ipswich contrive to hit." That was an exaggeration. His actual scores were 7 and 2. But it can be stated for the poet that the celebration after the match, in which both teams participated, might well have made his memory a little shaky. "I hardly recollect," he writes, "as my brain was so much confused by the heat, the row, and the wine I drank, that I could not remember how we found our way to bed."

But to return to cricket in Corfu—the game is not played elsewhere in the islands. That must have been partly because Corfu was the seat of the Residency, and because it was always a great place for games, as Old Alcinous proved when he wanted to do honour to Odysseus, his mysterious, but evidently well-born, guest. For after the company had eaten and drunk their fill, and the famous minstrel, Demodokus, had sung to them to the accompaniment of his lyre—"Let us go out of doors now," cried Alcinous, "and try our hands at various sports, so that when our guest has reached his home he can tell his friends that at boxing, wrestling, jumping and running there is no-one who can beat us." There is no reference to cricket in the narrative, and perhaps the game had not been created by then. But it will be recalled that hockey, at all events, was known as early as the beginning of the fifth century. For there is a famous relief in the museum at Athens, excavated in 1922 from the Themistoclean circuit-wall of Athens, which shews a team of six youths indubitably playing hockey. Two youths balancing their sticks stand on each side, while two others stoop towards each other, their sticks crossed on the ground, the ball lying between the hook of the sticks. The attitude, the style, is so perfect no girls' school at Cheltenham could improve on them.

If there was hockey in the early fifth century, might there not have been a rudimentary cricket some centuries earlier in the court of Alcinous? Admittedly, there is no reference to it in the Odyssey, but, at all events Phaeacians were very ball-conscious. There is, of course, that momentous game of ball which the maidens of Nausicaa were playing at the mouth of the stream while their mistress was singing to them; and before long Odysseus emerged from the copse,

naked and shaggy. There was also the game that Halious and Laodo-
mus played to entertain the stranger a little later on, with a beautiful
purple ball which was so special that even the name of the craftsman
who had made it is given. "And one of them, bending right back,
would throw it up towards the shadowy clouds, and the other,
leaping up from the ground, would catch it deftly in his turn before
his feet touched earth again." The game did not seem to involve any
other equipment than the ball, but it obviously called for a prowess
in fielding equal to that of any cricketer in ages to come.

For these reasons it would have been gracious, I thought, if the
Corfiotes had celebrated the memory of that early sports patron by
coupling his name with that of Lord Byron. But the opportunity has
been missed. There is a second club on the island which also plays
cricket, the Corfu Gymnastic Club, though that is only one of its
activities. I suggested with diffidence to one of their officials that
they might call themselves the Alcinous Gymnastic Club and they
promised to look into the matter.

However, the two clubs, which can summon up some twenty
cricket-playing members apiece, play each other week in, week out,
month after month, with a devotion and vigour worthy of Messrs.
Hutton and Trueman. They go on playing without pause till such
time as a British man-of-war will anchor off the island. Then forth
goes a challenge, which is accepted, for the Royal Navy is an
organization which has never yet been known to turn down a
challenge. So a matting pitch is laid down (even in this greenest
of the Ionian Islands there is no turf suitable for cricket). And
amid wild excitement and a band playing, and a tremor of parasols,
and small boys with eyes like saucers, and small girls licking ice-
creams like trumpets, the game begins, smack, ball on bat, smack,
ball in palms! The islanders always win, I am informed. Always.
For after all it should be said that on the deck of a corvette, or even
of an aircraft-carrier, the British sailor does not find it easy to keep
his hand in. There was one uncomfortable occasion when the Navy
team accused the Corfu team of putting stones under the pitch; but
before the day's play was over, it was admitted all round there was a
mistake somewhere. So the Corfiotes wipe the Royal Navy off the
face of the island and celebrate the victory in a tipple they call
zinzin-bira, which is, in fact, our own familiar ginger-beer, and must
be ranked as still another of the British legacies to Corfu, for it is
drunk nowhere else in all those regions. The Navy team prefers to
salve its wounds in *ouzo*, a more emphatic liquor. And the sea
chafes and strains among the rocks where Odysseus landed, and the

Princess Nausicaa, who was supervising some washing that was long overdue, came and smiled to him, in the way no self-respecting Corfu maiden would dream of doing to-day. And the Greek cricketers drink more *zinzin-bira*. And the Royal Navy cricketers drink more *ouzo*. And the moon comes out, and the caiques, laden with fish and water-jars, glide into the harbour, which is quite deserted now, what with this merrymaking among the cricketers.

III

I don't suppose that Sir Thomas Maitland's tasteful and discreet Residency can have looked very much like that somewhat over-whelming palace of Alcinous with the bronze walls and the blue enamel tiles that Homer describes, not to mention its golden doors hung on posts of silver, its gold and silver watch-dogs, and its golden youths, fixed on stone pedestals, who held flaming torches in their hands to light the banqueters in the hall by night.

Perhaps the Achilleion, the vast villa several miles southward down the coast, which the Empress Elizabeth of Austria built in 1890, had more of the necessary opulence and grandiosity. The style is late nineteenth-century classical, like most of the pictures, the statuary, and the furniture, and when Kaiser Wilhelm II acquired the villa in 1907, probably he did not make many changes. Then as now, the gardens around the villa were of great beauty, though to-day only three gardeners tend them, whereas the Kaiser had fifty. Or so I was told by a melancholy old man, who had been a gardener's boy in the Kaiser's time, and was head gardener now, though what satisfaction is that when there are only three of you? What chance has a garden got, anyhow, he wanted to know, when they are always taking you off from your potting-sheds and your greenhouses to fight wars? He had himself fought in the Salonica, Smyrna and Greco-Italian wars, and perhaps one or two others, he was getting a bit hazy. Still, his roses, at least, were as good as they had been in the old time, and these carnations, too, big as grape-fruit.

It was a beautiful garden, and perhaps it had a sort of beauty with three gardeners, that might have been missing with fifty. The same applies to the artificial grottoes, which look almost natural now. They used to be very spick-and-span once, with mirrors to surprise you in the nooks and crannies. I told him about the gardens of Alcinous, that earlier gardener, how "there was a large orchard of four acres, where trees hung their greenery on high, the pear and the pomegranate, the apple with its glossy burden, the sweet fig and the luxuriant olive". He had all these trees in his own garden, he insisted. "But listen!" I told him. "The fruit never ran short at any season of the year. There was also a vineyard, and the same applied there. While the grapes were ripening in one part of the garden, they were treading them out in another." The head gardener refused to credit it. I agreed it was hard to believe, however green your fingers were. But the gardeners of Alcinous had gods to help them, so it wasn't so strange, after all.

I suppose it is quite impossible for a garden to be devoid of beauty. If it has fifty gardeners to tend it, it will have one sort of beauty, if it has three, it will have another, if it has none at all, it will merely pass with increasing momentum into still another. Even if the fifty gardeners devote most of their time to straitjacketing flowers in rhomboids and parallelograms, of the sort I found so detestable in the council parks of my childhood, one can constrict one's vision to a single flower, and there is the beauty of all the world. Even if all the gardeners are colour-blind, they can make no unbeautiful juxtapositions, for in nature there are no antipathies of colour.

On the other hand the interior of a house can be so devoid of beauty that you feel its contents must have been assembled for a wager. That is how I felt about the Kaiser's villa, with its dreadful frescoes and tiled murals, its colossal "classical" canvases, its cyclopean desk where the war-lord sat writing up his notes on the archaeological inquiries he was so laboriously engaged on. From the study I wandered to the bedroom, from the bedroom to the bathroom, and there, as I idly turned on the taps in the gigantic marble bath, I was seized by a sudden overwhelming sense of the futility of the careers of the super-men, who fill the air with thunder and a smell of sulphur, and then, a few years later, are dispersed like the dust of a puff-ball. With a contraction at the base of the scalp I recalled that not many years earlier I had found myself in Mussolini's bathroom in his villa in Rome. In a large hall near by, a handful of soldiers from the British regiment quartered in the villa were playing cricket with a tall ormolu clock for wickets, a clock that must have been the pride of the Dictator's eyes. There in the bathroom, I turned on the taps from which the water had coursed down upon the semi-divine flesh. Only a year later I found myself in Hitler's bunker in the riven courtyard of the Chancellery in Berlin. Idly I turned the taps on. No water came. There had been no water with magic enough to

sluice the guilt of that Beelzebub mind. A long-legged spider spread
out all her legs there, and was at ease.

And now, once again for a third time, in Kaiser Wilhelm's
palace in Corfu, I found myself fulfilling the same pattern. I turned
on the *Süsswasser*, the *Seewasser*, but no water came. So, too, the
Kaiser had been here once, but he had gone. And years later the
Fascists and the Nazis came and went. And now once more, and for
ever I trust, the island belongs to its own Greeks again. Long may
the lovely dark-eyed Corfiotes press their olives in their olive-presses,
and the grapes beneath their feet in the time of the vintage!

The island of Corfu was colonized from Corinth as early as the
eighth century B.C., that is to say, a century, almost certainly not
more than two centuries, after the time the Odyssey was written.
In the very earliest days the settlers seem to have identified it with
Scheria, the Phaeacian land, for more than one reason. First of all,
it made sense geographically. Homer was already part and parcel
of the lives of all Greeks, and even so soon Greeks must have been
asking themselves which place was where. The recently-colonized
island of Corcyra—as they called it—must have seemed to them
(as it has seemed to most students ever since) plausibly located between the unfixed point of Ogygia, over to the west somewhere, and
the fixed point of Ithaca, the *terminus ad quem*. Further, they found
that the place they had settled in, a mile or two southward from the
site of the present city, fulfilled one of the major specifications of
Scheria, as Homer gives it us through the lips of Nausicaa. "Our
city is surrounded by high battlements," she tells Odysseus, who is
to follow her to her father's palace at a seemly distance. "It has an
excellent harbour on each side and is approached by a narrow causeway, where the curved ships are drawn up to the road." Well, old
Corcyra had two harbours right enough, one to the west of its
isthmus, anciently called the Hyllaic Port, and the other on the
east, called quite firmly the Port of Alcinous. That being established,
it would not be difficult to find the other elements in the general
landscape so delightfully sketched in the poet's description. And if
they were there when the Corcyrans found them, they ought to be
there to this day, barring geological convulsions, so off we went to
find out how the land, and the water, lay.

We started off nicely, for we were skirting the Port of Alcinous.
The mountains of Epirus and Albania beyond the channel looked so
ethereal as hardly to belong to this world at all, ranges of mist
melting into mist. The water was more solid than the land, it was
like a vast length of blue silk stretched tight between two rollers,

excepting at the very edge in the off-shore shallows, where through a Nile-green translucence the submerged rocks glowed like copper pans. On either side of the road the sprawling olive-groves were bordered with hedges as untidy with roses as the litter on Hampstead Heath after a Bank Holiday. About half-way along the peninsula, the driver had a small parcel to deliver at a farmhouse; then, re-calling that we had brought up the names of Alcinous and Nausicaa and Odysseus several times already during our brief acquaintance, he conveyed to us that here, where we stood, at one time stood the palace of Alcinous. Either the driver was being accommodating, or he was voicing a local belief. Anyhow, we entered the farmhouse by a gate almost obscured by such heavy tangles of honeysuckle, blackberry and dog-rose as would furnish half an English county. There were dogs and chickens and children and pigs and a young male farmer, but there were no female farmers. If there were, they hid themselves as bashfully as Nausicaa's maidens when Odysseus emerged from the copse. There was a farmhouse, too, of course, which may have been put up no more than a century or two ago, but heaven knows how many civilizations had contributed to the build-ing materials out of which it was assembled. Behind the house a path led through a thorny thicket to an out-building. Two walls at rigid angles to each other were still intact. Most of the two other walls were fallen into a welter of ivy and nettle, thistle and bramble. The long wall retained evidences of a fresco which was perhaps late Byzantine. The short wall had been built up round a beautiful marble portal, Roman, I suppose. Standing in the dark compound, the young farmer shoved his heel through the weeds and dislodged half a dozen cubes from the edge of a Roman mosaic which even yet had beauty. A few yards further away, among a litter of Greek drums and capitals, a tethered goat was grazing. By and large, it was easy to believe that a fragment or two of material salvaged from the ruins of the palace of Alcinous had gone into the building of that farmhouse.

The Phaeacian road commanded the two harbours, and through a region thick with laurel we made our way towards the more westerly one, once called the Hyllaic Port, and still called the Bay of Kalikiopoulo, though it is now shut off from the sea by a dyke and converted into a fishery. We noted the laurel with interest for we had been assured in Corfu that laurel grows thick where the marble of ancient cities lies not many feet below ground-level. Some little distance from the shore of this more westerly harbour, we came across a deep stream in a lush region of farms and meadows called

the Gardens of Alcinous. Needless to say the stream is held to be
the stream of Nausicaa, though unaccountably it is called by the
name of Cressida, whose associations are rather with Troy than with
Scheria. But as I gazed on the grey stone bridge over the stream, the
convolvulus and lilies, the flags and the poppies, that grew upon its
bank, the willows that hung over it and the thick reeds and rushes
that impeded its flow, I was compelled to think of still a third lady . . .

> *There on the pendent boughs her coronet weeds*
> *Clambering to hang, an envious sliver broke;*
> *When down her weedy trophies and herself*
> *Fell in the weeping brook . . .*

The stream is quite a distance from the bay, and I gather it
disappears before it reaches the shore. It is not at all a picture of the
stream as Homer paints it, but the land has probably been silted
over for a kilometre or two all round the bay. Discussing the identification of Cressida with Nausicaa's stream, a learned traveller, who
visited the place in 1862, writes:

> "There is nothing either in the position of the fountain or the
> circumstances of the narrative to render it improbable, though,
> on the other hand, there is certainly a wonderfully small amount
> of evidence in favour of the assumption."[4]*

The learned traveller was certainly not one for burning his boats.
For my part I was prepared to accept as prima facie evidence the fact
that there was a fair amount of laundry lying around on bushes,
spread out to dry. But Edward pointed out that it was Monday, so
there would have been laundry lying around in any case. A couple of
berry-eyed small girls lessened my disappointment by bringing round
a handful or two of tiny strawberries. They also plucked a yellow
flower which they called *asphaka*, and indicated that was good to
eat, too. I took it from their hands a little nervously and proceeded to
chew it, and that sent them into peals of laughter. No, one wasn't to
chew it, but to suck it, and to draw out its sweetness. I was expecting
any moment they would bring out a ball, and start playing with it,
and a young lady would sing to them while they played.

There was no ball, but I was ready, for the time being, to give
them the benefit of the doubt. I told them they were little Phaeacians,
and they seemed very pleased about it. So we turned in our tracks
again round the head of the bay to the point on the Phaeacian
road where we had turned from it, and continued to the tip of the

* For reference see D. T. Ansted, p. 238.

peninsula, which is called Kanoni, because there was once a one-gun battery there. Perhaps that was in the Venetian time. It does not seem to have been there during the British Occupation, the most halcyon period in the island's history; certainly not towards the end of it. Doubtless the Italians had a battery there again. Again it has been dismantled. Again Kanoni is merely a name. The type of battery that will be useful in any war to come is not likely to be placed on the Kanoni hill-top.

From the platform of Kanoni one looks down on a narrow causeway which connects the point with the Convent of Vlacherni, where four black-vested nuns pray out their days and nights. From the Convent a row-boat takes the traveller out to the small island of Pontikonisi, impaled with cypresses, that thrust themselves up from a compact grove of pines. At the heart of these black trees, you may glimpse the white walls and steeple of a minute hermitage. The romantic Bavarian painter, Boecklin, whose painting "The Island of the Dead", has made Pontikonisi as familiar among islands in a million coloured reproductions as Van Gogh has made sunflowers famous among flowers. It is all so swooningly beautiful a spectacle that one would in any event have hesitated to make an assault upon it. Boecklin has put in his debt all writers who travel to Corfu. My interest in Pontikonisi is that the island has been impressed into the Odyssean picture.

Through a descending wood of oleander, the path zigzags to the causeway below. In the shallow water on either side hermit crabs push their houses forward, prawns throw up a little trouble in the sand, small sacs of sea-mucus heave and contract, shoals of tiny fish dart forward, stop suddenly, dart off again obliquely, as if they were nerve-endings of a single nervous system. A small boy on the inner side of the causeway launches a handful of paper boats into the water. They are not paper boats. They are chicks that seem only a few hours old. Quite unperturbed by the curious new element, they peck away at insects in the scruff by the water-side. The small boy, whose name is Dzimmi, he tells us, has the part assigned to Charon in Boecklin's painting, he has the concession of rowing travellers to the Island of the Dead. He strikes a much keener bargain, for Charon was content with the payment of a single obolos, which had been placed for him in the mouth of his passengers just before their burial. Perhaps, if Charon had been in a position to argue, like the doe-eyed Dzimmi, he would have demanded a stiffer fee. Young Dzimmi stands in the bows in an attempt to look like Boecklin's Charon, but he is not tall enough to bring it off.

M

On close inspection the island is not quite so funereal as it looks from the shore. There are not only cypresses and ilexes, but a few olives, and a few fig-trees, and great sprawling bushes of geraniums. There are rose-trees run to seed, and scraggy broom in flower, and ficchi d'india, and a tall snapdragon, and white-flowering mis-embryanthemum.

But it was very lonely, or, perhaps, not so lonely as it ought to be. The hermit who once lived here had died only a few weeks ago, but he did not seem quite dead somehow. He had been here so long, it was difficult for him to get away. There was still a lamp or two burning in his tiny chapel, which the nuns will replenish with oil so long as they are alive. And what will happen when they are dead? I asked. Dzimmi will keep them burning, he assured us. He stood for a moment in front of a fairly new eikon, painted a century ago, perhaps. This one was the especial friend of the dead hermit, we gathered. He was Saint George, the one from Janina. He had large downward-drooping whiskers, a great scarlet *chitonio* (a cloak, that is), wore a *fessi*, a fez, an embroidered bolero, a blue cummer-bund, a white fustanella, and woollen leggings. Altogether a dashing saint. In one hand he held a cross, in the other the palms of martyr-dom. The Turks had hanged him. On the top left of the eikon there was a scaffold, with the noose dangling.

"*Kalo!*" said the small boy, Dzimmi.

"*Kalo!*" we agreed. He was such an attractive character, it helped one to understand why the dead old man was finding it so difficult to tear himself away from his hermitage.

I return to Odysseus. A long time before any of the Saints George, the people of Corcyra had fitted the island of Pontikonisi into the Homeric tale. Some held it to be the rock to which Odysseus, at the suggestion of Athene, clung so desperately when he was within reach of the Phaeacian shore; and still the malice of Poseidon tugged madly at him, and "pieces of skin stripped from his sturdy hands were left sticking to the crag, thick as the pebbles that stick to the suckers of a squid that is torn from his hole".

That is one school of thought. Others hold that Pontikonisi is the ship which Poseidon turned into stone on its way home after landing Odysseus in Ithaca, for the god's bad temper was quite un-bounded. It would have been a very large ship, of course, but one shouldn't go around in such contests measuring things with a foot-rule.

But that wasn't the reason why I found it difficult to accept all

this. As I have said earlier, it is more logical to believe that Scheria
is on the east coast of Corfu than on the west. Moreover, Homer's
narrative demands there should be a high mountain above Scheria;
for Poseidon, not content with petrifying that ship, had thrown up
a high mountain behind Scheria to shut it off from the rest of the
world. Is there, then, a site on the west coast, with a causeway
separating two harbours, and a place where Alcinous might have
had his *agora*, and his gardens, and his city, and his palace? And
if there is such a place, is there a high mountain shutting it off from
the rest of the world?

There is, proclaims Victor Bérard. He is not the first to do so,
but he is the most learned and circumstantial. It is called Palaeokastritza. And what is more, he continues, there is a stream for
Nausicaa to do her washing in, at just about the right distance from
Palaeokastritza, a stream called Ermoni.

So off we went next day to see.

IV

Off we went, then, under a phantom moon, to try and seize
the phantoms of Odysseus and Nausicaa, whom the art of the poet
has made as alive as the next door neighbour, and a good deal more
permanent. The country westward is largely cypresses on sheer
crags and olives in the valleys between, as if one of the powers that
followed the Phaeacian and the Greek wanted to make of it with those
funereal trees an elegy for the beauty that had gone. But the
cypresses are so numerous, I understand, because cypresses flourish
in limestone, and the olives are so numerous because the Venetians,
when they were lords of the island, gave a premium of one sequin for
every olive-tree planted. The Corfiotes are not very industrious
people—and who *would* be if they didn't need to be?—so they
planted the olives, pocketed the sequins, and left the trees to their
own devices. In certain places the trunks of the olives were so
inextricably and massively intertwined that a whole grove seemed
one tree. We noticed a fig-tree, too, that had mistaken a telegraph-
pole for another fig-tree, and had wrapped itself round it with a
similar asphyxiating fervour. Here and there, to add to the cemetery
aspect of the landscape, judas-trees flared like purple banners in
Lent. But to brighten the melancholy, on the edges of the infrequent
villages the great roses rioted drunkenly, the poppies flared like

blowsy slatterns among the bean-stalks, and the underside of the bean-leaves was silver as the wind bent the stalks.

At last we arrived at the lower reaches of the still-malarial Val di Ropa which runs below the north-south range which overhangs the western coast. We crossed it, and, even in that old automobile, we were aware, before we could see it, that the sea was quite close at hand. We got out of the car where the road stops, and trudged forward across fields of mud so thick it was necessary to stop every few yards to slice it off our shoes, which at once became as heavy as they had been, two sacks of potatoes each. Now and again a huge green lizard walked ahead, yellow underneath, its tail a dirty grey like a rat's. As we stood still, the lizard too stood still, pretending not to be there, just paddling with its left front leg and claw. Only when our shadows touched it, was the creature away, quick as the bird it feared. A grazing donkey broke into a frenzy of braying on our approach, banging together all its four legs, like a comic donkey in a circus, concocted out of two men. After a long half-hour, in which we seemed to have advanced only a couple of hundred sticky yards, it occurred to us to take our shoes off. We had advanced no more than a few yards when we flushed an adder, which stared at us from a stone, licking its chops. We put the shoes on again. So crossing one or two false unpalatable brown Ermonis, and in the increasing clamour of diesel cranes and pneumatic drills, we came upon the true Ermoni, a sizable stream. It was evident that the beneficent American dollar was at work here, too, and that the whole soggy countryside was to be drained and sweetened.

As we advanced downstream, the mechanic clamour lessened behind us, the banks steepened, and another sound assailed our ears, the roar of the sea beating against cliffs and jagged rock-inlets. Then we became aware of the singing of women, and found that the stream leapt towards sea-level in a series of three small falls, each of which at its foot had a rock-basin of the sort that women in these countries use for the washing of their linen, exactly such basins as the maidens of Nausicaa used. At this moment the wind changed, so that the clank of the machines behind us became inaudible. Instead a gust of bells from a flock of sheep drifted towards us southward was shaken out upon the air. Between the walls of golden cliff the sea drove across a bright yellow beach towards the stream-water, the salt and the fresh mingling. The flotsam of uprooted seaweed now thrust towards the land, now heeled over towards the open sea again. Immediately on the edge of the shore the water was malachite green creaming over the shallows, further away it was an innocent azure,

on the horizon it was a thick line of indigo. And all the time
the waves boomed, and boomed again. If the Odyssey is a sea, I
told myself, if the Odyssey is a sea that surges and thunders, then
here about the mouth of Ermoni the surge and thunder of the
Odyssey and of the sea are one and the same thing.

That was the first moment in a series which was continued that
day in Palaeokastritza, and found their culmination in the more
prolonged experience of Ithaca, a series of moments in which I felt
the actuality of the Odyssey as I had not felt it before. I don't mean
I now felt that there had been an actual Cyclops who had his eye
poked out by Odysseus, or that Odysseus landed here at Ermoni
with a magic veil round his middle that had acted as a sort of life-
belt. I mean I felt certain now, as never before, that there had been
an Odysseus, and there had been a Homer some time later; and this
Homer had been charmed and amused and excited by accounts of
the adventures of this same Odysseus, of which he knew some were
factual and many mythical; and that Homer had described these
adventures against a background of places of which he had known
some at first hand. He may have lived in some as boy or man. He
may have gone to some of them in later life to see what they looked
like after he had begun his career as a poet, and later worked them
into the fabric of his two principal works. I felt all this that day at
Ermoni with the same sort of bland certainty as that with which
peasants accept their saints. In exactly this place all that the poet
describes of the adventures of Odysseus landing on the Odyssean
shore, could so easily have happened. And let the shades of all the
Wolfs come gibbering up from Lethe to Ermoni to convince me to
the contrary—if they can. They will have no luck.

I said that a group of maidens were beautifully and obligingly
there at work by the rock-basins not far from the point where
Ermoni drops down into the sea. Let me say instantly they were not
doing any washing. They had not been brought down to the stream-
bed in a mule-waggon as far as I know, like Nausicaa and her
maidens. They were not lifting the clothes by armfuls from the cart,
like Homer's maidens, they were not dropping them into the dark
water and treading them down briskly in the troughs. That would
have been too much. If they had been, I might even have said to
myself that it had all been cunningly arranged by the Office of
Tourism on the other coast. But the troughs were there, the dark
water and the maidens. And they were doing exactly what those
Phaeacian girls would have been doing if their king, Alcinous, had
given orders that the Val di Ropa was to be drained and the flow

of Ermoni controlled. They had bright smiles on their teeth and pads on their heads and, chattering and giggling for all they were worth, they were collecting stones in baskets for the work in hand. Unlike their progenitors, who, at the sight of Odysseus, scuttled in every direction, these girls held their ground when we appeared, though, of course, our appearance was a good deal more respectable. They went on chattering and giggling, and we took photographs, and handed round cigarettes, and had lots of fun. Then we went down on the beach and sat down where the sea and the stream meet. I looked round on the harsh cliffs north and south. How exactly Homer had described it! "With an angry roar the great seas were battering on the ironbound land and all was veiled in spray. There were no caves, no harbours that would hold a ship; nothing but headlands jutting out, sheer rock, and jagged reefs." Then at length, what does Odysseus see? His progress has brought him off the mouth of a fast-running stream; he realizes this is the best spot he can find, for it is not only clear of rocks but sheltered from the winds. Ermoni, in fact. . . .

Well, we know the rest of the story; how Odysseus went to sleep in the copse there in the shade of a cultivated olive and a wild olive inextricably entangled (they still tangle up in Corfu in that same way). How Nausicaa came down to do the royal washing. How she threw a ball to one of the girls, who dropped it in the water, and all the girls squealed, as girls will. How Odysseus was awakened, and wondered what it was all about, and came out of his hiding-place, holding an olive-bough before him. How the other girls ran like fawns, but Nausicaa fell for the godlike stranger. The exquisite tact with which Odysseus, despite the state he was in, addressed the young lady, comparing her to a fresh young palm-tree he had seen in Delos. We know how Nausicaa thereupon fell head over heels in love with him, and addressed him in a series of innuendoes which would have turned the head of practically any man alive or dead, but not the head of Odysseus, who had had enough of extra-marital complications by this time, and really had a longing to rest up in a familiar bed, with a familiar head beside him on the pillow. We know how Nausicaa got into her waggon, and told Odysseus, as long as they were passing through the country and the farmers' lands, to walk quietly with her maids behind the waggon and the mules, following her lead. But that, she said, would not do when they got to the town. What would people say in the market-place if she turned up with a total stranger? He was to let her go on ahead towards the causeway that separated the two ports of her father's city. Soon he could come upon her father's lovely gardens, just near a fine poplar wood sacred to Athene, with a meadow all around. There he was to tarry for a little while. In an hour or so, he must find his way to the palace, which he would have no difficulty in recognizing, for none of the other dwelling-places was in the least like it. Having got there, he must address himself at once to her mother. "For, once you have secured her sympathy," Nausicaa assured him, "you may confidently expect to get back to your mother-land and to walk once more into your own fine house and see your friends again."

So Nausicaa got into her royal waggon, and flicked the flanks of her mules with her whip, and rumbled off. A few yards behind the waggon walked Odysseus and her maids. A few yards and three thousand years behind Odysseus and her maids, walked Edward and I. We had left our waggon a mile or so away, where the firm road begins again.

When Nausicaa got up on the morning of the day which was to prove so eventful for our hero, it was Athene, staunch patron of Odysseus, who had put into the girl's head the idea of doing a day's washing by the river. Athene was up to her old tricks, of course. She was pretending to be somebody else, probably because Nausicaa would have been frightened, or sceptical, if the goddess had just appeared as herself. Anyhow, she suggested that Nausicaa should get herself a mule-cart, and do it in style. "It would be much more comfortable," she said, "for you yourself to drive than to go on foot, as it's a long way from the city to the washing-pools."

Yes, for a royal princess to walk from Palaeokastritza to Ermoni and back again would be a long way, ten kilometres this way and that. Her maids would have to walk, of course. But twenty kilometres wouldn't kill them. In other words, the distance is about right, just as right as the river was, with those excellently adapted washing-troughs. Possibly there might have been streams nearer to the palace, and there certainly would have been malarial pools in the valley, as there are to this day. But the streams were probably dry most of the time, and standing water is left well alone. They certainly wouldn't do the trick anything like so well as Ermoni, "the noble river with its never-failing pools, in which there was enough clear water always bubbling up and swirling by to clean the dirtiest clothes".

In the car in which we had followed Nausicaa's party we traversed the length of the Val di Ropa a little quicker than they did. Doubtless the valley was part of the domain of Alcinous and as rich then as now in figs, fruit-trees, vines, and above all olives, which were larger and more venerable than I have seen them elsewhere. Near the head of the valley is the tiny village of Liapades where two roads meet. One goes westward to Palaeokastritza, and the other precipitately northward up the slope of Mt. Arakli, that is Heracles. Now what is Heracles doing in these parts? Why name the mountain after him? Is it because the legend that Palaeokastritza is the domain of Alcinous is a good deal older than we know? For certainly Arakli shuts off Palaeokastritza from the rest of the island very much in the way that Poseidon vowed he would shut off the Phaeacians, as part of their punishment for transporting Odysseus safely home to Ithaca. And if Poseidon had to move a mountain, who would he call on more readily than Heracles, that doughty performer of strong-arm deeds?

Well, then (we decided), if Mt. Arakli is the punishment-mountain we ought to get a first-rate view of the whole Phaeacian land from somewhere high up on its flanks, so we decided to take the mountain road first. It is a very steep and ill-made road, bordered by ancient vines and gnarled fields of olive. During the time of the Occupation the British did a fair amount of road-making, but I am sure they had had nothing to do with that one. Higher and higher we climbed, by hairpin bends so frightening I taught myself to eliminate them by shutting my eyes and saying this was the Great West Road. Once, when I opened them again, judging we had reached Hounslow, I found myself looking into a familiar face, the face of some female poet, though I could not give a name to her. Almost in the same instant I realized it was not a female poet, but a goat, though I could not see how a goat managed to balance herself there, with two legs on the road and two legs hanging out over the void. At last we arrived at the village of Lakones, a primitive, dusty, wind-ravaged place. I looked at the inhabitants with interest, for I was told that they were a proud people, who insisted that Lakones was a corruption of Lacedaemones, and they themselves were practically the only pure Spartans anywhere. I am not aware that history records any invasion of Spartans into Corfu, but I was ready to believe that if they had settled here, and they had survived, there was no place likelier for them to survive in. Certainly no existence could be more Spartan than theirs in Lakones, particularly in winter. And if their stock went back even further than the Spartans, back to the Phaeacians, it could be said Poseidon had had his way, and had barred them off effectively from the rest of the world. The road led beyond Lakones to a terrace slung out over the immense sea. There was a hut there, and a small

boy named Evthemios who served us with *ouzo*, and lucky we were
to get that, so far from anywhere. We went further still and higher,
along a road more outrageous, till we reached a village called
Makrades, where the men and boys came running towards us in a
state of almost idiot excitement. Only the women retained their
dignity, stooped over their labours in the field, or moving erect as
young trees, swaying slightly under the enormous loads balanced
on their heads. Rarely outside a Sahara oasis have I seen children
so squalid and trachomatic. I could almost feel that Poseidon himself
had infected them in this way, having decided that he had not
punished the original Phaeacians sufficiently. We got out of the car,
which surprisingly seemed to possess as many component parts as
it had set out with, and went still further, and still higher, till we
reached the ruins of the thirteenth-century convent, now called the
Castle of St. Angelo, from which the still extant convent below gets
its name, Palaeokastritza.

Leaning over a rock which seemed as far from earth as from sky,
there it all was, the Phaeacian land, so reduced in scale by our great
height that it might have been drawn for us by one of the cart-
ographers of Alcinous himself. From the Bay of Liapades the coast
runs east to west and slightly north so far as Angelokastron, the sheer
cliff whence we were gazing now. From the centre of this coast two
snub-nosed promontories project southward. On the promontory
further west the convent of Palaeokastritza stands, its walls and
steeples white, and about as small as a gull's wing, amid that small
patch of dark trees that give shade and nourishment to its monks. It is
the other promontory called Haghios Nicolaos, which corresponds
so excitingly to the picture so clearly painted in the poem; for it has
a harbour on each side where it projects from the coast, named
respectively Port Spiridion and Port Alipa, and the promontory
itself is narrow enough to be the causeway where the curved ships
were drawn to the road. The *agora*, the market-place, which Odysseus
would have come upon on his way to the palace, would be the area
on shore between the two harbours. As for the gardens of Alcinous
where Odysseus was to take his ease for a while, they would be the
green slopes lying further back under the face of Mt. Arakli, almost
as rich with figs, vines, and olives, as they were then. The small
boy, Evthemios, knew very well what was expected of him, for when
he saw us looking round for some boat-shaped island which we might
identify with the ship that Poseidon had petrified, he pointed far off
to an island in the north-west called Karavi. Though Bérard confirms Evthemios in this, it seemed to us unlikely, for what on earth

would a boat returning from Ithaca be doing so far up in the north-west? Perceiving our dissatisfaction, he suggested that a small rock just east of the entrance to Port Alipa might suit us better, which it did.

It should be said that though so far the archaeologists have not discovered any antique ruins, Mycenaean or any other, on this promontory of Haghios Nicolaos, one need not be put out by that. In a region of so much seismic disturbance, the whole palace might have slid into the sea, where it is awaiting exmarination, if that is the right word. It is also possible that the only architect Alcinous ever had was the poet Homer, and we know that that architect's blueprints are as fresh and clear as the day they were first set down.

I had not yet been to Ithaca, and though my instinct and my reading urged me in that direction, I had not yet been compelled by first-hand experience to believe that the author of the Odyssey must have visited the island at present known by that name, and spent a fair amount of time there. But looking down on the places to-day called Port Alipa and Haghios Nicolaos and Port Spiridion and Vigla, the whole complex of Palaeokastritza, the sense of certainty I had at Ermoni once again took possession of me. For an instant I wondered if the poet himself might not have climbed up to this cliff-top eyrie, where then as now the eagles slowly circled the great vault of sky, and then as now the air was as intoxicating as the wine of the gods, and the sea swung its huge blue carcase against these red cliffs—I wondered if the poet had looked down on all this, and said to himself: "Where else than here can Alcinous, of whom certain of my predecessors have sung—where else than here can Alcinous have had his palace, where else can our redoubtable Odysseus have been so splendidly entertained, with running and wrestling and discus-throwing and the game of the purple ball? It must have been here and nowhere else. I think I know just how the verses are going to shape up," said old Homer to himself. "I must go back at once to my lodgings and try them out on the lyre. This place is less fit for man than for gods and eagles and I will leave it to them."

We descended the mountain and walked a little while in the *agora* at the base of the Haghios Nicolaos promontory, where the Scherian captains and ship-builders and fishermen would go up and down discussing the day's topics. Then we went over to the further promontory, where the monastery is. The convent is on that spit of land, and not on the other, presumably because there is more room for it there, with its encompassing olives and fruit-trees, than there is on Haghios Nicolaos, and one would have found it easier to believe that the palace of Alcinous was there, too. But Homer seems to indicate that the city and palace were on the spit of land with a harbour on each side. We will not dislodge them, then, from Haghios Nicolaos, where the poem and the landscape and Bérard have jointly succeeded in planting them.

There was nobody visible at the monastery save an incredibly old monk who acted as janitor. There must have been at least three or four other monks somewhere, in their cells maybe, for the fruit-trees, the oleanders in tubs, and the flowering plants in petrol-tins, were well tended. I have rarely seen a man older, smaller, shabbier than that janitor, his grey hair disorderly as a swallow's nest, his eyes pink and rheumy, the hair behind his neck like a ball of frayed string, the breeches shoved into stockings full of holes, and the whole of him swathed round in an enormous cape of shoddy sacking. For all that there was a smile of great sweetness on his face as he unlocked the chapel-door with an ancient wooden key almost as large as himself. He took his eikons for granted, though some were beautiful and several so quaint an Illyrian Bosch might have painted them. But his special pride was the midriff bones of some huge sea-beast, cinder-dry, that looked as if it might have been washed up centuries ago. He had been almost completely silent till now, but now he spoke, forming his words with difficulty, like a child almost completely deaf. We gathered that this was the skeleton of the whale which had swallowed Jonah, and later, spewed him forth on this beach here, the beach of Haghios Spiridion. We exchanged gifts as we left. For us there was a bunch of sweet-smelling wall-flowers, these late blooms from the gardens of Alcinous.

There is a pink-painted little inn called the Café Zephiros over against the bay of Spiridion where it curves round towards Nicolaos. One would take this to be about the place where the *agora* was, which Odysseus would have passed through on his way up from Ermoni. He would not have lingered here, for fear of awkward questions from the natives. Besides, Nausicaa had already suggested to him that he would be better off whiling away half-an-hour further up, in her father's gardens.

There are oleanders on each side of the doorway of the Café Zephiros and vine-roofed pergolas behind it. There a cloth is spread for you and you drink wine, and you eat lobsters. But before you eat them, you choose them for yourself, from the little rock-pool which mine host has stocked with them, down there in the elbow of the bay. If once in a lifetime you are privileged to drink wine and eat lobsters at the Café Zephiros, with the Odyssey open on the tablecloth beside you, and the bays and the causeway and the gardens of the Phaeacian land spread out before you, and the musky odours of juniper and myrtle coming down from the steep mountain behind you, and the sheep-bells and goat-bells ringing all round you, and the sea hissing along the sands—if these things happen to you once in a lifetime, you are as lucky as anyone deserves to be.

We sat down happily under the pergola, looking at the place where the palace of Alcinous had been. The waiter came and set down our lobsters before us, bedded in bright green leaves.

Over in the palace, the waiters were serving the great dishes of roast meat, and mixing the wine and water in due proportions. For Alcinous had summoned the best people to a great banquet in honour of their far-travelled guest. Twelve sheep were to be slaughtered, eight pigs, two bullocks. Homer is very specific, as usual, about the meat course.

What else beside the meat and wine? There will have been honey for sweetening, and "certain dainties", but it is not clear what the "dainties" were. Apparently no vegetable but onions, which were eaten to give flavour to the wine. And fish? According to Gardiner, "fish is caught and eaten in the time of Homer, but only by those who can get nothing better; a reduction to a fish diet is regarded as a painful strait, in great contrast to the ideas of later times". The very mention of fish seems to produce acute nausea in Homer. Again and again the adjective for the sea is "fish-infested". In the passage where Achilles admonishes the body of a Trojan he has just killed: "Lie there," proclaims Achilles, "among the fish, where they can lick the blood from your wound in comfort." A little further on another hero is left lying around, "busily attended by the eels and fish, who nibbled at his heels and devoured his fat".

No. Homer had no use for fish. And presumably that went for the crustaceans and the molluscs, too. But they were eating oysters, at all events, in Homer's time, and Priam's time, too, according to the most incontrovertible evidence, namely the excavations at Hissarlik, which turned up oyster-shells at every level of Troy's history. I myself kicked up an oyster-shell at the heart of the diggings. Who, I asked myself, who had winkled out that succulent morsel? Was it some Roman tax-collector? Some minor rhapsodist from Ilium? Was it perhaps one of the knights of Paris or Hector, using a small bronze pick?

Homer certainly knew all about oysters, though the single

reference he makes to the creature is as nauseating as all his references to the fishy things of the sea. It is the occasion when Patroclus hurls a stone which dislodges the eyeball of Cebriones. "Ha!" jeers Patroclus. "Quite an acrobat, I see, judging by that graceful dive! The man who takes so neat a header from a chariot on land could dive for oysters from a ship at sea in any weather and fish up plenty for a feast!"

But how enthusiastic the poet and all his heroes are about meat! Was it a taste they had brought with them from the vast cattle-herding territories from which they originally came? In a famous passage the very words sizzle like meat-juices spitting over a fire:

> "So the old priest burned the pieces on the faggots, while he sprinkled red wine over the flames and the young men gathered round him with four-pronged forks in their hands. When the thighs were burned up and they had tasted the inner parts, they carved the rest into small pieces, pierced them with skewers, roasted them thoroughly, and drew them all off!"

Exactly the way they prepare *shishkabab* to this day, anywhere between Istanbul and Corfu!

The waiter removed the broken shards of lobster. He set oranges and figs down beside us, and snow-white cheese. It would be time for us to go soon.

Over there, on the slipways of one of the Phaeacian ports, Odysseus, too, would be embarking soon. As far as can be deduced from the narrative, he had spent three days and two nights as the guest of Alcinous and his gracious wife, Arete. But what crowded days and nights these had been! There had been royal banquets and ceremonial games, and Odysseus himself had been given the opportunity to tell the breathless story of his adventures, which have been so famous since that day. At length the festivities were at an end. Over by the quayside a Phaeacian ship was drawn up, stacked with the magnificent gifts his hosts had heaped on him. Of all ships that have cloven the blue sea, none have ever been more remarkable than the ships of the Phaeacians, which had no steersmen, nor steering-oars such as other ships possess. "Our ships know by instinct what their crews are thinking and propose to do," proclaimed Alcinous. "They know every city, every fertile land, and hidden in mist and cloud they make their swift passage over the sea's immensities with no fear of damage and no thought of wreck."

Fifty-two of the best young men of Scheria sat down at the

rowing-benches, but they were there rather as an honorific escort than because there was any work for them to do, beyond the initial launching which gave the ship its impetus. On the ship's deck, well aft, Odysseus lay himself down to sleep, a sheet under him, and a fine rug over him. And no sooner had these young men touched the water with their oars, than "a sweet oblivion sealed the eyes of Odysseus in sleep delicious and profound, the very counterfeit of death". He will not open his eyes again until he is back in his own land, after all his wanderings.

I have been to the land of the Phaeacians, I said to myself. For me, too, only Ithaca remains, after all these many years. From the western coast of the Phaeacian land, no ships sail any more anywhere. The harbour works of the twin ports of Scheria have been dismantled long ago, and have slid into the sea, and they lie very deep down under the sea's bed. Well, then, back to the east coast, where the harbours are nowadays.

We got into the car, and advanced fifty yards. That was all we advanced for about an hour. We tickled and coaxed her, beat and abused her, but she would not move. Then suddenly she was off, alone and stately, nobody at the wheel, mistaking herself, I suppose, for a Phaeacian ship. With splendid presence of mind and with Olympic speed, Edward sprinted after her, vaulted into the driver's seat, and pulled the hand-brake, after which the driver and I climbed into the vehicle, and off we went. The Val di Ropa was flooded with sunlight like a golden water. *"Kal 'esperas!"* the peasants called, their faces gleaming lustrous as bronze apples. It was late evening as we reached the outskirts of Corfu. The whole air was full of points of fire. Most were stars, many were fire-flies. It was an enchanted night and very still, the sea was as breathless as the land. Nothing would disturb the slumbers of Odysseus where he lay well aft in the Phaeacian ship, with a sheet beneath him and a rug to cover him, the finest handwork of Arete, that gracious queen.

V

There was one final diversion, positively the last of the final diversions. I found that the steamer made a stop at the small port of Samé, on the west coast of Cephalonia, looking over towards Ithaca. I felt it would be an impertinence to the gods, whichever they may be, that have kept my keel afloat during my long Odyssey, if I did not touch the soil, and breathe the airs, of the demesnes which Odysseus ruled from his central keep in Ithaca.

The poet has told us in the Iliad that Odysseus was the overlord of the Cephallenians who lived not only in Ithaca itself but in certain islands close to it, including Samé and wooded Zacynthus, and the mainland opposite. There is another reference to these Cephallenians, later in the Iliad, a substantial force, apparently, whom the choleric Agamemnon finds standing around, doing nothing in particular. Agamemnon is rude to Odysseus, then the Cephallenians go to it. At the end of the Odyssey, when Odysseus has disposed of the Suitors, his father, Laertes, is terrified that the cry of revenge will go out to every town in Cephallenia. As for Samé, presumably an important place in this maritime Cephallenian confederation, Odysseus talks of it nostalgically at the court of King Alcinous, when he is asked to give an account of his origins. "Our landmark is the wooded peaks of windswept Neriton. For neighbours we have the many peopled isles with no great space between them, Doulichiom and Samé and wooded Zacynthus."

It is a long time ago since Homer wrote his poems, and it would be exciting if only one or two of these place-names were still extant in the group of islands he is manifestly describing. But Ithaca is still Ithaca; Zacynthus, having been Zante during the centuries of the Venetian occupation, is Zacynthus again; the Cephallenians still occupy the largest of the islands that once were subject to Odysseus, though their name has been slightly modified, and they are called Cephalonians to-day, dwellers in the island of Cephalonia; and, finally, Samé is still Samé, though as these passages make evident, Samé was once the name of the whole island, as well as of its chief town—exactly as to-day the island and chief town both of Corfu and Chios are called by the same name.

I say that Homer is manifestly describing a group of islands in the Odyssey which we know to-day by the same, or similar, names, just as he is describing a landscape in the Iliad where several of the Homeric names to-day persist *in situ*. In other words we have left the fairylands behind us, the lands of the Lotophagi, the Laestrygones, the Phaeacians. We are on the map. We are on the list of steamer-sailings. We can disembark at Samé. We can meet the "proud" Cephallenians face to face.

Two tickets for Samé, please!

It was a blustery day of driven rain, nothing visible anywhere except grey sea, grey rain, and an occasional fishing-boat that came up so suddenly from nowhere, looking at once so ghostly and so archaic, with her sharp prow, her small foresail, her tall mast, the little wheel-house at the stern, that you said to yourself: She must be one of the twelve ships that Odysseus is taking up to Aulis, and she has lost her bearings, and she is sailing north, and sailing south, trying to find the captain-in-chief, but he died long ago. Later in the day, a pale sulphurous light suffused the cloud-ceiling, making the liquid sea curiously solid and dull and wrinkled, like . . . like . . . I racked my brains . . . yes, like all the world's lead-foil, crumpled and creased in Poseidon's fist.

At length we entered the narrows between Ithaca and Cephalonia. "Our landmark is the wooded peak of windswept Neriton," I recalled. The mountain there on our left must surely be Neriton, still half-veiled in cloud. It occurred to me that I had been as close as this to Ithaca once before, and it had slipped through my fingers. Many years had gone by since then. Please, Ithaca, I thought, let me not lose you again! An hour or so later we had turned a dark promontory that stood out in the sea like a block of ebony, excepting where a long froth of foam nagged along its base. We were now at last in the Bay of Samé, where a valley split an overhanging pressure of mountains. On the port bow a mole extended, its extremity marked by an iron pylon on which a red lantern gleamed. Two lights, three lights, winked on the foreshore; then four lights, five— hardly more than that. There, then, was Samé.

We were further away from the harbour than usual when the ship blared forth its three blasts, short and sharp, as if she came to this place under protest, and the sooner she got away the more she would like it. A small row-boat came out to us, and carried us off, the only passengers to disembark. Very forlorn the place looked, squalid and forgotten. Distributed along the waterfront in small groups, the inhabitants watched us in perfect silence as we climbed ashore. There was an air of incredulity about them, as if they wondered what it could possibly be that had brought strangers to so unrewarding a place. We stood about a few moments, our bags at our feet. Still they all watched us. Nobody moved a step in our direction. From far out behind us the ship hooted, this time once only. It was a derisive sound, as if to say: "If that's the sort of place you like—it's all yours." We turned. There she was, a shining and friendly thing, moving away from the darkness into the darkness, leaving us, and the silent men, and the tiny port, to our own devices. I felt very melancholy, all of a sudden, in a way that I have never felt melancholy in any other of the Greek Islands. It seemed almost as if

Palace of the British Governors

Corfu: Girls on route to Nausicaa's stream

Corfu: Old ladies of Canoni

a cold invisible finger touched my forehead. The melancholy left me rarely during the short time we were in Cephalonia, and in remembering this during later months I permitted myself to speculate whether I was the victim of a presentiment of the tragedy that was to befall Cephalonia not more than a few months later. For I think it is true to say that even the most matter-of-fact amongst us, the most cynical, are now and again in a lifetime troubled with such presentiments of trouble to come. Certainly it has happened to me more than once as the years have gone by. But if that was the explanation of the mood in Cephalonia, I should have reacted in the same way in Ithaca, where, on the contrary, all was limpid joy from the first moment to the last. Or perhaps that is a *non sequitur*? I don't know. Perhaps there is quite a straightforward explanation of that grey mood in Cephalonia. Compared with Mytilene or Santorin or Chios it is a grey island, without brilliance in its history, with little beauty in its villages and public buildings.

But I go too fast. I am on the quayside at Samé. The bright ship is far off, but still in sight. On the quayside no-one moves, no-one says a word. It is very unnerving.

"Wait a moment, ship!" I feel like crying out. "I didn't really want to get off here! Come back, can't you? Come back!"

There was no more ship to see. The headland had extinguished her. There was only the tiny port, and the silent men, and away behind us, on each side of the dark valley, the ruins of a great city, rarely visited or talked about, a city as old as Troy or Mycenae, a city of which to-day almost nothing is known, except that Homer sang of her, and Livy has a tale to tell of how a Roman soldier, the consul Marcus Fulvius, laid siege to her and captured her and laid her low.

Suddenly the silence snapped. The inhabitants of the new town of Samé were all about us, bickering, arguing. Automóbile, automóbile. The word came up again and again. It seemed that everyone in Samé had an automobile. It seemed that nobody ever came to Samé without making preparations for an immediate escape from Samé over the mountains to Argostoli, the present-day chief city. So many drachmas. So many drachmas. Which automóbile to choose, which driver? It seemed not only invidious, it seemed dangerous, to make a choice. I remembered the system with which I choose my Derby winner. I closed my eyes, turned round three times, and stabbed the air with an outstretched finger. The finger touched a waistcoat-button. "You!" I said. It was Spiro. Half-past four in the morning, he said. Too late? Apparently no time was soon enough to get away from Samé. I shuddered. Too early, I said.

N

Another Spiro took our bags from us. This one kept the inn, as primitive a sleeping-place as I have ever seen. The beds were like concrete and the one blanket as hard as sheet-metal. We washed in an enamel basin from which nearly all the enamel had gone long ago. It was a Giorgos who kept the little restaurant hard by. We ate some fried fish which was chiefly bone. Our meal being over, we walked the length of the minute waterfront, past the pollarded acacias that looked like the inside-out skeletons of umbrellas, past the mole, then down the minute waterfront again, past the pollarded acacias, planted with marguerites around their bases, in a spasmodic fantasy of decoration. From an invisible window the strains of some familiar piece of music floated out across the soot-black water. What was it? Could it be? It was. It was Mozart's G Minor Symphony wildly, tearfully, irrelevant, like those marguerites around the acacias. Every now and again, at intervals calculable as the drippings of a tap, Mozart was punctuated by the mindless churr of a night-bird. Tic! Tic! Tic! What bird is that? I asked. *Kukuvaya*, said one of the Spiros. Some sort of owl, I thought. It was a curiously comfort-less sound. To the Samé women long ago it was just as comfortless and fatuous, the night the contingent of Samé ships drew out from this same port, to join forces with Odysseus, over there in Ithaca.

A hand clutched the blanket, which fell to the ground with a clatter. It was Spiro, the driver. As far as I knew I had just dropped asleep. But no, it was four o'clock, and Spiro wanted to make quite sure I would not be late. I rose and got into my clothes, and was aware of a dim atavistic impulse towards a morning wash. There would be no time for that. I went downstairs, and was aware of another impulse, towards a cup of coffee, a glass of milk, anything would do. But the inn was not open, there was only sea-water to drink. We could, however, have bought Athenian newspapers a week or two old, for the old man who kept the kiosk by the water's edge had let down his shutters and was ready for business. Or perhaps he had not gone to bed all night? In a state of somnambulism Edward was already down there, by the car that was to take us to Argostoli. It was also to take six proud Cephallenians, some baulks of timber, a goat, and several sacks of grain lashed to the mud-guards. Was it night still? Was it to-morrow morning? Were we dreaming all this? *"Avanti!"* demanded Spiro. Then I remembered I had come to Samé in order to see Samé. "Later!" I insisted. "I want to go there!" I pointed to the misty slopes of the twin peaks behind the port, where the ruins of ancient Samé lie. Spiro wept, and wrung his hands, and tore his hair, then, without warning, the tantrums stopped. A sweet smile was on his face. He had a brother, Athanasius, at that moment in Argostoli. Athanasius would take charge of us later in the day. He drove off, his car hugging the ground as close as a cow-rake. We returned to our quarters, slept a little, washed a little, and had a cup of goat's milk with some dark colouring matter, then went off to explore Samé.

I will admit that Samé was a pious rather than an exhilarating experience. It was a grey morning, the hill-slopes were damp, and the ruins in Samé consist chiefly of sections of ruined walls, which are perhaps of all ruins the least compelling. The walls run up to the ancient Acropolis, and from the Acropolis to the summit of the adjoining hill, covering the vulnerable trough of ground between. Some of the surviving blocks are of most impressive size, as old Ansted noted a little breathlessly, declaring them to be "a feat fully equalling, if not exceeding, anything recorded in Egypt, or gigantic works in other countries, where human labour has been ruthlessly employed to accomplish objects". And indeed, what enemies were these defence-walls of Samé built to keep out? Were they built by these Cephallenians of whom Odysseus was overlord? Or by the predecessors of the Cephallenians, who found them as useless against the Achaean invaders, as later the Hellenic citizens of Samé were to find them useless against the strong-jawed no-nonsense Romans? Judging by the ground covered by these walls, and the vast number of ancient shards that still lie about on its surface, it is clear that Samé must have been a great city once. How is it that those factors which operated to produce so great a city have never operated since? Was it because Samé was a seaboard emporium for a kingdom among the islands of which in Homer we catch only a fitful glimpse? What has happened to the titan mass of material which once constituted the walls of Samé and the temples and walls they enclosed? Who has spirited it all away, and how? And yet, fortunate Samé, if all her walls had been intact and the altar-stones of her temples had been still in place, how much more fragile than egg-shell they would all have been, if the poet had not found room in two of his verses for her two syllables!

We were still beating the bournes of the prehistoric town, when Athanasius, the brother of Spiro, came running light-foot up the hills after us. Somehow Spiro had managed to convey an air of acute crisis to our visit to Cephalonia. Had we made his acquaintance some weeks later, we would have found it not wholly impossible to believe that he had had private notice in advance of the wrath to come.

"Quick! Come! Argostoli!" demanded Athanasius breathlessly, as if at any moment fire might consume it, or it might slide into the sea.

"*Kaló!* Fine! We come!" we observed temperately, and turned down-hill towards the shore. Here to one side the hillside had been banked up, perhaps to hold the foundations of a house. Here, perhaps, had been the manor of one of the suitors of Penelope, who knows, perhaps the house of the egregious Antinous, of whom Telemachus himself said he had the bitterest tongue of all; or did Antinous hail, maybe, from Zacynthus?

"Argostoli! *Moline di Mare!*" urged Athanasius. "*Vengono tutti gli professori per studiare!*"

I had, in fact, read in the book that there were two mysterious sea-mills at Argostoli, which receive their power from streams of sea-water thrusting *inland* under the shore-side shingle. It was so mysterious, apparently, that all the professors came to study it. I had a sudden acute vision of professors racing down the railway-platforms, jumping on gang-planks, their gowns streaming, their mortar-boards awry. At Victoria Station the last professor of all came trotting up breathlessly, only to find the barrier shut in his face.

Yes, I wanted to visit the strange sea-mills of Argostoli, if only to see if there were still one or two professors about, with their tables and instruments.

"*Molto interessante!*" I said. Conversation was in explosive spurts of Greek, Italian and English. My thoughts returned to Odysseus. I wondered whether as liege lord of the islands, Odysseus would sometimes tour among his dependencies. Was that heap of stones all that was left of a temple of Athene where he would make offerings on his arrival in Samé?

"Also is the home of the Lordos Vyron in Metaxata!" gasped Athanasius, tugging at my sleeve.

Indeed, yes, I remembered that, too. Somewhere on the southern coast of the island was the small peasant house where Byron stayed for two or three months, awaiting the call to Missolonghi and the tragic *dénouement* of his tale. He had been to Ithaca during that period and had been enchanted by it. He had had the idea of buying up the island, lock, stock and barrel.

I resumed control of my sleeve. "*Molto interessante!*" I again endorsed. At last we reached the scrawny little quayside of old Samé, where once there had been great warehouses of Mycenaean ware, and markets for the goats of Ithaca, of which there must have been plenty for the export trade, and grain from Doulichion, wherever that might be, and jars of olive-oil from old Nestor's city of Pylos. Ah, but here was the car of Spiro and his brother Athanasius, already loaded with a good deal of what the elder brother had left behind of the human and animal population of Samé. None the less, and despite appearances, room had been left for us in the front seat beside the wheel. Edward had already ensconced himself, I had a foot on the running-board, when suddenly, loud and long, the siren of the incoming steamer roared among the headlands.

"Ship for Thiáki!" said Athanasius, a little foolishly.

Loud roared the siren again, totally unanswerable.

"Edward!" I called out. I removed my foot from the running-board. Edward knew already. So it had been before, so it would be now, and for the last time. He was already out of the car.

"What is?" cried Athanasius in anguish.

"Ship for Thiáki!" I said.

His face was contorted with grief.

"*Moline di mare!*" he implored. I was already moving away. "The house of the Lordos Vyron!" he wailed. I turned my eyes towards the water and the advancing ship. I was for Ithaca.

CHAPTER EIGHT

Ithaca

I

WE were for Ithaca, over there across the narrow channel. "You are quite sure?" I asked on the Samé quayside. They looked at me oddly. "*Malista!*" they said. "Thiáki!" As if they were saying Shoeburyness, which it was to them in a sense. I asked again at the head of the steamer gangway, before I stepped off on to the deck. I was not going to be taken to Patras, or anywhere else, as had happened to me long ago. They took the bags aboard. They seemed to have no doubts about it. After all, they did it two or three times a week.

That was Ithaca there, those long cliffs running north and south. The sun was hot and hard on the peaks. The scrub on the slopes moved faintly in the heat-haze like seaweed anchored in rock-pools. We were round Samé headland now, we were round the cape of Haghios Johannes, the south-eastern point of Ithaca, we were steaming northwards now. A prince had once said to Alcinous, his host: "I am Odysseus. My home is under the clear skies of Ithaca. Our landmark is the wooded peak of windswept Neriton." The skies were clear now as then. Surely that was Neriton, that great cone of a mountain rising in the east sheer from the sea, though all the rest of the island was a mountain, or two, rather, divided by a high neck of land? As for the woods of the windswept peak, doubtless they were there once, but earthquake and the peasant's axe and the goat's tooth must have cleared them long ago. "It is a rough land," the traveller declared, "but a fit nurse for men." No wonder he spoke with such love, having the picture of this place sharp and lovely in his mind, sharper and lovelier as the years went by.

We were moving more southerly now, into the long Gulf of Molo which almost bisects the island; now we were making westward into the profound Vathy fiord. We were well in the gulf by now. Far off, then not so far, beyond the small island where the ruined Lazaretto, a one-time quarantine station stands, you could at last see the houses of the small port of Vathy running round the horseshoe that closes the bay. Loud cried the hooter three times, and three times back came the echo from the mountain walls. Now the Lazaretto was

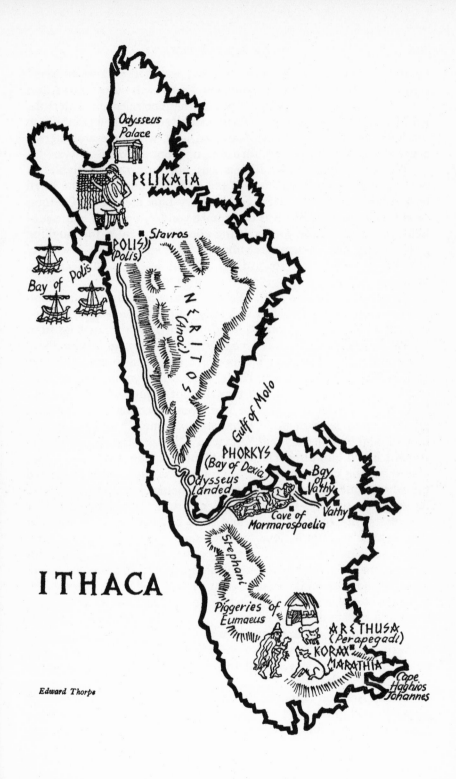

Odysseus
Palace

PELIKATA

Stavros
POLIS)
(Polis)

Bay of Polis

N
E
R
I
T
O
S
(Anoi)

Gulf of Molo

PHORKYS
(Bay of Dexia)

Bay of Vathy

Odysseus
Landed

Vathy

Cave of
Marmarospaelia

Stephani

Piggeries of
Eumaeus

ARETHUSA
(Perapegadi)

KORAX
MARATHIA

Cape
Haghios
Johannes

ITHACA

Edward Thorpe

behind us. Ahead of us, clear in view, was a flotilla of coloured caiques that seemed all hugger-mugger across each other's bows, and beyond them, the blue and pink houses that encircled the waterside, withdrawing at their centre to form a small square, then climbing to the lower terraces of the scrub-covered hills, with here and there a cypress, and a belfry or two, thrusting up from the olive-groves.

We were ashore now. Ithaca was not only three syllables of poetry, she was the hard stone of the quayside underfoot, the small boys scrabbling for the baggage, the navy-blue men of the Customs prodding at parcels. She was the square yonder, a well of white sunlight, the men and the youths sitting about in the cafés, the laughing girls strolling arm-in-arm three abreast, for it was Sunday. A wave of friendliness rolled over towards us, almost washing our feet from under us.

"Actaeon!" a voice said. We had heard already that Actaeon was the name of the only inn in Vathy, in the whole island. At that same moment two small brown hands reached to take our bags from us. We looked down. It was a youngster, bare-foot, in a threadbare vest and a pair of tattered trousers which had been snipped short for him with a pair of scissors. There were other youngsters around, and he was not the largest, but they did not dispute us with him. He had an air of authority, as if he had been expecting us. A pleasant grin was on his large mouth. "What is your name?" I asked. "Spiro," he said, and had already said "Actaeon". Those were about the only words I heard him utter. He was as silent as a faun, swam like a fish, almost as long under the water as on top of it, and smiled to himself the whole time as if the world were a delicious joke. The eyes were large, green. usually, with brown flecks, but they changed colour frequently, not only by night and day, but according to whether there was or was not a cloud over the sun. A curious little creature, lonely, self-sufficient, in that intensely amicable island hugging to his own bosom his private incommunicable delights. He was the son of the only bad man on the island, as far as we ascertained, a drunkard, a man who always beat Spiro when he returned home. It was like beating a stream as it flowed by.

"All right, Spiro, Actaeon!" we assented. But he was already on his way, past the almost Hawaian café slung out over the sea, with its ceiling of palm-leaves, and the milky-green water shimmering under the floor-boards.

Is the Actaeon standing at this day? I don't know. It almost certainly collapsed in the earthquake like ninety per cent of the houses in Vathy. But if there has not been time to rebuild it yet, it will be rebuilt sooner rather than later. I am not going to permit myself the luxury of misery regarding Ithaca. As I evoke the island during the enchanted days and the roystering nights we spent there, it has a perfection of aspect, mood and experience such as I have rarely known. I am not going to throw my imagination forward across the month or two which separated the island from the earthquake, and superimpose on the Vathy we saw, the broken Vathy it was after the earthquake dealt with it. I will not think of the Ithaca folk gazing down from among the stripped olive-groves on the ruins of their homes. If I do, it will invest with wretchedness a memory which is all delight, and what good will be done to old Odysseus, who kept the café on the square, and periwinkle-eyed, soft-voiced Anastasia who kept the Actaeon, and old Katsamos, the retired inspector of mathematics from Athens, who was as clear about the location of every incident in the poem as an estate-agent about the properties on his books? I say again as I said earlier. There are two Ithacas. There has always been a second Ithaca alongside Homer's. One of these, the temporal Ithaca, was badly scarred. She cannot ever be the same again, but she will recover. Said this same gentle and rock-like Anastasia (as it has been reported to me) to her fellow-islanders whitefaced among the olive-groves, looking down on their ruined homes—said Anastasia: "Courage! We will build a better Ithaca!"

As for the other Ithaca, it is immune from earthquake or tidal wave or pestilence; it will endure so long as there is poetry on this planet.

So Spiro took us along to Anastasia's Actaeon. Anastasia is an oldish lady, of Roumanian origin, still very loyal to the memory of the Roumanian Royal Family, and particularly to Queen Marie, whose photograph adorned her little sitting-room and each of the bedrooms. She herself, wearing that wimple round her head and the large cameo brooch, looked not unlike the distinguished lady, with not so much dignity but more sweetness. Nothing was too much trouble for Anastasia, less a landlady than the kindest of aunts, whether it was to sew the hanging seat back on to a pair of trousers, or to get up to make coffee and a pannier of food to take with us on the mornings we went out to fish in the breathless grey gulf waters long before the sun rose. The bedrooms themselves seemed to be almost as much on shipboard as on land, with the fishermen and boys talking to each other from their decks only a few yards away, and the reflections of the water dancing hand over hand on the white-

washed ceilings, so that as you stared upward these seemed themselves like the sea's bed, and in a half-daze you could not remember
which was which.

The square was tugging at us irresistibly. Over there, if anywhere, we would hear the latest gossip about the famous laird who
had been away from the island for so long that practically every one
had given up hope of his return, excepting his wife, though probably
even she would take a lot of convincing it was really he if he should
turn up. The lady herself, as far as one knew, never left the Palace,
where she was being courted night and day by a battalion of Suitors
from all over the place, if courting is the proper word, for they
seemed to spend a good deal more time junketing and carousing
than turning pretty compliments to the lady. We might perhaps
meet her son over there at one of the cafés, unless he had already
gone to the mainland on the excursion that had been suggested to
him. He was not tied hand-and-foot to the Palace, as his mother
was, though from a West European point of view he was a rather
spineless young man. What prevented him from taking over his
father's estate, sending off that mob of Suitors with a flea in their
ear? If he wasn't of age yet, he certainly was in his late teens.
Perhaps his father's colossal legend was too much for him, as it had
been too much for his father's own father? Well, that was the sort of
thing one might learn something about at the café tables.

Very sketchily we washed and stowed our things away, then,
making a salutation in the direction of Anastasia and Queen Marie,
we issued from the Actaeon. Outside, a lizard petrified in the sun,
lay Spiro on the low sea-wall, the sea under him twinkling like a
tarantella of fire-flies. Only the eyes moved, between our eyes and a
small row-boat close by. "*Ouzo!*" I said. That was an adult affair.
He was a lizard again, a lump of rock. We walked on towards the
square, the sea so close under foot, and in your nostrils, and in the
ears, you felt your blood, too, was salt-water; past a store or two, a
box-like house or two, with black and scarlet rugs hanging for
an airing from the first-floor windows, past Panni's friendly and
scruffy little restaurant, past the café on the water, loosely swinging
on its piles, past the proud public lavatory with which some successful
Americo-Ithacan had endowed his home town. And we were just
about to turn into the square itself, where the sunlight stood up like
thick curtains of white heat in front of a room, and you must pull
them aside before you enter, when a cry went up from the crowd of
small boys and girls at the quayside:

"There they are! There they are!"

In a moment everybody strolling about or sitting at the café-tables was running towards the water.

"It's old Nicolaus!" they were calling out. "Look! There he is! There!" They pointed to a caique approaching, her sail filled, her engines chugging for all they were worth. "The Phaeacian ship!" I said to myself. "And the old boy's pretending his name's Nicolaus!"

But it really was his name, I suppose. Anyhow that was how the people of Vathy knew him. The small deck was crowded with passengers of all ages, it seemed there would scarcely be room for a wine-jar. Even at a distance, I could make out that the men seemed to be formal in their attire, the women bright and flowery. Then, as the boat swung to edge in closer, the mass shifted and one could see a woman dressed crown to heels in white, with a man all in black standing as stiff as a board beside her. Of course the woman was a bride. The man was a bridegroom, the man was this Nicolaus. "Hoora! Hoora!" cried everyone on shore. "Hoora! Hoora!" cried the passengers, all but Nicolaus and the bride, who were far too aware of the grandeur of the occasion. How delicious it all was! Rousseau might have painted it, or Diaghilev made a pendant to "Barabau", his bebustled and bowler-hatted ballet. The caique had quite a bit of difficulty finding a berth, for there were a great many craft up and down along the waterside. But nobody minded that, least of all the bride, who wouldn't have minded if the berthing had taken an hour or two longer, for this was her lifetime's big day, and she had waited a long time for it, and if her bridegroom was no longer in the first flush of youth, neither was she for that matter, but very plump and proud and pretty she looked, the bouquet clutched tight in her hand. The wedding-party, I was told, had just come over from the tiny island of Atakos some miles away to the north-east, where the bride was born and had lived till now. The bridegroom had a small farm beyond Perakorio, on the high ground under Mount Stephani, and had been courting the girl from Atakos for a good many years. But they were both cautious people. A bride needs a dowry, and so does a farm. The bride had brothers in America who had promised to send her money as soon as they could spare it for her, but a number of years had gone by, and nothing had come from over the water. At last Nicolaus had proclaimed that he would marry the girl even without the dowry. No, said the girl, the brothers would keep their word sooner or later. And so they had. And here they were, the bride and bridegroom, with all their friends about them, stepping on to the quayside, stepping into the cars that

were to take them up to Perakorio. All in all, it was a heart-warming
‚thing to happen within an hour or two of the arrival in Ithaca. It
was as if the oldest of the Suitors had at last made up his mind that
he didn't believe one word of that story about the web Penelope was
weaving for her father-in-law, and it was high time he set about
finding himself a wife from one of the other islands, even if she was
less of a catch.

Before long the square was at its Sunday avocations again, the
older men gossiping at the pharmacy, the others at the café-tables,
and the bright girls wandering up and down in their lilac and
briar-rose and daffodil dresses. We had had no decent meal yet, but
we were too enchanted by the square and the people in it to go
chasing after one, so we made do with whatever old Odysseus of the
café could provide for us in the way of *mezes*, some bread, some olives,
some chunks of cheese and octopus. A group of young men, about
ten or twelve of them, were sitting at a little clutter of tables not far
from us, all in their Sunday suits. One had the feeling they were
the "best" people of the place, the upper crust. One was magnificent
in a draped fawn American jacket, a pair of Nile-green gaberdine
trousers, and a pair of piebald black and white shoes like those
affected at one time by Riviera gigolos. Everything and everybody
that I saw while we were in Ithaca rendered itself immediately
into Odyssean parallels, which, I think, is not surprising; it was
impossible, therefore, that I should not see these young men as the
Suitors, although there was no particular Penelope in hand whom
they were besieging, and they did not spend most of their time
guzzling goats' paunches stuffed with blood and fat, with great
chines of beef and ribs of pork. They were moderate eaters, if only
because there was not much to eat on the island, and a good haul of
fish was a real excitement. They were temperate drinkers, too, and a
few glasses of the good island wine would get them very merry. One
or two were happily married, and though several of the others had
girls somewhere vaguely in the offing, they did not press their suits
with great vigour, at least in public. Unlike northern youths, on the
whole they kept their love-lives to themselves. In the meantime they
preferred each other's company, and if they chanced to meet in the
square or on the road the young ladies that were assigned to them,
they made no song and dance about it. It was different with Giorgos,
who much preferred to be called George, the young man in the
American jacket, a dark fine-boned youngster, a scion of one of the
oldest families in the island, one of whose forbears a century ago had

written a rare and learned History of the Isle of Ithaca. They had
owned olive-groves for generations both in Ithaca itself and on
one or two of the adjacent islands, and to-day, at all events, a good
deal of their land was hired out to the poorer peasants, who paid
their rent in terms of the kids and goats whose flesh you saw on the
slabs of George's father's shop. Young George had spent two years in
the U.S.A. with an uncle, and had acquired a less oblique attitude
to the other sex. It occurred to me that in their preference for each
other's company these contemporary Suitors were not at all unlike
the earlier ones, who would probably have been extremely irritated
if Penelope had finally given up her husband as a bad job, and
decided on making that choice among them which from time to
time they asked her, rather half-heartedly, to make. They knew
when they were on to a good thing, all those lashings of wine, and
the ribs of beef and the great roasted hams from the piggery of
Eumaeus. And, of course, Penelope was not as young as she had been.
Besides, if Odysseus should turn up again, it would be awkward. He
did. And it was.

The young men were obviously very interested in the two
strangers, exactly as their predecessors had been, when the disguised
chief appeared looking like a down-at-heel foreigner. We looked like
that, too, but nobody threw any cow-heels at us. On the contrary,
they were charming.

It was George, born Giorgos, who finally made up his mind to
address us.

"Hi, you English?" he called out.

"That's right."

"You been to America?"

One of us had, one hadn't.

"I've been to America!" said Giorgos.

"Fine! You should go to England some time!"

That was intended as a simple statement of fact, but it evoked a
gale of applause and laughter among the Suitors.

"You come here and have a drink!" said the eldest. (He was
Dimitrius, the great comic, the self-made draper.)

"Have one with us!"

"With *us*! With *us*!" the others insisted. One could not argue
with such geniality. We went over and sat down among them.
Names were exchanged, hands shaken, drinks ordered.

"You come to collect bones?" asked Telemachus. (He was one of
the two Telemachuses in the group. There was also an Odysseus.
They doubtless had a saint's name apiece, too.) "You take *my*

bones, too, to nice girl in England?" He tapped his ribs to indicate
his own skeleton was available for export.

"Well, no," I said. "I'm not after bones, really." I assumed that
was a reference to the activities of the archaeologists, who often
enough found bones as well as sherds and jewels and other objects
during their diggings. It was, in fact, a reference to bones of a much
later epoch, as I was to learn next day. No, I said, I was not in the
bone-collecting business.

"You sell anything?" asked Dimitrios. "What discount you give
for cash?" He had a quick eye for business.

"Holiday may be?" asked another.

"In a way, yes. But it's more than that." I knew I was not
making myself clear, so I produced my Greek "papers" and laid
them on the table. Heads gathered and scraped against each other.
Other heads craned over from adjoining tables. Passers-by came
close to be in on it. There were too many pairs of eyes to take in one
set of papers, so Dimitrius read out the salient passages. He finished,
and there was a brief silence. Then suddenly "Bravo! Bravo!" they
cried. There was a great slapping of backs, and more glasses of *ouzo*
appeared out of the air. It was clear they took it all very personally,
this Odysseus business, and Homer, and the whole story. It was not
a perquisite, a tripper racket, like Shakespeare to the good burghers
of Stratford. Despite the ancient fame and the great beauty of the
island, there is no tourist traffic in Ithaca, or by now there would
have been a great deal more accommodation than Anastasia's
humble little inn. You can't buy a single postcard of the place. The
islanders tend their vines and press their olives, they herd their goats
or go out fishing. If anybody feels like working, he works. If not, not.
If the store-keepers in the little streets behind the square come over
to the cafés for a drink or a card-game, leaving their shops un-
attended, it is impossible not to know where they are in case you
need a pound of candles or a pair of slippers. Sometimes one or
another of the young men takes a job in the merchant navy, or
finds his way to relatives in America. Then he comes back again,
partly because he can't get a permanent visa, and partly because he
prefers Ithaca. It is as if there were two theophanies in the island,
which are in no competition with each other, and they almost as
readily call their children after the Homeric *personæ* as after the
Christian saints.

My new friends wanted me to expand on the subject of the
"papers", so I told them of my devotion to the leading citizen of
their island, and how long I had been *en route* for Ithaca. "Bravo!

Bravo!" they cried again. One or two wiped tears from their eyes.

Then suddenly an idea struck them. This was Sunday, the day off (though they didn't seem to work very industriously when it was the day on). Sometimes on a Sunday morning they would go fishing, or take a caique, a *benzina*, to one of the beaches. Or they would pile into a taxi and take a ride. But though there was a kilometre or two of road in two other directions from Vathy, the only place where a car could go to stretch its wheels, so to speak, was Stavros, the chief village of the northern peninsula, and they had arranged to drive up to Stavros in an hour or two. "We will take you to Pelikata," the young men said, "which is just above Stavros. You know, of course, that that is where Odysseus was born? We will shew you the walls where his big house was. Also his grave, where he was buried."

"Pelikata?" I repeated. "You *did* say Pelikata?"

"Yes, Pelikata!" they endorsed. "We will go to Pelikata, and we will see the other things of Odysseus up there; then we will go to the restaurant and have wine and eat meat, and sing songs. You come, yes?"

I turned to Edward.

"You remember Pelikata?"

"That's where they've done some digging, isn't it? They think the house of Odysseus may have been there."

"These chaps don't *think*. They *know*. They say they're going to eat meat, and drink wine, and sing songs, up there near the house of Odysseus. Like those other young men used to do, all those many years ago, till the Chief came back, and put an end to it all."

I turned to my friends.

"Yes, yes!" I proclaimed with joy. "Let's go to Pelikata!"

For if I was going to the place of the house of Odysseus, I was going to the beginning of it all. I was going where I should have gone when it all started for me, in 1916, but it would have been rather awkward then.

II

Pelikata is not a name in Homer's poem, but a name on the present-day map of Ithaca. If we talk of a possible house of Odysseus in Pelikata, we mean that to-day's Ithaca is Homer's Ithaca. I am not going to consider the question whether Homer's Ithaca is actually some other island, say Leukas, or Madagascar, even though the German scholar who raises the issue was as learned as German scholars have the habit of being, and in the erudite Miss Lorimer he enlisted a formidable lieutenant. After all, the association between the two Ithacas goes back with a brief remission in time, and a slight verbal modification, for some two thousand years, at least. The *Lives of Homer*, one of which purports to have been written by Herodotus, are at their latest nearly as old as that, and they of themselves leave the identification in precious little doubt. The traveller who visits Ithaca with the Odyssey in one hand and in the other (or, maybe in a suitcase) the stout volumes of the *Proceedings of the British School in Athens*, containing essays devoted to the excavations in Ithaca, will have no doubt at all.*

To proceed with the considerations which lead the traveller to Pelikata. If Ithaca is Ithaca, it is to be assumed that the princes of Ithaca who lorded it about the time of the Trojan War, had a royal dwelling and a city on the island, whether or not one of these princes was actually called Odysseus. That was exactly analogous to the line of thought which induced Schliemann to dig in the northwest Troad. He had, in fact, started digging in Ithaca, too, and had somewhat rashly concluded that the heap of stones popularly called the Castle of Odysseus, still extant on Mount Aëtos, the isthmus mountain, indicated the site of the hero's city. For various reasons, some archaeological, some inherent in the poem, it was realized that the city, if any traces still existed under the ground or over it, must be sought for elsewhere than on Aëtos. Was there any significance to be drawn from the fact that the place-name "Polis", that is, "city", had immemorially been attached to a small bay in the north-west of the island? Did the name indicate that there might have been a port here once, serving a town climbing the slopes behind? And how about the country when you got to the top of the hill? Was there room up there for a palace and its out-buildings, for its vineyards and olive-groves? Were there any evidences of ancient occupation still visible? Did it seem a sensible thing to start digging up there? The answer to all these questions was in the affirmative. There was ample room up there. It was felt to be an ideal site for an ancient city, commanding as it does the whole undulating plateau which constitutes the most fertile area of a mountainous island. There were several promising ancient stones round and about. Finally, a Dutch archaeologist, one Vollgraff, had actually reported the presence of a few ancient sherds up there early in the century (exactly as there had once been reports of a few desultory finds on Hissarlik).

* For reference, see bibliography, page 240.

Corfu :
Canoni Bay

Ithaca: Bride brought to Ithaca

Ithaca: Cave of Marmarospaelia   Ithaca: View from the fountain of Areth

The name of the hill-top to which all these considerations led was Pelikata.

"Pelikata!" I repeated to the young men there at the café on the square at Vathy. "Let's go to Pelikata!"

"*Kaló! Kaló!*" they proclaimed, rising to their feet so heartily they almost threw their chairs back. "This way!" We raced over to the corner of the square where the three or four Vathy taxis usually stand. At the moment there was only one, for the wedding-party had gone off in the others. It had not occurred to us that a company as large as ours was now would be accommodated in only one car. But that was the idea. I had some time ago arrived at the conclusion that just as old elephants go off to certain jungle clearings to die, or so it is reported, so old cars go off and die in the Greek Islands. Excepting that there cars do not die, or if they ultimately do, they merely disintegrate like puff-balls. I realized at once of this old Ford in Vathy that it was the most notable, the most fearsome, of all the petrol-powered vehicles to which we had committed ourselves during our journeys. Compared with this one the cars that had taken us from Chanakkale over the Scamander plain to Troy, and up the mountain roads of Chios and Corfu, were Rolls-Royces and Bentleys.

Edward and I entered first. The young men then began to pile into the car, on to it, and round it, rather like rugby footballers piling up on the ball in a scrum. Several small wooden stools were introduced into the car for additional seating. A clobber of packages turned up from somewhere, and coagulated round us like swarming bees. There was a prolonged tussle with a starter. At long last there was a whisper, a sneeze, we were off. The road leads along the southern shore of the Bay of Vathy for a mile or more, then, cutting below a headland, runs alongside the small Bay of Dexia. A mile or so later the road reaches Aëtos, which is at once in itself a mountain and the isthmus that connects the southern and northern peninsulas. For a time the road climbs the mountains of Anoi, or Neriton, along the east coast, then switches over the saddle to the west. There the Strait of Ithaca extends below under the breaking precipices, and beyond the water, the vaporous lavender ranges of Cephalonia.

My first view of the island from within was a little spasmodic, glimpsed as it was over burly shoulders and through the crook of elbows. It was also a little distorted, I must confess, with fright. The road had no surface, and sometimes no edge to it. Now and again the wheels were hanging over empty space. The driver was a considerable raconteur, and often removed his hands from the wheel to emphasize a point. If I'm going to die, I told myself, I can hardly conceive of a lovelier place to die in, and pleasanter company. But I didn't want to see my death coming *at* me. So when it looked imminent, I merely closed my eyes, and counted ten. Then I opened them again, and if we seemed to be facing another crisis, I closed them again. It was easier that way.

None the less, even in those circumstances, I could see enough to approve the accuracy of the description of his native island given by Telemachus at the court of King Menelaus.

"In Ithaca," said he, "there is no room for horses to run about in, nor any meadows at all. It is a pasture-land for goats and more attractive than the sort of land where horses thrive. None of the islands that slope down to the sea are rich in meadows and the kind of place where you can drive a horse. Ithaca least of all."

He might have added it is not the kind of place where you can drive a car, either. Not that sort of a car. One might ask, in virtue of this thoroughly explicit description, how Herr Dörpfeld some thousands of years later could possibly maintain that Ithaca was Leukas, an island where in many places you can drive abreast half-a-dozen fours-in-hand.

I could see enough on that journey of another thing, the beauty of Ithaca, enough to know that for me, at least, there never had been, and never would be again, a place so beautiful, the ribs of golden hills, the magistral olive-trees, the cypresses black as coal-cellars, the sudden froth of a bank of wild flowers, the far-down bays as tiny as shells, the contours of the mountain ridges against a sky of which you could only say it was an abstraction of blueness, pure as mathematics, too pure even to be poetry.

And it was Stavros now, a high village pitched between the rising ridges, a small square where the car could manœuvre, a church, a restaurant, a café or two, a few houses, a few farms straggling among figs and almonds, a few goats, dogs, sheep and cats. The populace was already waiting for us in the square, the rumour of our coming having preceded us a long time ago across the baby-pure air. It was soon learned that two Englishmen had arrived who wished to see the things of Odysseus. The young men of Stavros followed in our wake, and two or three of the older inhabitants were miraculously added to our load, including a retired doctor who was very know-ledgable on Homeric matters. So the car lurched off and up again by stony paths, through rough olive-groves and fields of poor wheat, and everywhere white and pink and yellow flowers of cistus among the rocks, and gorse and broom exploding like fire-works, and close-cropping thyme, bee-haunted, under the outstretched green hands of the wild fig. After some minutes the track became impossible even for a Vathy Ford. The journey was continued on foot a little further, till we reached the small hut which serves as a local museum to house the finds of the British archaeologists. A minute further and higher, and we were on the top of the Pelikata plateau, and, turning north or east or west, looked down on three waters from the vantage-point where Homer, I do not doubt, looked down on the domain of the princes of Ithaca, one of whom was named Odysseus, whose tale he told.

To the untutored, or even to the tutored, eye there is not much to be seen in Pelikata, though the imagination has more than enough for a feast. First my friends showed me the small waste and rocky rubble which still edges the grass-grown pits and trenches dug in 1930 and later years. Here and there a few broken sherds lay about, possibly ignored by the scholars, perhaps dug up by local hands later. Some of them were large enough, and had clear enough markings, for even the unprofessional eye to realize their antiquity. They were clearly not bits and pieces of recent pottery imports from Patras. Then we went into the tiny museum, where the professionals have reassembled even such small sherds as these into jars and bowls and vases which go far, far back to the Early Helladic, the Minyan, and the Mycenaean time. Not even a surgeon who handles living skin and bone brings more piety and dexterity than these scholars do to the reassemblings of these broken sherds; and indeed it can be said of the scholars that in a like manner they reconstitute the skin and bone of civilizations fragmented under the weight of the collapsed millenia.

There was one sherd I had hoped to see, and saw; in itself an inconspicuous thing, a triangle in dun terra-cotta less than three inches in length. I had read about it in London, its importance had been emphasized in Athens. But if in the excitement I had failed to recall it, my friends would have seen to it that I did not miss it. "Look! You see? The name of Odysseus!" And there indeed the name of Odysseus was, scratched faintly in the rough terra-cotta surface . . . *euchin Odyssei*, offering to Odysseus. It is not an old sherd compared with many in the museum; it has been provisionally dated as between the second and first century B.C. But in some ways it was the most thrilling thing I saw that day among the "things of Odysseus". However, it was found not on Pelikata, but down in the cavern in Polis Bay. I will speak of it again shortly. I was shewn certain other Odyssean "things", up there on Pelikata. These included a number of roughly-carved prehistoric stone blocks which, it has been conjectured, belonged to a circuit-wall enclosing the summit of the hill. There were also various other chunks of masonry of the same age, both *in situ*, and worked into terraces and modern walls. There was also an isolated rock-tomb where, I was assured, Odysseus had been buried. I felt that that was probably a tradition that lacked substance. A little further away I was shewn a School of Homer, as might be expected; just as you expect to find, and do in fact find, a School of Homer in Chios. It is true Homer was believed to have been born in Chios, whereas the early biographers do not go further than to say he sojourned for a time in Ithaca. But there it is, a little distance north of the Pelikata diggings, a platform of ancient squared masonry on which to-day the small church of Haghios Athanasios stands; and there amid the olive-groves and the vine-terraces Homer instructed the aspiring poets of Ithaca, or so they have believed in Ithaca, though not for more than a century or two, so that this also can hardly be considered one of the more impressive traditions.

There were also three fountains presented to me in the area. I was permitted to choose which of the three was the Pool of the Black Fountain, the Melanhydros of the Odyssey, where the palace handmaidens went to fill their pitchers. Whichever it was, the Young Men resident in Stavros were also convinced that it was not only Melanhydros, but the Fountain of Arethusa where (it will be remembered) Eumaeus, the faithful swineherd of Odysseus, found the right fodder for his pigs. That very nearly precipitated a fight with the Young Men of Vathy who declared that the Fountain of Arethusa is close by the Raven's Crag, still known as Korax, and Korax, as everybody knows, is on the south shore of the other peninsula, under the plateau called Marathia. And the Vathy men were right; for if the city of Odysseus is to be located at Pelikata (which the Vathy group yielded, though with reluctance) then the Fountain of Arethusa must be sought for not a few minutes walk from the fountain, but (for one or two reasons I will discuss later) a good many hours away.

The altercation came to nothing, and we were taken along to another Melanhydros, without the issue being raised that this fountain, too, was Arethusa. It was over against a terraced inn that

bore the friendly name of Apolausis, or "Enjoyment", and its name
was Kalamos. On purely aesthetic grounds I would have endorsed
its claims. Three springs of water leap glancing from three spouts
in an elegant triple archway, their cold dark waters assembling in a
sculptured trough below, with a shady plane-tree on one side, and a
line of cypresses stalking up the hill. This ignored fountain must be
the loveliest monument, so far as I know the only one with such style,
surviving from the Venetian time. The other survivors, the blue and
pink houses, the little churches, are homespun in comparison.

What have the archaeologists who conducted the excavations in
Ithaca to say of their bearings on the historicity of Homer? Talking
of the cairns at Aëtos, a few miles south of Pelikata, Heurtley says:
"As far as the Homeric associations are concerned, if our conclusions
based on purely archaeological grounds are correct, the ashes
covered by the cairns may include those of men who were alive
during and perhaps took part in the war against Troy." (It is now
suggested that the "cairns" may have been the hearth-stones of
dwelling-places.) Miss Benton is more reserved. "It would be rash,"
she says, "to date the amorphous scraps from Pelikata at all closely.
Fabric and shape seem Mycenaean, but as archaeological evidence
for a Palace of Odysseus, they fail to carry conviction."* It would be
a good deal to expect, of course, that the fragments should accur-
ately pin-point the palace of a hero whose existence in sober history
is still to be established. But a layman allows himself to believe that
Miss Benton is unduly reserved, particularly in face of her own
terra-cotta fragment, the votive offering to Odysseus. It is true that
the object is dated one thousand years after the presumed date of
our hero, but it should be remembered that that is two thousand
years *before* our own time. A relic which proves an association
between Odysseus and Ithaca two thousand years old, makes it
possible for us to believe that on that same island an actual Odysseus
once lived, and that the fields of the "amorphous scraps", some of
which are exactly contemporary with his war, are the fields where
his house once stood.

With such encouragement, proferred so cautiously by the
archaeologists, it was not only possible, but easy, I might even say it
was inevitable, that I should believe. Somewhere here then, I told
myself, as I wandered among the roots of olives and the fading
asphodel, Odysseus was born to Laertes. Somewhere here he
brought his chaste bride, Penelope, and built a house for her. Or if

* For reference, see bibliography, page 240.

he inherited a house from Laertes, he at least built the nuptial chamber here, and the bed in it, for he describes the building at length.

> "Inside the court there was a long-leaved olive-tree, which had grown to full height with a stem as thick as a pillar. Round this I built my room of close-set stonework, and when that was finished, I roofed it over thoroughly, and put in a solid, neatly fitted double door. Next I lopped all the twigs off the olive, trimmed the stem from the root up, rounded it smoothly and carefully with my adze and trued it to the line, to make my bed-post. This I drilled through where necessary, and used as a basis for the bed itself, which I worked away at till that was done, when I finished it off with an inlay of gold, silver, and ivory, and fixed a set of purple straps across the frame."

There were a number of long-leaved olive-trees around on Pelikata, with stems as thick as pillars, but it would need a bride-groom as cunning as Odysseus and a bride as rare as Penelope before such a bed could be built again, and where will you find them?

In that bed, Telemachus, the son of Odysseus, was born. To that house a distinguished visitor came, no less a king than Agamemnon of Mycenae, to persuade Odysseus to add his strength to the Achaean forces in the great onslaught that was being prepared against Troy. It is said that, reluctant to leave his young wife and son, Odysseus pretended he was mad, and went out to one of his fields, sowed it with salt, and ploughed it with an ass and an ox yoked together. But the warrior, Palamedes, suspecting the stratagem, exposed it by laying the small Telemachus in front of the plough. There was nothing for it. It was the war for Odysseus, a reluctant starter but a late stayer. Down this hill to Polis Bay a messenger ran, skirting the vine-terraces and the long-leaved olives. "Get the ships ready, the scarlet and the blue ships! The Lord Odysseus sails for Troy!"

And now, having refreshed ourselves in the café called Enjoyment with some interim flagons of wine and a tree-load of *nespoli*, in the steps of that same messenger we descended to the Bay of Polis under the hill. To my friends it was as much the Polis of Miss Benton as it was the Polis of Odysseus; and perhaps some day a votive tablet inscribed by these contemporary Ithacans will be disinterred in the same cave to take its place alongside with the tablet to Odysseus (which, I am happy to learn, has survived the recent earthquake and now reposes in the village library of Stavros).

I should say that my friends were dashed to learn I had not met
the lady. They talked of this devoted scholar with something of
superstitious awe, as if she had stepped straight out of the remote
heroic world whose material traces she had helped to bring to the
light of day. Indeed, she seemed to rank second only to Penelope
herself in the female section of the island Pantheon. I promised that
when I went back home I should seek out Miss Benton and give her
their respectful greetings.

The cave lies under a steep cliff on the end of a bay on the north-
west coast of the island, less than half-a-mile below Stavros. It was
first discovered, or at least it was first rumoured that antique fragments were to be found on the site, in 1864, when the man who
owned the land, a certain Louisos, began digging a pit there for a
lime-kiln. It happened that Schliemann was around, in a state of
such excitement to be treading Homeric earth for the first time that,
as he tells us, he quite forgot heat and cold, and without the least
self-consciousness on anyone's part, read out to the assembled
islanders great stretches of the rolling incomprehensible hexameters
of the Odyssey, the tears pouring down his cheeks. When the
ecstasy abated, he devoted most of his attention to the so-called
"Castle of Odysseus" on Mount Aëtos, which he wrongly accepted
as the remains of the Homeric city. Certainly he did not attach any
importance to the obscure goings-on at Polis, or he would have got
to work on the sea-shore cave in Ithaca with the same enthusiasm as
he shortly brought to the hill-top in the Troad. It can be imagined
with what excitement he would have alit upon the votive mask to
Odysseus. However, Schliemann went further east, and Louisos
disposed of the gold and bronze fragments he had discovered,
which, like the more sensational "Gold Treasury of Priam", have
now disappeared, leaving no trace. The Dutchman, Vollgraff,
conducted an excavation in 1904, and discovered a quantity of
Mycenaean sherds, which in one swoop took the history of the cave
back to the second millenium B.C., all the way back to the time of
the Trojan War and beyond. It was later stated that a complete
bronze tripod-cauldron had been discovered by one of Louisos's
workmen at this time, and that it had been melted down to escape
seizure. If this were true, it would have confirmed what seemed
already probable, that the cave had been an ancient shrine presumably of Athene, seeing that inscriptions to the goddess had
already been located there.

Miss Benton conducted her excavations in the summers of 1930,
1931 and 1932. The floor of the cave is certainly lower than it was in

antiquity and is now covered with water, both from rock seepings and from the sea. With the burning sun overhead and the water infiltrating so deep and fast that it was necessary to have recourse to pumps, the excavation was a trying piece of work. It was abundantly worth while.

The earliest finds are by many centuries earlier than the time of the Trojan War. The cave is likely to have been a shrine of some sort, rather than a dwelling-place, for caves have always been invested by primitive man with a supernatural awe. The discovery of pieces of at least twelve tripod-cauldrons (one of which is beautifully reconstructed in the little museum at Vathy) amply confirms the sacred nature of the place. To the Odyssean traveller the most thrilling discovery was the fragments of about a hundred second-to-first century female masks, evidently local products. As I wrote earlier, on one of these fragmented masks are scratched the words: "votive offering to Odysseus", and, in another direction, "so-and-so" (name absent) "dedicated it".

While speculating on Hissarlik hill on the nature of Odysseus, whether he was myth, or man, or merely a figment of the imagination of poets, I expressed the hope that some day a stone might be disinterred which might confer upon Odysseus the actual validity of history. I referred briefly to the find of this votive mask in Ithaca, but stated that it was by some thousand years too late to be contemporary evidence of his existence. I stated also that it was rather a theological than a historical document.

One thing, however, the fragment *does* make clear. Whether Odysseus was merely myth or not, whether he had once been alive or not, it is now certain that some six or seven centuries or so after the time of Homer, and undoubtedly directly as a consequence of the Homeric poems, a cult of Odysseus actually existed, at least in Ithaca. He has become a divinity in his own right, though his cult may not have been widely diffused and may not have endured long. Until a similar tablet has been unearthed in Leukas (the island to which I hoped to make no further reference) we must reconcile ourselves to accept Ithaca as Ithaca, and, in the way most proper to us, inscribe on a votive tablet our devotion to Odysseus.

The tripods and the votive mask between them make it as certain as such things can ever be, that the cave at Polis was the Odysseion, the shrine to which an inscription unearthed in Magnesia makes a casual but exciting reference. The same inscription refers also to a ceremonial athletic festival, an *Odysseia*, which (Miss Benton concludes) will most likely have been celebrated on the foreshore of this very bay.

Ithaca: Fountain of Melanhydros

Ithaca: Vathy

At all events, while several of us that evening were exploring the cave and examining what remains of the wall that at one time protected it, and of the diggings of the British scholars, the Suitors of Stavros and Vathy, with that sense of the fitting I had come to expect from them, began to play games among the rocks and the shingle of the foreshore, the blue sea-holly and the purple sea-lavender, for my special benefit enacting the latest Odysseia in history. They ran races, duly impeded by obstacles, between a rock and an ilex-tree. They wrestled. With a ball that had mysteriously appeared from somewhere they played a ball-game such as, for all anyone knows to the contrary, the earlier youths may have played in those early Odysseias.

I was more grateful to them than they knew.

But it was getting dark now. I felt that the hospitable young men had devoted to us too much of the time that they had proposed to devote to their revels up in the restaurant on Stavros. The human games were at an end. The bats took over, circling about our heads like the lassos of cowboys. On the terraces the fireflies turned and turned again their silent rattles of silver light. From the edge of an olive-wood a thin flat sound, totally unmusical, repeated itself again and again, like a hammer tapping on stone. *"Kukyvaya!"* the young men said. It was an owl, maybe Athene's own owl, the small big-headed creature of the monuments, the creature we had heard in Samé. The place was getting a little eerie. Some of the youths had left already. Now the rest of us climbed to Stavros again.

Before we went, I turned and faced the dusking sea. Far off I saw twelve ghosts of ships, the fleet of a famous islander, who had been summoned with the bravest of his fellow-princes to fight for the Greek princess, Helen, far across the seas in Troy. He would be away a long time in Troy, and even longer on the return to his house in Ithaca.

People had been saying that that house had been on the top of the hill there, beyond Stavros, on the plateau called Pelikata. I had been to Pelikata once that day, and Odysseus had not left for the wars yet. I would come back later, I told myself, when the wars were over, and all the long wanderings. Blood would flow, and heads would roll in the dust.

In the meantime, this very evening, we were to join the Suitors at their party in the Stavros inn. So we did, and indeed it was a grand party, with a great deal of golden wine flowing, and dish upon dish of mutton laid before us, cooked in oil and tomato and rich in spices, and an accordion puling and moaning as if it was not Stavros but Montmartre. Half-way during the merry-makings there was breathless excitement when a trio of distinguished guests joined us. They were a man and wife and their daughter, the three leading actors of a fit-up company from Patras, who had been preparing a large room somewhere for the performance next day of a play: "The Girl Likes a Walk round the Sea this Evening." In the days when they were still current, I rarely saw a leading actor look more like a leading actor, than M. Janitsa, with that broad-brimmed black hat, that nose like a large but slightly unripe strawberry, that flowing cloak, that immense Yeatsian bow, and the hand thrust into the waistcoat whenever it was not raising a glass. His wife was plump and vivacious, with eyes darting like birds under the hedgerow brows. Every now and again her chest expanded to a hiccup and all her jewellery tinkled like the lustres of a chandelier. The daughter was lovely in a more classical manner, an exact incarnation of Byron's Zoë as I have always imagined her, the moon-pale skin, the broad white forehead, the full lips, the broad chin. At all events she was too lovely for the impressionable George, who, as I surmised earlier, must have been over-sensitized by his experiences in America. The moment the girl appeared his jaw dropped and his eyes glazed over. He was not able even to take his wine properly, and it dribbled down the chin again. Love happened like this to George. It was like being under a brick wall when it fell. His friends ragged him unmercifully so long as the spasm lasted; on this occasion it was to last three days, then he was heart and soul in the fold again. The proceedings went on for a long time, and everybody got very gay indeed. It was requested that everybody should sing a solo song, and I contributed my party number, the first four lines of the first verse of "Drink to me only", which I can execute without going sharp or flat once. Toasts were drunk to the two ladies present; also to Penelope, a lady of long ago, and to Miss Benton, a contemporary lady. My glass was filled again. And still again. There was dancing to the accordion up and down and around, in between the tables and the simmering open stoves. There were many more young men than ladies, but we made do. It was very gay and noisy and rather stifling, so I went out into the night air and walked among the olive-trees. An owl called, and another called again. The sea below was dark and still like the Underworld itself. Like the Underworld. The words reverberated behind my skull. Like the Underworld, where these earlier young men descended when their long junketings were over, and their Doom befell them, and among the old ghosts their newly-arrived ghosts squeaked and gibbered.

It was the night when Odysseus settled the account. It was not the Odysseus I had known before, in whose wake I had wandered far and long, the adventurer among enchanted islands, among lotus-eaters and sirens and anthropoghagi. It was an Odysseus I had hardly glimpsed before, not even on the fields of Troy, when, after all, he was fighting man to man in open battle. It was an Odysseus hardly yet arisen into the white light of poetry from the sooty primordial depths, an Odysseus burning with a grimmer blood-lust than the Hebraic proponents of the eye-for-an-eye. On the night of the revenge of Odysseus, there were women dancing here on this hillside, then as now, not many yards away, maybe, the women who had been cronies of those insolent Suitors. "I swear I will not give a decent death," swore Telemachus, "to women who have heaped dishonour on us all." For Telemachus, who had been a rather milk-and-water young man till now, was suddenly as fierce as a lion now that his father had come back from abroad. And when it came to a parcel of young women his valour knew no bounds. So he made a ship's rope fast to a bedding-post, and twisted it into a series of nooses to take the heads of the women; then he hung the women at such a height that their feet could not touch the ground. And so they danced there for a while. But not, the poet tells us, in a phrase as sardonic as any in all literature—not for very long.

Then, when the bodies of the slain Suitors and their paramours had been cleared away, and the blood scrubbed from the floor, and the whole house purified with sulphur, there was more dancing, and there was music. For it was feared that the relatives of the dead might learn of all this killing before Odysseus had had time to establish his authority again, and it would be awkward for everyone. "So strike up a merry dance-tune on your lyre," commanded the prince, "as loud as you can play it, so that if the music is heard outside by anyone in the road or by one of our neighbours, they may imagine there is a wedding-feast!"

It was a dreadful night, all in all, that night of the earlier party up above Stavros. The boughs creaked. The owls hooted. The sweat was like ice between my shoulder-blades. So I went back to the restaurant and pushed the door open. The warm air stood up like mattresses.

"Where you been, Mister Lu-iss?"

"A long way!"

"Hi! More wine for Mister Lu-iss!"

I was glad to drink more wine. The accordion squeaked and gibbered. The women danced as if their heads were in nooses. I will be glad to get away from Pelikata, I told myself. I will not come back again. Another glass? Yes, yes. The man opposite me, who was he? The face was vaguely familiar. Who was he? He had drunk so much he probably didn't know himself by now. Then I remembered who he was. He was the driver who was to take us down the wild road to Vathy, the rough and rocky road, with the ghastly precipices first to the right and then to the left.

Who cared? By now I didn't. I knew exactly what one did. One shut one's eyes. One might open them in Vathy, or, failing that, in Heaven. We were in the car again, rather more of us going down than coming up. The car had a running-board on the left, but not on the right. We were driving away, and we were driving down, and there was a soldier or a gendarme or something squatting on that left-hand running-board. It seemed to make a bit of difference to the steering, but drivers can make adjustments. We were singing at the tops of our voices, we were a solid lump of song. And very ribald song, too, not at all the sort of song you should have on your lips at the moment before the moment in which you may present yourself to your Maker. Ah, well, your Maker would understand. Those were rocks, far, far, down, ragged rocks, and by the edge of the rocks that was the engulfing sea.

The electric moment was when the red fox jumped down out of the scrub on to the road, and stood staring coldly at our headlights for a moment or two. "*Ai, ai, ai!*" cried the driver, and the policeman, and all the young men. The red fox turned quickly and ran. He did not jump into the scrub above or below the road. He ran *along* the road, very quickly and easily, and the car followed him, left, right, left, on the road that twisted beside the steep precipices.

"*Ai, ai, ai!*" roared the young men. For one moment the fox turned and stared at us, his eyes like shining topazes. Then he vaulted into the thick myrtle, below and out of sight.

So, after all, we reached Vathy.

III

There was a knock at my door next morning. "Come in!" I said. It was probably Anastasia with the sheets. Or one of the young men come to propose some project or other.

The door opened. It was neither of these. A somewhat older gentleman stood there, in a panama hat and a light beach suiting. He was brick-red in complexion, heavy and competent in hands and feet. He was carrying a shopping-basket. I had seen him on the boat yesterday, but we had not spoken, and I was not aware he had landed in Ithaca. He paused for a moment, then bowed from the waist.

"Sakharof!" he said. "I'm in the room next door!" That was clearly a Russian accent. Those were Russian cheek-bones. "How do you do?"

"You're British? You write books?" He laid down his shopping-basket.

"Yes, I do."

"I work for the British. It may interest you. I've come to collect bones."

"I see." What I meant was that I saw what the young man in the square was talking about yesterday, the one who had asked me if *I* had come to collect bones. At the same moment another memory, grotesque in its inappositeness, floated up from the drowned depths of my childhood mind. "Any rags? Any bones?" The little old man in the green flapping frock-coat who used to wheel a handcart outside the front doors. You gave him the soup-bones, he gave you the blue-stone cubes with which the women scrubbed the front steps.

"Bones?" I repeated. "How very interesting!" But M. Sakharof was evidently not *that* sort of a bone-merchant. He was an archaeologist, or a palaeontologist, or something. My heart quickened. Had there been a recent discovery of a Mycenaean shaft-tomb in Ithaca complete v. ith bones? Were they even speculating whether they were the bones of Odysseus himself, and the members of his family? Was it intended that this very shopping-basket should contain those princely bones? "Are the bones in a good state of preservation?" I asked. "Did you find any bronze and gold pieces, too? When did all this happen? I didn't hear a word about it in Athens."

M. Sakharof scratched his nose.

"I don't think you understand," he said. "Not Greek bones. British bones. People who died here during the British Occupation."

"Of course!" I adapted myself to the changed picture. "There must have been a garrison here in the last century, as well as in the other islands."

"That is so. I have come for their bones."

"But what do you want their bones for? Where are they? Surely they're all right where they are?" I must have looked and sounded rather cross.

"I suppose they are," he said, shrugging his shoulders, and

splaying out his great hands. "Don't blame me. You see, I am an official of the Imperial War Graves Commission. It's my job. I don't only look after graves. I move bones when they have to be moved. I get orders from London."

"Then you must be a colleague of Mr. Millington, in Chanak-kale?" He was, of course. "I see. Ah well." It was my turn to shrug shoulders. But I did not think it at all well.

"I thought," said M. Sakharof, rubbing his hands, "seeing you are British, you might like to be there while we open up the graves. You are welcome. We start work in an hour."

"Where *are* these bones?"

"In the Gardelaki churchyard. That's just behind us, up the hill. You can see the belfry from the terrace at the back here. I'll show you. You can come later." He picked up his shopping-basket.

"What's that for?" I asked. The bag was not empty. Had the job, in fact, started? Did the bag contain some poor little drummer-boy's bones which, I am sure, had been quite happy where they were?

"It's my lunch," he said.

By now I was getting a little fractious.

"What's it all *about*?" I asked. "Suppose somebody did it to you?"

"Peh!" he went. He pursed his lips and ejected from between them a sharp explosion of breath. It was clear the performance meant: "Orders are orders! And bones are bones! Don't be senti-mental!" His actual words were: "It's a matter of finance!"

"Is it?" It seemed to me other matters were involved, too.

M. Sakharof went on to explain. The matter is in the hands of one of the major departments of State, though nobody had ever been quite certain which. Perhaps that is why the bones had been undisturbed so long. The fact is there are several pockets of bones up and down the area which cost the British taxpayer varying sums of money for annual maintenance. The Ithaca bones cost the department no less than fifteen pounds a year. The present idea was to collect the bones in the Ionian area and bury them in a common grave in Corfu with a tablet to cover them all. The whole job of maintenance would then only cost some forty to fifty pounds a year. And what is more, the bones would be together from now on, and properly looked after. It seemed to me all very efficient and economical, but a little pedantic. I thought if the bones could have had any say in the matter, they might have preferred to stay where they were. I thought that if any of these British garrison dead had

had time to produce children and these children had any posterity, they would have had the same views, wherever they were now. And if it should happen to *me* (I felt like telling M. Sakharof) that I should die in Ithaca—in Ithaca!—heaven help anybody who should think of digging up *my* bones and carting them around.

Anyhow, I did not go to see the work in progress up in the Gardelaki churchyard till some evenings later, when I knew M. Sakharof and his workmen had gone. Better to be alone, I thought. It was a sad spectacle, the ancient trees uprooted that had once given shade to the graves, and the grave-stones, doubtless to be broken up soon, standing in lopsided heaps against the wall, and the gaping holes, the mounds of shifted earth. Two of the stones recorded the deaths of small children, one two years old, dead of a fever, the other an infant of some months. Three sacks stood up in an angle of the wall, crammed higgledy-piggledy with bones like potatoes, the bones that had long since got used to Ithaca. A hawk sailed indifferently on towards the summit of Aëtos. There was, he knew, nothing for him here.

IV

That evening in the square, Dimitrius asked us would we like to go fishing next morning. He had a small row-boat and you could put up a sail, too, if there was a bit of breeze. We said yes, that would be fine. He would call for us before dawn, he said. Later on the fish see just what you are up to.

"And I think I know where you like to go," he concluded. "To Dexia Bay, yes, where Odysseus go ashore, when he come back to Ithaca? And from there up to the big cave, you know, Marmarospaelia, where he hide the presents?"

"Yes, yes, to Dexia Bay," I repeated. "And after that Marmarospaelia." Really, these young men were kind and intelligent. How beautifully they were making the end of my Odyssey their affair as much as mine.

Homer tells us that in Ithaca there is a cove named after Phorkys, the Old Man of the Sea, with two bold headlands to protect it from wild weather. That in itself does not help us much in the identification. On so rugged a coast any cove or bay will almost of necessity have a bold headland at either extremity. "At the head of the cove," the description continues, "grows a long-leaved olive-tree and near by is a cavern that offers welcome shade and is sacred to the Nymphs whom we call Naiads." The long-leaved olive-tree will obviously not help very much. But the cavern might, for Homer goes on to describe it minutely. It is, of course, a highly poetical description. Yet if there is a bay with a cave near by of which thîs is a pretty accurate description, however poeticized, it seems likely that that is the bay which Homer had in mind. Exactly such a cave, in fact, exists, up in the hillside over against a bay in the southern peninsula, a bay with a shelving beach such as the narrative demands. The name of the bay is Dexia, the name of the cave is Marmarospaelia. It is true that the poet states the cave is "near" the long-leaved olive-tree which marks the bay for Odysseus, while Marmarospaelia is a good half-hour's climb away, so that Odysseus must have found it something of a grind to cart his load of gifts up that rocky slope. But "near" may still mean a good deal further than that, and Odysseus was strong as well as cunning. And it is not unlikely that his patron, Athene, who was hard by, helped things along. Finally, the cave is stated to be sacred to the Naiads, who are the deities of upland places and mountain springs; if it had been a cave by the sea's edge, it would have been sacred to the Dryads. All in all, these considerations make it difficult to believe that Homer did not have Dexia and Marmarospaelia in mind when he wrote of Phorkys and the cave of the Naiads, and that he did not have personal knowledge of Ithaca, having been a mere ship's boy, as I dreamed earlier, or a wandering poet, like the minstrels in his own tales.

The before-dawn world was devoid of form and colour, with water and sky and mountains all fused into a pearly-greyness. Now and again from left or right a headland thrust forth, and then was withdrawn again, like a piece of scenery which is moved on-stage before its cue. No-one spoke. There was only the whisper of parted water, and far away along the shore, a cock crowing, a dog barking. Spiro was there, but he could have been the wooden bow itself, so silent he was.

I was too drowsy to take much interest in the fishing, for we had gone to bed very late, and, as it seemed, had been awakened almost immediately after. The bait we used, like the mist solidified, was dead-white, too, small cubes of octopus-flesh. We would throw out the line, and move on after a minute or two, if the fish did not bite at once. The sea-god, Phorkys, is looking after his own, I thought. To move was almost as motionless as to stay still. Now and again I threw in a line, too, and felt the electric thrill up my fore-arm as a

fish bit. But when I drew my line up, my only catch was the palm of
my hand. I returned to my reveries.

It is fitting, I mused, that I should approach Phorkys-Dexia in a
drowse, like that earlier traveller lying wrapped round in his rug in
the Phaeacian ship with his darling presents around him. It is fitting
that the island should be so obliterated in mist, that it might be any
place at all, island or mainland . . . as it was to Odysseus awakening
on the beach at Phorkys Bay. At length to the mist the sun succeeded,
blazing, though it was still so early in the morning, in the fulness
of its noonday heat, for the mist was merely refined, not blown away,
and the sun's rays were condensed through it as through a burning-
glass. The water now was transparent for many fathoms, in this bay
whose name is "Deep", the silver line exploring endlessly down like
a nerve. The fish in the boat's bottom that had been Grimsby-grey
were a slither of brassy silver and coppery gold.

Soon we were ashore, the Phaeacian ship and the Vathy row-
boat. Somewhere on this pebbly strand the Phaeacian sailors laid
the sleeping Odysseus down by the roots of a long-leaved olive-tree
with his gifts beside him. They took care to put him a fair distance
from the path, behind a broad tree-trunk, so that he should not be
robbed by passers-by. So doing, they ran their ship down into deep
water again, and turned to make for their own land, fated never to
reach there. The path exists to this day, with a fair likelihood of
passers-by, for it is the road from Vathy to Aëtos and Pelikata. As
for the olive-tree, you may take your choice in a whole grove, any one
of which may be standing where the other one stood.

At dawn Odysseus woke, but his old friend, Athene, had been
up to her tricks again. She had veiled the whole scene in just such a
mist as had enveloped us all that morning. "Where am I?" the hero
wanted to know. "And what has happened to my presents?" he
cried out in panic. So he checked them over, and they were all
there, his fine tripods and cauldrons, his gold and his splendid
fabrics, perhaps here, in the spot where now lay our more pedestrian
possessions, our haversacks with cheese and eggs and bread, our
rather warm wine-bottles.

Now a shepherd appears on the scene; and surely Odysseus must
have recognized it was really Athene, even though he was too polite
to say so. "You ask where you are?" asks the shepherd. "You must
be a simpleton or have travelled very far from your home to ask
what country this is. It has a name by no means as inglorious as that.
I grant that it is rugged and unfit for driving horses, yet narrow

P

though it may be it is very far from poor. It grows abundant corn, and wine in plenty. The rains and the fresh dews are never lacking; and it has excellent pasturage for goats and cattle, timber of all kinds and watering-places that never fail." Ithaca, in fact. Athene rolls the obscuring mist away, and proceeds to identify the place. This was the bay of Phorkys, hard by was the long-leaved olive-tree which, apparently, he knew well. Up the hillside was the Cave of the Nymphs, visible then, but concealed from view now, by the tree-grown terraces which have been dug and planted since that time. Finally she points to the great cone of Mt. Neriton, the most conspicuous landmark of the island to the traveller by sea, and only from Dexia among the island's southern bays seen to stand up so singularly clear to view.

All doubt now is thrust from his mind. This is Ithaca at last, at long last. This is the great moment to which he has strained through so many tribulations across so many years. He kneels down to kiss the beloved soil, then lifts his hands to invoke the nymphs of the cavern. A modern transported across the gulf of time to that scene might have expected him to make solicitous enquiries regarding his wife, his son and his parents, who might long ago be dead for all he knows. He does no such thing. Athene herself rebukes him for his oversight. But life has toughened him, and he was tough enough to begin with. He is quite ready to wait till he sees with his own eyes how things are.

"To the cave!" says Athene of the flashing eyes. "Let's stow these gifts away, then we'll talk things over, for things are at a pretty pass up there in your palace."

So under his load of copper and gold and fine fabrics Odysseus staggers up the hill. Like a bird, like a thought, the goddess flies above.

It is hot. My friends and I will take our ease by the water's edge and follow them in an hour, or two, or three. One is not pressed for time in Ithaca. We bathe in the waters green as grass and soft as snow-flakes. Half in, half out of, the olive-tree's shadow, we break our chunks of bread and cheese, peel hard-boiled eggs, swig deep draughts of Ithaca wine. The shadows sway gently over closed eye-lids. Only Spiro does not rest, pure as flame, and as active. Now he is visible on the water, now for endless stretches of time invisible under the water, suddenly he is high in the branches of a tree, having climbed there with less noise than a squirrel.

The two or three hours have gone by. The sun is high over

Neriton, but there is a slight breeze from the north. We leave a bundle of our things in the roots of a long-leaved olive-tree, for there are no passers-by. And if there should be, none will covet them. We climb the hill at last, by terraces of fig and vine and wheat, up scrubby slopes of arbutus and ilex, until we reach a broad terrace spangled with white and yellow daisies, and fox-gloves peeping out from among broom and bracken, and here and there the last bee-orchids and grape-hyacinths. The hill is cloven here as with an axe to give an entrance to the cave, an isosceles wedge of blackness, flanked on each side by water-pocked slabs of limestone. This is Marmarospaelia. You enter the cave across a narrow portal, and descend almost at once by a natural slope which seems at some time to have been carved into a rough stairway. It is not at all easy going, for the stairs are steep, and the rock by your hand and under your feet is thick and slippery with the kind of deposit which often forms in these caves. You perceive that the place is not so dark as you might have expected. More light enters than by the narrow portal on the northward face of the cave. There is an aperture in the roof open to the sky. The place is littered with great boulders, and hung with slimy stalactite pillars. Here and there in the rock-ledges the drip of water through the aeons has hollowed out a number of receptacles not unlike small holy-water stoups. As you turn away from the dark clumsy stairway and inward into the recesses of the cave, you come upon a flat recess which has certainly been levelled by the hands of man. In a cave, and in a cave in this island, it must be believed that this is the altar-stone of some ancient cult.

So much then for the actual cave of Marmarospaelia. Let us come to Homer's description of the Cave of the Nymphs:

"It contains a number of stone basins and two-handled jars, which are used by bees as their hives; also great looms of stone where the Nymphs weave marvellous fabrics of sea-purple; and there are springs where water never fails. It has two mouths. The one that looks north is the way down for men. The other, facing south, is meant for the gods; and as immortals come in by this way it is not used by men at all."

It is extremely difficult to believe that the correspondences between the poem and the facts are a series of mere coincidences. When Homer visited Marmarospaelia, perhaps to lay an offering on the very altar-stone we saw there, the wild bees may well have been nesting in these stoups hollowed out by the endless drip of water, as they sometimes nest to this very day. It is more than probable that he saw a number of two-handled jars lying about which the celebrants had brought to pour wine on their sacrifices. In Homer's intensely anthropomorphic eye the translation of the stalactitic whorls of limestone into the great looms of stone where the Nymphs weave their fabrics, would have been immediate and inevitable. As for the two entrances, there they both are, clear for all to see. The entrance facing the north is about as tall as a small man and not much broader. We are told that after Athene had found a safe place to stow away the Phaeacian presents—in the dark corner, one presumes, where the altar was carved—she sealed the opening with a stone. That is just about the size of it. As for the other entrance in the roof of the cavern, even to this day only a god or a bat could come in that way. A mortal would need a rope ladder.

And finally, regarding the "springs where water never fails". There are no springs there now, and the water has failed at last. But there must have been aeons of water seeping into the cave when the face of the island was shaggy with forest. That is the water that has whirled and twisted those looms of stone. In that black slime that coats every surface the last drops of that once-shining water is held in an apparently eternal suspension.

"This is your cave, Nymphs!" I murmured. "Let no-one dare to doubt it."

I turned to Edward and suggested that it would be improper to visit the Cave of the Nymphs, and to place no offering on their altar.

"A goat?" he suggested. "There was one just near the mouth of the cave."

"It might lead to complications," I thought. "A pity! We should not have come unprepared!"

At that moment a shower of green hazel-nuts descended on us from the aperture in the roof of the cavern. It might have been Spiro, who was missing, or it might have been the Nymphs, ready to help us out of the difficulty. We collected the hazel-nuts and piled them upon the altar.

"We'll need some twigs, Dimitrius, for a fire!"

"Some twigs!" repeated Dimitrius, raising his head towards the entrance of the immortals. "Some twigs!" the roof and walls of the cavern echoed. "Some twigs!"

Only a few moments later a bundle of twigs was hurled down towards us, and then another. Whether it was Spiro or the Nymphs, they worked quickly.

So we collected the twigs, heaped them on the altar-stone, laid the green hazel-nuts on the twigs, and made a fire. As the fire blazed, I recited certain hexameters from the Odyssey, not because they were intrinsically apposite, but because they were those I knew by heart. But they were the Odyssey. I had known them since my boyhood. If the Nymphs were still around, they may have derived some enjoyment from the incantation. I for my part issued from the cavern into the gold-and-blue light of day with a sense of duty done.

V

Having disposed of the presents in the recesses of the cave, and brought up a stone to hide its entrance, Athene and Odysseus sat down to discuss plans for the destruction of the Suitors and the return of the prince to his heritage. That done, Odysseus turned his back on the bay of Phorkys, and took a rough path up into the mountain behind, which led him to the place where his old servant, Eumaeus, with rare devotion, still tended the royal sties. Athene had given Odysseus exact instructions as to how to find the place. It was near the Raven's Crag and the Spring of Arethusa, she told him, and later the narrative adds a further detail. We learn there is an over-hanging rock there, sheltered from the north wind, where Eumaeus is in the habit of spending the night out of doors, to make certain nothing happens to his beasts.

If Phorkys is Dexia, then the mountain Odysseus ascends is to-day called Stephani. Travelling along the crests of Stephani, will Odysseus sooner or later come upon a level place broad enough for a swineherd to pasture his beasts? And will that level place be near a spring, a high raven-haunted crag, and an overhanging rock giving shelter from the north wind? He will, indeed; a level place called Marathia, a famous spring hard by called Peripagedi, and a famous crag called Korax, the very name we meet in the Odyssey. There will be more than one overhanging rock giving shelter from the north wind, now as then without a name. Is this merely a cluster of coincidences?

But there are some other considerations which make the identifi-cations unescapable, at all events once the archaeological evidence for Pelikata as the site of the palace of Odysseus is agreed. It is to be gathered that the pastures of Eumaeus were a long way from the palace, as distances go in Ithaca, for when Eumaeus goes off to advise Penelope of Telemachus's return from the mainland, it takes

him a whole day to get there and back. If Marathia is the place of
the pastures, the distance is, in fact, twelve difficult miles each way,
very much up-hill and down dale, a tough day's work for an old
man. Then, further, there are the circumstances involved in the
landing of Telemachus in Ithaca. Athene had appeared in a vision
to the young man, sleeping in the portico of his host, King Menelaus,
over in Argos. She had warned him that the leading spirits among
the Suitors were lying in ambush in the strait between Ithaca and
Samos, that is, explicitly somewhere along the west coast of the
island. To frustrate them he was to land in Ithaca at the first point
he reached, and send his ship round to the city port. On his way
north-west from the mainland to the island, the first point he would
reach in Ithaca would be the cape to-day called Haghios Johannes.
He would disembark, therefore, on one of the small beaches on either
side of the promontory, probably at the beach to-day called by the
same name as the fountain, Peripagedi. At this day a rugged path
leads up from Peripagedi to the plateau called Marathia. Having
done as the goddess commanded, Telemachus duly arrives at the
farmstead early on the morning after the arrival of his father, and
there father and son after long years are at last reunited.

Up there on Marathia, by the Raven Rock and Arethusa's
Fountain, the two tracks converge, the track taken by Telemachus
climbing from Peripagedi, the track taken by Odysseus climbing
from Dexia. Being in Dexia some time later, it would have been
proper for me to follow Odysseus up the steep escarpment of
Stephani. But it was hot, it was getting late, and we had left on the
beach the boat that had brought us, and must be taken back again.

So we returned to Vathy, and set off two mornings later for the
pastures of Eumaeus up on Marathia. (We will not niggle over these
identifications a single instant more.) Marathia was once again to be
a meeting-place for father and son, and there I should meet Odysseus
for the last time. From Marathia Odysseus must return to his house
in Pelikata to settle his accounts, as he and his patron, Athene, had
arranged between them. In Pelikata he had been born, he had
married, and his son had been born, and to that Pelikata I had paid
my dues. I had had a nightmarish glimpse of the Pelikata where
Odysseus wrought his frightful vengeance, and to that Pelikata I
would not follow him. What happened there is told in the best-
known and the most vivid story-telling in all the world. Did Odysseus
die in Pelikata? Homer leaves his death obscure, even a little
sinister. On the ambiguous lips of the seer, Teiresias, when Odysseus
meets him in the Underworld, we learn that Death is to come to

him out of the sea, Death in his gentlest guise. What Death was
that? Was it the sea itself? Was it a sea-god or sea-monster (though in
Homer's mind all those are one and the same thing)? Was it, as some
imagined, Death at the hand of a son of his own begetting, Telegonus,
child of Circe? Let us console ourselves by the other half of the
prophecy, that when Death was to take him at last, it would find
him worn out after an easy old age and surrounded by a prosperous
people.

Well then, from Marathia, let Odysseus take his way along the
hill-tops and the Anoi-Neriton range home to Pelikata. I too would
make by Vathy and by Athens to my far hyperborean home.

It was not our last day in Ithaca by a radiantly happy week or
so. But it was the last day in the wake of Odysseus. Our companions
were the elegant George, now out of love for a little time, and the
volatile Spiro. Like a puppy Spiro was now two hundred yards
ahead, now a hundred yards behind, now invisible down-hill, now
outlined on a crest against the bright sky. We covered a fair distance
as it was. Spiro must have covered the distance three or four times
over. He looked as much like a small animate bronze at the end as at
the beginning.

After a mile or so the track became so rough with ankle-twisting
boulders, it was evidently the dried bed of a torrent. The intention
was to descend on the Bay of Peripagedi, to bathe there, then
ascend to the Fountain of Arethusa by a track shown on the map. So
up we went, high and high, then down we went, low and low, among
odours of broom and myrtle and rock-rose and thyme as thick and
musky as incense in a church with all the windows shut. I am pretty
sure George had already lost the way. He revealed a fine faculty all
day long for losing the way—almost as if his sojourn in America had
blunted the open-air talent which was so sharp in all his friends.
That was certainly no goat-path down the final almost vertical
descent to the small bay, and though George swore it was Peripagedi,
it could not have been, if the map was anything to go by. It was the
smaller bay just to the north, and it seemed to have no name.

I am glad it had no name. The hour or two we spent there, or at
least one part of it, was outside that type of space which has names on
maps, and that type of time which is measured on clocks. Without
delay the others took to the water, swimming far out. I swam the
exiguous distance which is far enough for me, and then lay down on
a rock beside the glassy green stillness under Homer's sky. It seemed
easy to believe as I lay there that a creature would emerge any

moment out of the water, her hair dripping on her shoulders; or there might be a faint whistle from rock to rock, a dryad calling to another.

At length the others were back from their bathe, and soon we were climbing up the mountain again, where it hung over the further, the southern, side of the bay. There was a trickle of a path for some few hundreds of yards or so, but then it dried up. The going was steeper and steeper. It became very precipitous, and it was getting hotter all the time. The sweat poured down the cheeks and rested in the small of the back. At last the mountain turned in upon itself. We were in a deep gorge, undoubtedly the gorge in which the Fountain of Arethusa had cracked open the mountain-side. We scrambled down on to the boulders in the ravine below, hoping to use them as a causeway to ascend to the fountain and the cliff. Very little water got down as far as this, a spoonful here and there. Still struggling upward, we came to a muddy yellow pool on which insects scuttled and spawned, or dizzied above the surface in a whining cloud.

"Arethusa Fountain! Here she is!" proclaimed George.

"Oh no!" I said resolutely. "Not *this*!"

"O.K!" agreed George, always anxious to oblige. "Not this! We go!"

Immediately ahead of us, blocking the gorge, was a boulder, clammy, steep, and as large as a house.

"And this isn't Korax, either!" I insisted. For the winged creatures here were not ravens, but midges.

"No? No!" George accommodated. There was no way round the boulder on either side. The way onward was up and over it. I did not see how it could be managed without climbing-irons. The others managed it, I tried and slid back, only with extreme luck avoiding the noisome basin. There was nothing for us to do but to climb out of the gorge again, and haul ourselves up slopes which at that moment were practically perpendicular, and very loose in texture. It was very important to make sure as you tugged at a root or grabbed a boulder that it was not going to come away from its moorings. Sometimes it did, but luckily each time I found a hand round my wrist just as my own handhold gave, or a shoulder under my lunging feet, as they scrabbled upon nothing. It was humiliating, but I could put up with it. At last, panting and bleeding, I was aware that the gorge was invisible, we were now out on the open hillside again, which here seemed convex, but I presume was not.

At all events, I took not more than one horrified look down into the swimming void below, and henceforth kept my gaze sternly upward. This continued for some time. It seemed a very long time indeed. Then the glad cry went up: *"Odos! Odos!"* It was the path that George had been hoping to hit upon. It could not be a path to anything but the Fountain. Perhaps Eumaeus had taken this path when he wanted to fill his goat-skin gourd. Perhaps Telemachus had taken this path when he came up from the bay. Anyhow, it was a path, not a tangle of ankle-slashing thorn. The path at length turned the boss of the mountain, and led round into the gorge again. Then it turned still again and became a rock shelf, and the rock shelf ended in the great purple-grey cliff of Korax that stood out stark and severe against a violent sky; and there were birds taking it easy in the wind-stream that the confined hot rocks discharged into the upper air, birds that should have been ravens, but probably were hawks, but they would do. And already as you approached Korax you heard a faint chuckle of water and in your nostrils was the smell of maidenhair fern damped by rivulets coursing down the rock. This then was the Fountain of Arethusa, not at that moment in terms of water a spectacular thing to see, though certainly in ancient times when thick woods bordered the pastures of Eumaeus, and particularly so in a rainy season, the waterfall must have been a noble sight. But Arethusa it was, and Homer's music upon the ear. So we lowered our faces into the stone troughs which the water had hollowed, and washed the sweat and dust away, and drank deep; then filled our very British Army felt-jacketed water-bottles, and straightened up, and drank deep still again, this time not for our own comfort, but in honour of Korax and Arethusa. So we turned at last and looked far down below on to the glittering sea, and on the forehead of the sea an island lifted out of it, floating rootless, like a nautilus, or blown dandelion-seed.

Some half-hour later we had reached the crest of the mountain and found ourselves upon the plateau of Marathia, the eastward thrust of Mt. Stephani. Yes, yes, there was ample room for that homestead of Eumaeus, with its wall of quarried stone and its hedge of wild pear on top; ample room for the twelve great sties where fifty sows slept on the ground and had their litters, and for the boars that lay outside. (Though there were far fewer animals than there should have been, we learn, for the Suitors had been making deep inroads into the stock. Oh greedy Suitors, miserable Suitors, knowing so little of the dreadful fate that is about to march down upon you from the heights of Marathia!)

"You look for something?" asked George, a little dashed. We had not eaten, and we had all been very active, and were hungry. But the day's work was not finished yet.

"I want another rock," I said, and gave the specifications. "There doesn't happen to be one called 'the Rock of Eumaeus' anywhere around?"

George shook his head. Local tradition had not pronounced on the point. We spent some minutes trying to locate it, and we found a satisfactory one, but it did not have the certainty and awe of Korax there, under the mountain's broken edge.

"Hi! Hi!" came suddenly from behind the hollowed hand of George standing outlined against the sky, gazing into the blue north.

"Hi! Hi!" faintly came back again. It was a goatherd far off. The wind veered and brought the tingle-tangle of goat-bells. Then not merely sounds, but words, totally incomprehensible, went outward, came back again, across the great vacancy, over the tops of rock-rose and asphodel.

The goatherd came closer.

"My man! My goats!" explained George with satisfaction. It might have been Telemachus boasting of a herd that his father had assigned to him as a birthday-present.

"His name isn't Eumaeus, is it?" I asked.

George knew all about Eumaeus.

"No, it is Andreas," he smiled. "But let it be Eumaeus, if you like."

Or, in fact, Laertes, I said to myself. He looked more like Laertes than anybody, at the moment Odysseus, his son, went over to reveal himself to the old man after the massacre of the Suitors. He was wearing the same sort of stitched leather garters round his shins to protect them from the brambles, and just such a patched and disreputable tunic, though the goatherd's tunic had covered a lot more ground, all the way from Bradford to Ithaca. He was for all that an impressive fellow, with raven eyes, and a nose like Korax. We greeted him with the immemorial Greek word of greeting, and asked him to take wine with us. He, for his part, took a lump of goat's cheese out of a cloth wallet slung round his shoulders, and broke off a portion for each of us. There was also bread, eggs, olives, raisins and dried figs. It was a good meal, I thought, to be taking on the plateau of Marathia, with the rock of Korax below, and below that the Fountain of Arethusa.

But before we got down to it I thought it proper to pour a libation of wine on to the warm and thirsty earth. For this was the

end of it, the moment to which the road had led across the four
decades of my Odyssean adventure.

At that moment I could have sworn I saw a traveller some
distance along the plateau. He was dressed in beggar's rags, but he
was the lord of this island, not quite the demigod but more than
mortal. Apparently aware that there were strangers in the pastures
of Eumaeus, his old servant, he turned and looked at them. How had
they come here, from what land? Were they hostile? Were they
friendly? The lord of the island was not perturbed. He turned again
and was on his way home.

It was still dark, but there was a sense of morning in the air,
when, a few weeks later, we stepped down from the Ithaca quayside into the boat that would carry us over to the Athens-bound
steamer. It was dark again, and again there was a sense of morning
in the air, when in Athens air-port we entered the London-bound
plane.

Only one full day had gone by. The outward thread between
England and Ithaca had meandered mazily through many a
convolution over nearly four decades. The homeward chain, arrow-
straight, was to be forged between Ithaca and England within a
morning and a morning and an evening.

It happened that I was acquainted with the pilot of the aeroplane, and in the terminal we had time for a cigarette and a few
words together. He told me about the girl he had recently married,
I told him about the conclusion, so few hours ago, of my Odyssey.

Not long after we left Athens the young man sent me a note
inviting me to take a seat beside him in the cockpit. It was light
already. The dawn was lapping westward like a surf along a flat
strip of sands as enormous as half the world. In not many minutes
we were over the Acarnanian escarpment. A few minutes later it
was the sea, still as glass, but already flame-blue, excepting for the
white fringe that edged the coasts.

"I'm going to give you a last look at Ithaca," the pilot said
casually, as if it was nothing to him to have the godlike faculty of
unrolling at will the map of lands and seas, of obscuring them by
cloud if cloud was there, or flying at such a distance that they were
reduced to the dimensions of a painting on a wall.

The pilot turned the machine slightly off course. In hardly any
time all the principalities of Odysseus were spread out below us—
Doulichion and Samé and wooded Zacynthus, and that famous
island, Ithaca, his home. We came down a thousand feet or so and

circled on a wing-tip directly over Aëtos. There it lay, seen as
Athene herself might have seen it when she came winging over from
the top of Olympus to descend on the beach of the bay of Phorkys.

The island seemed to lie in a trance of sleep, like Odysseus
himself that morning, wrapped in his Phaeacian rug by the roots of
the long-leaved olive-tree. What perfection of shape it had, the
northern and the southern mountains and the mountain between,
the delicately scooped-out bays, the now golden promontories! In
those toy villages and the minute blue and pink blocks on their outskirts some of my friends were just stirring. The fishermen, perhaps,
and the bakers, and those goatherds who, like Eumaeus, had spent
all night beside their beasts?

It was only so few hours ago, and it was already so long a time
ago . . .

"O.K.?" said the pilot.

I nodded. Certain syllables of verse droned in my head:

> *the perfect hills stood in the seas*
> *the minute seas curl under them,*
> *even as if Praxiteles*
> *had carved it on a gem.*

Ithaca was now invisible. Swift and straight the aeroplane went
thrumming north-westward on its way.

ACKNOWLEDGEMENTS

I have used throughout the admirable translations of the Iliad and the Odyssey by Dr. E. V. Rieu, as published in the Penguin Classics, and here express my gratitude to the publishers and the translator. I would also like to express my gratitude to Mr. John Mavrogordato and the Hogarth Press for permission to quote some stanzas from Cavafy's poem, as translated by Mr. Mavrogordato (Hogarth Press, 1951); to Mr. H. T. Wade-Gery and the Cambridge University Press for permission to use some lines from Mr. Wade-Gery's version of the Hymn to the Delphian Apollo (*The Poet of the Iliad*, C.U.P., 1952); and to Lady (Marie Noële) Kelly, for permission to quote from her translation of an essay by Professor Kuehn, originally published in the *Allgemeine Zeitung* of Mayence. ("Turkish Delights": *Country Life*, 1951.)

The endpapers and charts have been drawn by Edward Thorpe. Some of the photographs were taken by the author. Acknowledgements are due for photographs kindly loaned by Mr. Zoltan Glass, the Italian State Tourist Office, the Greek Government Department of Information, and the Turkish Press Attaché.

REFERENCES

1. H. PEAKE and H. J. FLEURE. *Corridors of Time*. (Oxford University Press, 1927–33.)
2. Messrs. BLEGEN, CASKY and RAWSON. *Troy*. (University of Princeton, 1950.)
3. L. DURRELL. *Prospero's Cell*. (Faber, 1953.)
4. D. T. ANSTED. *The Ionian Islands in the Year 1863*. (W. H. Allen, 1863.)

BIBLIOGRAPHY

H. Peake and H. J. Fleure .	Corridors of Time (3 Volumes). (Oxford University Press, 1927–33.)
H. Schliemann . . .	Troja. (Murray, 1884.)
H. Schliemann . . .	Ilios. (Harper and Bros., 1881.)
M. and C. H. B. Quenell .	Everyday things in Homeric Greece. (Batsford, 1924.)
M. and C. H. B. Quenell .	Everyday things in Archaic Greece. (Batsford, 1931.)
V. Bérard	Introduction à l'Odyssée. (Les Belles Lettres, 1924.)
V. Bérard	Calypso et la Mer de l'Atlantide. (Librairie Armand Colin, 1929.)
V. Bérard	Ithaque, etc. (Bibliographie Armand Colin, 1927.)
E. V. Rieu	Homer. The Iliad, a new translation. (Penguin, 1950.)
E. V. Rieu	Homer. The Odyssey, a new translation. (Penguin, 1946.)
M. P. Nillson . . .	Homer and Mycenae. (Methuen, 1933.)
W. H. D. Rouse . . .	Homer. (Nelson, 1939.)
Blegen, Casky and Rawson .	Troy, Vols. 11a, 111a, 111b. (University of Princeton, 1950.)
M. Bowra	Tradition and Design in the Iliad. (Clarendon Press, 1930.)
L. Whibley	Companion to Greek Studies. (Cambridge, 1913.)
E. Ludwig	Schliemann. (Putnam, 1932.)
Ventris and Chadwick . .	"Evidence for Greek Dialect in the Mycenaean Archives". (Journal of Hellenic Studies, Vol. LXXIII. 1953.)
H. T. Wade-Gery . . .	The Poet of the Iliad. (Cambridge University Press, 1952.)
P. Argenti and H. J. Rose .	The Folk-Lore of Chios. (Cambridge University Press, 1949.)
Fernand Robert . . .	Homère. (Presses Universitaires de France.)
Marie Noële Kelly . .	"Turkish Delights." (Country Life, 1951.)
R. Warner and Hürlemann .	Eternal Greece. (Thames and Hudson, 1953.)
R. Liddell	Aegean Greece. (Cape, 1954.)

239

G. W. ORKNEY	. . .	*Four Years in the Ionian Islands.* (Chapman and Hall, 1864.)
LORD RENNELL of RODD, W. A. HEURTLEY, SYLVIA BENTON		Papers by. (*Annual of the British School at Athens,* 1933, 1949, 1952.)
W. W. HYDE		*Ancient Greek Mariners.* (Oxford University Press, 1947.)
W. LEAF		*Homer and History.* (Macmillan, N.Y., 1915.)
J. E. HARRISON . . .		*Myths of the Odyssey.* (Rivington, 1882.)
L. DURRELL		*Prospero's Cell.* (Faber, 1953.)
L. COTTRELL		*The Bull of Minos.* (Evans, 1953.)
C. W. CERAM		*Gods, Graves and Scholars.* (Gollancz, 1952.)
SMITH and BLAKENEY . .		*Smaller Classical Dictionary.* (Dent, 1910.)
D. T. ANSTED . . .		*The Ionian Islands in the Year 1863.* (W. H. Allen, 1863.)
BOISSONAS . . .		*Dans le Sillage d'Ulysse.* (Colin, 1933.)
H. FESTING JONES . .		*Biography of Samuel Butler.* (Cape, 1919.)
SAMUEL BUTLER . . .		*The Authoress of the Odyssey.* (Cape, 1922.)
R. D. BARNETT . . .		*Journal of Hellenic Studies.* (Vol. LXXIII, 1953.)
W. SMITH		*Dictionary of Greek and Roman Biography and Mythology.* (Taylor and Walton, 1844.)

INDEX

A

Aaea Island (Circe's Island), 14, 80
Abbazia, s.s., 24, 25, 26
Abraham, 22
Abydos, 26, 27, 56 (*see also* Chanakkale)
Achaea, 77
Achaean fleet, 98, 99
Achaeans, 28, 45, 49, 52, 62, 74, 75, 77, 79, 115, 126, 137, 195
Achilleion villa, Corfu, 172
Achilles, 65; tomb of, 69; 74, 75, 188
Acre, 32
Acropolis, Samé, 195
Actaeon Inn, Ithaca, 200–1, 202
Aden, Gulf of, 162
Aeëtes, King, 28
Aegadean Islands, 88
Aegean, 67, 69
Aegina range, 135
Aeneas, 50; flees from Troy, 67
Aeolia, 13
Aeolian Islands, 13; settlers, 69
Aeolus Island, 88, 96
——, Lord of the Winds, 13, 76, 101
Aëtos, 208, 209, 213, 215, 223, 225, 236
Affray, H.M.S., 27
Agamemnon, King, 22, 69, 71, 73, 74, 76, 77, 78, 79, 98, 99, 100, 137, 191, 214
Agathocles, tyrant, 159
Agora, Santorin, 127
Ahhiyava, 76, 77 (*see also* Achaea)
Aipos Hills, Chios, 147
Ajax, tomb of, 68, 74, 107
Akaba, 117
Albanian mountains, 165, 174
Alcaeus, poet, 138
Alcinous, Phaeacian king, 87; palace of, 88, 172–3, 175, 187, 188; 93, 163, 167, 170; Gymnastic Club, 171; Gardens of, 176, 185; 179, 181, 183, 184, 185, 186, 189, 191, 198
——, Port of, Corcyra, 174
Aldershot, 169
Alexander, 69
Alexandria, 126
Allah, 33, 35

Allgemeine Zeitung, 237
Amazons, 26
Amphitrite, 114
Anastasia, hostess, Ithaca, 201, 202, 206, 219
Anatolia, 47
Andreas, modern name, 234
Andreus, 77
Andromache, 71, 74
Aneas flees from Troy, 67
Angelokastron, Corfu, 185
Ankara, 37, 50, 52, 63
Anoi mountain, Ithaca, 209, 231
Antinous, 196
Antipaxos Island, 94
Anubis temple, Santorin, 127
Anzac, 51
Aphrodite, 62, 146
Apolausis Inn, Ithaca, 213
Apollo, 137
—— Carneios, 125, 127
Apollo's Ephoboi, Gymnasium, Santorin, 127
Aragon, Courts of, 58
Arakli Mount (Heracles), 184, 185
Arasimandros, Santorin, 128
Archomenos, 77
Arden, Enoch, 144
Ares, God of War, 62, 146
Arete, wife of Alcinous, 189
Arethusa, Fountain of, Ithaca, 212, 229, 230, 231, 232, 233, 234
Argenti, Ur., 147
Argives, 137
Argonauts, 26, 28, 114, 115, 162
Argos, 75, 230
Argostoli, Samé, 193, 194, 195, 196
Artemidoros, Temenos of, 126
Artemidoroses, 126
Artemis, 22, 150
Asia Minor, Greek cities of, 69
Asius, 56
Aspronisi Island, 116
As-su-va (Asia), 61
Asy (Asia), 61
Atakos Island, 203
Athanasius, a Spiro, 195, 196, 197
Athena, temple to, 69

5/5/59

N-e

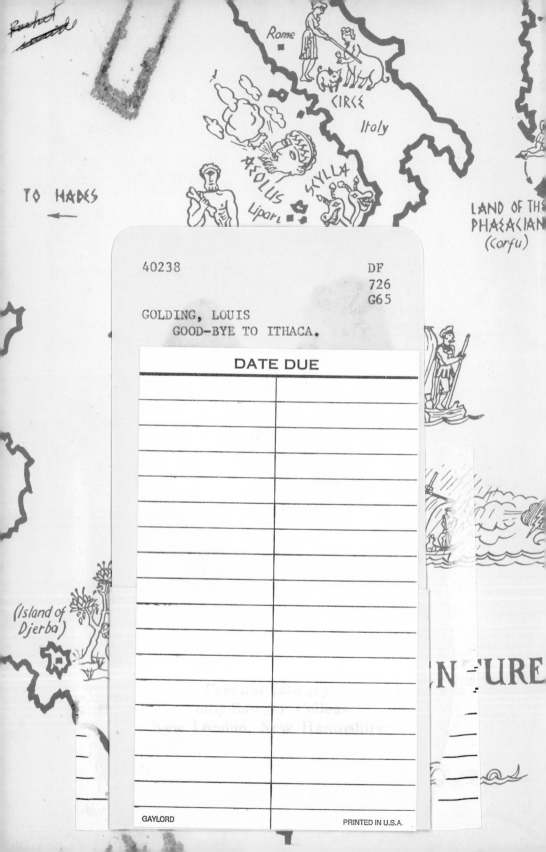

Rome

CIRCE

Italy

TO HADES

ÆOLUS
SKYLLA
Lipari

LAND OF THE
PHÆACIANS
(Corfu)

(Island of
Djerba)